PUNISHMENT WITHOUT CRIME

BOOKS BY S. ANDHIL FINEBERG

Punishment without Crime
Project in American Jewish History
Biblical Myth and Legend
Overcoming Anti-Semitism

S. ANDHIL FINEBERG

Punishment without Crime

WHAT *YOU* CAN DO ABOUT PREJUDICE

DOUBLEDAY AND COMPANY, INC.

GARDEN CITY, NEW YORK, 1950

The extract from Rabbi Cohen—*First Citizen of Texas*, by Webb Waldron, is reprinted from the February, 1939, issue of *The Reader's Digest*.

The extract from *The Walls Came Tumbling Down*, by Mary White Ovington, is reprinted by permission of Harcourt, Brace and Company, Inc.

TO HILDA,
THE BETTER HALF OF ANDHIL

Contents

Introduction

This book was written to finish a conversation.

We were talking about community relations. My friend, a divinity student, sensitive to the cruelties inflicted by prejudice, was eager to work for the elimination of intolerance. He saw, however, only a single means to that end, one hope, and only one. Again and again he said, "There is only one way to eradicate prejudice—through the power of love."

"But what of today?" I asked him. "What of the critical daily problems which plague human relationships? How can any simple formula apply in all of the thousands of cases wherein people refuse to be kind or just—or even merciful?"

My young friend was undismayed. He had accepted a rigid program and was determined to cling to it regardless of consequences. "The more acute the problem," he insisted, "the more necessary it is that we preach love, teach love, practice love."

"Let's take a specific case," I said, "one uncomplicated situation. A few years ago in the town where you attend college there was not a single barber willing to serve Negro students. Not one of the barbers could be persuaded to stop the discrimination, though there had been many attempts to convince them. Most of the barbers contended that they themselves were unprejudiced, but that they would lose their white customers if they catered to all races. Tell me, how would you have applied your formula to such a situation?"

"I have already told you. Wherever a difficulty exists we must keep on repeating the message of love until it has the desired effect."

"I respect your motives," I said, "but even the most philosophic of us should not expect others to wait that long for a haircut. Let me tell you how the problem actually was resolved. A group of white students finally approached one of the barbers—the least prejudiced of the group. They promised him their own trade and as much more as they could send him if he would also accept the trade of Negro students. That plan worked."

I cited other examples of prejudice in action, so varied that to me, at least, it was clear that no one formula, however inspired, could possibly suffice for all of them. But still my young colleague held firmly to his original thesis of the efficacy of love alone.

I retired from the conversation, determined to write a book which would discuss in detail the intricacies and perplexities of racial and religious prejudice. It would be a book about the futility of easy generalizations and about the constant need to take concrete, practical steps on the way toward ultimate goals. It would describe a multiple, variegated plan of attack against prejudice and show how such an approach proves beneficial where inflexible formulas fail.

Punishment without Crime is that book. It is the conclusion of one conversation—and of hundreds of others which differed from it only in time and place. Containing the substance of what I have learned in ten years of professional work in the field of community relations, it sums up what I would like to have told my friend and what I am still trying to say to others who too often work with more zeal than wisdom.

Intolerance persists. The professional worker in the field of community relations deals with it, not in a philosophic vacuum, but in an imperfect world in which intolerance is already entrenched. Faced with the consequences of his decisions, he learns to scrutinize with meticulous care his own methods and those of others. He must cope with explosive situations demanding immediate action as well as with deep-seated difficulties which can be resolved only through a broad program of long-range activity. He encounters theorists and daydreamers, practical thinkers and zealots. Among the ardent workers he finds those who can only swing a club and those whose only approach is with a cookie jar. Some wear a perpetual scowl, while others have a permanent, propitiating smile. Too often when the psychological moment has arrived for friendly mediation the fire-eaters smash ahead with their axes; and when the situation demands a forceful advance despite opposition, the Pollyannas refuse to do more than beam affably.

Intolerance is not a great stationary block of solid evil. It is a shifting, moving fog, a paradox and an enigma. Those of us who deal with it must understand why. There are times to fight and times to avoid battle, times to dash briskly ahead and times to wait and reconnoiter. Without the willingness to speak and act forcefully when the occasion demands it, we are unlikely to dent even the periphery of bigotry. In other instances, against the cherished prejudice of a dominant majority, fiery assault tactics bring disaster. Unless we manage to inject friendliness and compassion—what my young friend would call "love"—into the battle against intolerance, we may inflict as many wounds as we heal. We must somehow destroy this protean evil and at the same time promote the enduring harmony with which it is to be replaced. While laying the groundwork for a society free of intolerance we must manage to find the right answer to the challenge of the moment.

Intolerance has a double aspect—the personal and the communal. The difficulties which prejudice creates for an individual now and then are inextricably intertwined with the major scourges which corrode communities. This book deals with intolerance as it affects both the individual and the group. In specific concrete terms it discusses both *what you can do alone* and *what you can do in co-operation with others.*

It presents a unified thesis; an attitude and a program which, to be of use, should be understood as a whole. The various manifestations of prejudice which are here treated separately are actually interrelated even when the relationship is not apparent. Much of the material which appears under one heading is equally pertinent to another and might as readily have been used there. Though the arrangement of the book is such that you will find it a useful reference when a problem arises, whatever lasting value it may have lies in the total thesis and not in the parts.

I cannot claim to be the originator of more than a minimal part of the content of this book. I have had a hand in the working out of some of the methods presented here—the "quarantine treatment" for rabble-rousers, for example, and the plan for striking at the root of prejudicial scurrilities instead of attempting specific refutations. In a very real sense the suggestions offered and the principles advanced in these pages are the product of literally hundreds of capable persons engaged in the daily tasks of improving group relationships, as practitioners or as researchers. A host of people will recognize in the episodes described in this book events in which they themselves participated. It was their experiences which created the strategies presented here. They are the witnesses that these methods have been used successfully. I have drawn freely upon what they have told me or have written to me, and from the books, pamphlets, and brochures which describe their activities.

To mention by name the scores of colleagues whose efforts in community relations have had a continuous, direct effect upon my own is obviously impossible. Perhaps I can make some partial acknowledgment of my indebtedness by expressing my gratitude to the personnel of some of the organizations with whom I have worked. Among these agencies are the American Jewish Committee, the Anti-Defamation League of B'nai B'rith, the American Council on Race Relations, the National Conference of Christians and Jews, the Bureau of Intercultural Education, the National Association for the Advancement of the Colored People, the Urban League, the New York State Citizens' Council, the Mayor's Committee of New York City, and the National Community Relations Advisory Council and its member agencies.

My thanks are also due to Mel Evans, Ralph A. Beebe, George J. Hexter, and Edward H. Cushman, whose assistance in the preparation of this book has been invaluable.

No organization and no individual other than myself bears any responsibility for the views expressed here. I am fully aware that on a subject of this sort no one has ever written a book with which all informed people, motivated by the highest ideals, have *completely* agreed. I can only ask those who may at first disagree with some of the conclusions stated here to bear in mind that at one time I, too, would have rejected some of them. But through my own experience and that of others I have learned that first thoughts and normal emotional responses are deceitful guides in difficult situations—most especially those which involve prejudice.   S. A. F.

PART ONE

Where Are We Now?

CHAPTER 1

How Would You Solve These?

To get started let's take four case studies, in each of which certain people were confronted by serious problems due to intolerance. As you read what happened in each of these four instances ask yourself, "What would I have done had I been confronted by that problem?" Compare your own decision and its likely consequences with the course actually taken. Would you have done something less effective, equally helpful, or even better?

In 1940 the Nazi Propaganda staff launched a rumor that American merchants were discharging American employees and hiring German-Jewish refugees to replace them. The story was a complete phony, sent here from Germany by short-wave broadcast, but native hate-mongers picked it up and promoted it by a whispering campaign. It went the rounds speedily, and soon people were saying that merchants in their own cities were firing Americans and employing German refugees. That accusation was not circulated publicly. No newspaper would carry it. But the dirty work was done by word of mouth. Many phone calls to store proprietors and even the falling off of sales indicated that damage was being done.

During the height of this whispering campaign a large department store received phone calls every few minutes asking whether the rumor was true. Some inquiries came from frightened Jews greatly disturbed by the rumor. Some were from malicious persons who wanted to be annoying and who would not accept denials. Still others were from decent, honest souls who wanted to find out the truth. The number of calls increased and became increasingly troubling.

The problem became so acute for Jewish merchants that several thought seriously of denying the rumor in the newspaper. Those who consulted me were told that it would be a grave error to publish a denial. Many people whom the malicious rumor had not reached would learn of it for the first time. It would become the talk of the town to far greater extent than before. As do many mistaken attempts to combat prejudice and the lies it circulates, a public answer to this canard would be a boomerang.

But still those phone calls kept coming in.

What would you have done had you been a merchant barraged by these devious, Nazi-inspired rumors? What would you have told those who made the insistent phone inquiries?

Most Jewish merchants faced the situation with grim fortitude until it died down. Their replies to the phone calls were, "We have no Jewish refugees on our staff," or, "We have only one," "Only two refugees," or whatever the truth might be. One merchant would answer very patiently, "How long do you think I could stay in business if I put people behind the sales counters who can't speak English fluently?"

Would you have given the *best* reply? Probably not, unless you had had considerable experience with similar situations. Yet there was an effective technique which, wherever used, dispelled the rumor within a few weeks. This is the way in which it was done. All phone calls on the subject were directed to one person, who gave the same reply to everyone. "Please come in and see for your-self. Our employees are not invisible. You can see and talk to every one of them. Come in, look around, and draw your own conclusions."

If the inquirer persisted, "But why don't you tell me? Have you or have you not discharged American employees and taken on refugees?" the reply was, "We do not ask our employees their religion or nationality and therefore you will have to make your own in-vestigation. We'll be glad to have you do so."

Here was a response which was particularly effective because it did not reveal the fear implicit in other methods of denying the falsehood. In confronting a lying rumor nothing is more hurtful than to appear frightened by it, since that is interpreted as evidence of a guilty conscience. The well-considered reply threw the burden

WHERE ARE WE NOW?

of proof on those who promoted the slur. What could be fairer than to make the questioners the judges as to the truth or falsehood of the allegation?

Inspired rumors and vicious propaganda can be combated successfully, but it takes a great deal of know-how—too often more than most of us have.

Here is an even more striking instance of the important difference between ill-considered emotional reaction to prejudice and the more skillfully planned method of dealing with it. It involves a family of Polish origin who had moved into a new neighborhood. The father, Mr. R., spoke with a foreign accent but his son of ten and his daughter of eight, born in the United States, were in every respect American. The family was apparently accepted into the community, but two months after their arrival Mrs. R. was horrified when her children told her that one of their playmates had referred to Mr. R. as a "hunky."

The mother realized that this unkind attitude might be communicated to the other children. Her first impulse was to discuss the matter with the mother of the offender. In some circumstances that might have been the correct thing to do, but after some thought Mrs. R. decided that she needed advice if she was to do the *best* thing possible under these particular circumstances. She rightly chose not to "do something" but rather to do the *best* thing possible. She consulted a teacher whom she had heard address a parent-teacher meeting on the subject of intercultural education.

"I want my children to be Americans," she said. "And I don't want them to have to fight for that right. Tommie wanted to lick that boy. Perhaps he was right. Perhaps it is the best way to handle this."

"It certainly is not," replied the teacher, "unless you want him to go on using his fists all his life, even when his mind can do a much better job."

"Then what can I do except talk to the boy's mother?"

"How well do you know her?"

"I don't know her well, but we've met and talked a few times on the street. She seemed friendly enough."

"But we can't predict her reaction," said the teacher. "She might be the very person from whom her child learned that obnoxious word. Even if she agrees with you, your relationship to her will be strained hereafter. Nor do we know how well she handles her child. She may be very harsh and make him sullen. I think you can do something better. You can have the neighbors' children recognize your family for what it is. You can get them to accept you and your children on amicable terms with nothing concealed."

The teacher outlined a plan which the mother accepted. The next day she invited ten of her children's playmates, including the one who had used the nasty term, to attend a party at her home several days later. Until then her own children were to avoid the child who had insulted their father. Though there was, of course, a possibility that the culprit might not accept the invitation, the teacher rightly surmised that he would not miss a party where his friends would be enjoying themselves.

When the guests arrived they found the living room gaily decorated in American themes. There was a large picture of a military officer, and during the games an award was offered to the one who could make the best copy of it. They were told that the man in the portrait was Count Pulaski. When asked who he was, the mother explained that Pulaski had helped General Washington win the Revolutionary War. She told them that many people born abroad had come to the United States because they loved the ideals of our country. One of them, she said, was this Polish nobleman and soldier, Count Casimir Pulaski, who had given up wealth and a comfortable home in Poland to fight and die defending the young republic. After she had established the children's admiration for Pulaski, the mother mentioned that someone had once called him a "hunky." The children were appalled. They agreed that no one ought ever to use such a word. (Her own children had been cautioned to act as though they had never heard it before.)

Polish delicacies were served and, although no undue emphasis was laid upon the fact that the family was of Polish origin, that fact appeared in some of the chatter. Oh yes, they were very proud of Pulaski. But this was incidental. "Isn't it grand that in America we can all get together this way and enjoy ourselves so thoroughly!" was the feeling which predominated throughout the conversation.

These children were learning by doing—a basic principle of education. There was no further difficulty on the score of nationality. Social acceptance had been accomplished, not by a rebuke, more likely to prevent than promote friendship, but by promoting genuine fellowship, which assures the best relationships.

Let's look at another instance:

In a certain suburban neighborhood where no Negroes live there is a small church. It is not the fashionable one of that area and its little congregation supports only a visiting minister. The building and its grounds had been maintained by a part-time man who devoted about twenty hours a week to those duties. In 1943, however, this caretaker went to work in a war plant and before long the grass around the church became unkempt. Inside and out the building became increasingly untidy. Volunteers offered to do chores. But work connected with the war effort received priority and the church was increasingly neglected. A year slipped by and the church building was becoming an eyesore.

The minister who came to preach and attend to pastoral duties every other week end met in a nearby town a childless elderly Negro couple. The man had been injured in an accident and could not take on protracted heavy jobs. With his wife's assistance, however, he was quite able to perform the custodial duties required about the church and was willing to undertake the job in return for a small salary and rent-free use of a few rooms at the rear of the building. The minister proposed that the couple take up residence there. The comfortable living quarters, otherwise vacant, represented half the remuneration.

Had the church building been an institutional structure, obviously a church, it is unlikely that a problem would have arisen as a consequence of this arrangement. But it was a large, converted dwelling, resembling the other homes along the street. Within a week after the Negro couple had moved in grumbling broke out about "those d—— foreigners who should never have been allowed to make a church out of the place and are now bringing in Negroes (they used the insulting form of the word "Negroes") to live on our street."

By the time the minister paid another visit the members of his congregation living nearest to the church were in panic.

"We'll have to send them away," they told him. "They are creating so much ill feeling that we won't be able to stand it."

"Are they doing their work properly?"

"They're splendid people," everyone agreed. "Just look what they've done in a few days to fix the place up again, and they're as polite and self-respecting and respectful of others——"

"Then how can we tell them to pack up and leave?" asked the minister. "We told them they could be sure of a home and a job as long as they did the work properly."

"But, Mr. L., we're catching the very mischief. One neighbor has already told her children not to play with mine until we get rid of this man and his wife."

And so it went.

The congregation held an impromptu meeting. Most of the members were ready to end the matter then and there by discharging the Negro caretaker.

"Take my resignation at the same time," said the minister.

"Oh no, Mr. L.," was the immediate chorus. "We need you here and this doesn't involve you at all. You recommended this couple in good faith. None of us foresaw how it would be interpreted."

But the caretaker was not discharged. When last I heard of this matter a year after the ructions the Negroes were still on the job and there was no difficulty whatsoever. I wish that I could report that the people of the street, converted by a few good speeches, had said, "What of it? What do we care? Why shouldn't worthy Negroes be permitted to live on this street along with the whites?"

That, however, did not happen and in this instance could not have happened. Yet even the most intolerant persons on the block and those who were most troublesome had ceased to offer any protest because of an idea that emerged from that board meeting.

The caretaker canvassed the neighborhood for several days offering to mow lawns, do little paint jobs and the like at the prevailing hourly rate for such work. On the bulletin board bearing the name of the church, the minister, and announcements of services there was added, "John Wood, Caretaker." The accepted social balance was thus restored. Not a Utopian solution, but the best the situation would permit and a much better fate for an elderly couple who would otherwise have been compelled to rely upon public charity and have a more meager subsistence.

Here's a very different situation:

A Christian friend spoke to me about a play that was about to open in New York ten days later. "It's sacrilegious," he said.

"Yes," I agreed. "It is certainly theologically offensive to the overwhelming majority of Christians. It is regrettable that it is being produced."

"Well, what shall we do about it?" he asked.

"At present, nothing," I replied.

My friend became annoyed. "You would do nothing about a play that outrages the religious sentiments of your neighbors? Wouldn't you join a protest?"

"I'm not talking about my own personal reactions," I corrected him. "I'm thinking about the strategy of handling the problem. This play lost money when it was tried out in a summer theater. From all that I've heard about it, it consists of long speeches that are difficult to understand. Much of it is monotonous and boring."

"Then you don't object to a bad play unless it is interesting and appeals to audiences?"

"No," I assured him, "that is not the point. What I am thinking is that unless this play has much more popular appeal than I'm told it has, the producer cannot afford to keep it going. A play that is financially unsuccessful will soon close up. Let's give this one time to commit suicide."

"But in the meantime some people will see it."

"Yes, but only a few. If you get people of influence to attack it publicly, intense public interest will certainly be aroused and far more people will pay to see it."

"Then why not talk to the producer?"

"I don't know the producer," I answered, "and haven't the slightest idea who could influence him. He is a complete blank to me. But I do know that theatrical producers, managers, and theater owners are among the most stubborn people in the world. Show business is no place for anyone who won't back his own judgment to the limit. This producer probably believes that this show of his is the most moral, the most religious, and most uplifting project that ever came to New York. And being both a producer and theater owner, he has a double dose of obstinacy."

"So you don't think anything can be gained by bringing pressure to bear on this fellow?"

"Positively not. You *can* make him fighting mad. He may decry censorship, interference with art, denial of freedom, and the like. One of the best assets he has right now is that the play was banned in Boston. If it had not been prohibited there, it probably would have soon died there. It may have been taken to Boston with such purpose. There are many cities in which to try out a show which have no Watch and Ward Society. 'Banned in Boston' is a number-one selling card for books and plays no one would otherwise notice. It's the only *free* advertising that guarantees national coverage without a penny's cost to publisher or producer."

"But what if the play does succeed and attracts audiences?"

"That," I replied, "would present an entirely different situation than the present one. It would call for a skillful educational campaign to offset its ill effects. How to deal with a play or a book when it is still a possible dud is one thing. Dealing with one that is already becoming popular is another. We are now dealing with a new play. At this stage I count on its dying at birth. I urge that we avoid giving it the breath of life."

Eventually it was agreed that a public furor should not be created. The play opened in New York with no denunciation in the public press from those who considered it religiously offensive. The critics found little in it to praise. Their reviews, on the whole, were unfavorable. After sixteen performances before small audiences, the play closed.

These are rather simple case studies. The remedies were direct and uninvolved. In each instance, however, they were effective; innocent people were spared vexation, injury, or serious damage.

Unfortunately, not all problems involving prejudice can be so happily resolved. Many are complex and baffling. Before we probe into other emergency situations or into the lingering, malignant injustices inflicted by intolerance, we shall have to dissect prejudice itself. We must understand why many men and women who consider themselves intelligent, benevolent, democratically minded citizens and who hold their neighbors' esteem, indulge in racial and religious prejudices.

The first major question is, "Why do otherwise good people harbor something as evil as intolerance?" Let us see why and how the prejudiced are themselves tricked and deceived by their own prejudices.

CHAPTER 2

Introducing the Victimian

Have you heard of the social-distance scale invented by Dr. Emory S. Bogardus? Try it as a test of your own prejudices. Write down on separate lines the names of a dozen or more ethnic and religious groups. After each one write the numerals 1 to 8. Then consider each of those group names. According to your immediate reaction, encircle the numbers that correspond with the eight degrees of social acceptance listed below:

1. *I would exclude them from my country.*
2. *I would admit them to my country but only as visitors.*
3. *I would admit them to citizenship in my country.*
4. *I would admit them to employment in my country.*
5. *I would admit them as classmates in my school.*
6. *I would admit them as neighbors to my street.*
7. *I would admit them to my club as personal chums.*
8. *I would admit them to kinship by marriage.*

The highest numeral encircled for each group indicates your attitude toward that group. If, for example, you used the name of your own racial or religious group, your score on that line would probably be 8, the highest possible score. You might well rate "Americans" at 8. If you measured your feelings about "American Indians," "American Negroes," "American Jews," "American Catholics," "American Protestants," or "Chinese-Americans," would your score be equally high? Do you tend toward the lower or higher numbers? The higher your score, the less prejudice you harbor.

Dr. Eugene Hartley used the Bogardus Scale on students in eight colleges. Among forty-nine group designations used by him were "Danirean," "Pirenean," and "Wallonians." None of the students ever met a Danirean, a Pirenean, or a Wallonian. No one ever has. These are names of non-existent people. Yet the students who revealed a great deal of intolerance toward other groups had similar attitudes toward these none-such groups.

Conversely, the students who indicated least intolerance toward genuine groups were not intolerant to these fictitious ones. Dr. Hartley drew the logical conclusion: "The degree of intolerance expressed by individuals is a generalized function of the individual and is not completely determined by the specific group toward which the attitude is directed."[1] Gardner Murphy believes that "This means that there is really no such thing as anti-Negro prejudice or anti-Semitism—except as an expression of purely negative reality, like a vitamin deficiency. There is an acute absence of something, namely of the normal human interchange of ideas or feelings; there is a system of barriers." Disliking an individual *because of his own traits* is not prejudice. Any normal human being, including the members of his own group, would in all likelihood dislike him because of those objectionable attributes or misdeeds. But aversion to a certain group is racial or religious prejudice. There is a barrier between the prejudiced person and the group—a fence, as it were, with which the prejudiced person walls himself in.

Dr. Hartley's test and other experiments reveal a tendency to dislike, to suspect, and even to fear people whose race, religion, or culture is different from our own. There is always "our kind" and "the other kind." Those who happen to be members of our own groupings (and therefore quite like ourselves in language, customs, mannerisms, and the like) belong to our own *in-group*. All others (in relationship to ourselves) belong to *out-groups*. The innate capacity for disliking out-groups may remain dormant and insignificant. It does serve, however, as the tinder which prejudice sparks into a flame.

The primitive impulse to regard members of out-groups with dread or contempt appears least among little children. But they adopt the prejudices of their environment unless the demoralizing process is checked.

A Negro mother, who realizes the necessity of nipping budding

[1]*Problems in Prejudice*, Eugene Hartley, King's Crown Press, New York.

intolerance, told me that her son came home in an angry mood and shouted, "That Wop kid down the street bumped into me with his bicycle and knocked me down."

"Wop! What's that mean?" asked his mother firmly.

"Aw, you know! An Italian."

"I don't know," the mother insisted calmly, "why you should use a nasty name, insulting all the Italians, even if one ran into you."

"All right," said George magnanimously. "That Italian kid was riding along as if he owned the whole street and ran right into me. It wasn't funny."

"Now tell me," said his mother; "what did you do?"

"Called him some names."

"Such as?"

George's eyes lowered. "Well, I used that bad word."

"I don't understand," said his mother, "what this boy's being Italian had to do with his riding that bicycle or knocking you down with it. Suppose you explain to me why his being an Italian figures in this."

After some patient discussion George agreed that when angered by a personal incident he would avoid mentioning the group name of the offending party. Unsavory nicknames for groups were to have no place in his vocabulary.

In this instance the boy on the bicycle was guilty of carelessness and of inflicting undeserved injury. Yet because his group was unfavorably mentioned he became a "Victimian."

You ask, "What is a Victimian?" A Victimian is an individual whose conduct is appraised by others, not only on its intrinsic merit, but also on the fact that he is a member of a certain racial or religious group. In its restricted sense, "Victimian" means a racial or religious group habitually disesteemed and mistreated because of prejudice. In its widest sense, Victimian means anyone who in a particular situation and even for a moment is wronged because of racial or religious prejudice. A Victimian is psychologically related to the non-existing Danireans, Pireneans, and Wallonians. The mistreatment and the abuse he suffers result more—and often altogether—from antipathy against his group than from any fault of his own. He is at the receiving end of racial, ethnic, or religious hostility. In this book I shall refer to Victimians when the advice to be given in regard to a situation would be essentially the same, regardless of the group membership of the victim. The race or religion of a mistreated person will be furnished when needed to make the episode intelligible.

You doubtless remember the furore that reverberated from Washington, D. C., a few years ago when Marian Anderson was denied the use of Constitution Hall for a recital. Her fame, magnificent voice, and distinguished musicianship should have opened any concert hall to her. Yet the Daughters of the American Revolution, owners of the hall, refused to allow Miss Anderson to sing there. This humiliating injustice was not because of personal lack of character or want of artistic ability on the part of the Negro contralto. Racial segregation in our national capital made Miss Anderson a Victimian in this instance. In other localities she is welcome in all of the concert halls. The *place* is often a determining factor in respect to prejudice. A Victimian in one section of the country is often not a Victimian in another, and identical Victimians do not receive identical treatment in all localities.

Perhaps you think that native white Protestants in our country are never cast in the Victimian role. But even members of that group occasionally encounter prejudice against themselves. The majority group is composed of sub-groups, which are not free of intolerance toward members of other sub-groups within the main category. Moreover, members of minority groups are not always kindly in their judgments or reactions toward larger groups and sometimes make individuals of the dominant groups feel the slings and blows of intolerance. Indeed it would be difficult to find an individual anywhere who might not, in some circumstance, find himself cast as a Victimian.

Robert W., born in Boston, recently returned from military service, had never encountered serious prejudice. When his profession took him to a new locality he purchased a home, not expecting any objection to himself or his family. A few days after he had occupied the house he was shocked by a scrawled note thrust under his front door. It read, "Get out or we'll make trouble for you. We don't want your kind here." This might have happened to anyone of any racial or religious origin. This happened to a white Protestant whose family had resided in New England for more than a century and whose presence in a backward section of the deep South was resented by a few crackpots still fighting the Civil War. Where phobias and resentments are rampant the personal character of the individual victim does not elicit the good reactions he deserves.

Robert encountered animosity only because he had been born at some distance from the community to which he had moved. He had become a Victimian.

Robert's wife, who had discovered the note, became terrified. She wanted to sell the house and move out of the reach of those who had sent the warning. Her husband, however, was not the faint-hearted kind.

"Wish I'd found this instead of you," he told her. "Get it out of your mind and leave it to me. Let me have the *whole* worry on this. Say nothing about it and let me tackle the problem."

Robert mentioned the matter to none of his acquaintances or associates. He did not want to make them think of him as a Victimian. He called at police headquarters. "What do you make of this that was put under my door last night?" he asked the police captain.

The captain's brow puckered as he read and reread the scrawl. "Could be most anything," he said, "but I wouldn't take it too seriously. Probably it's a kid's prank."

"Probably. But my wife's upset. She wants to move away."

"I understand," said the policeman kindly, "but don't make this public, at least not now. We can handle it better if you don't. We'll be watching your house every minute. Don't even think of moving."

Robert turned grim. "I'm certainly not moving," he said doggedly, "unless you tell me the case is hopeless and that the amount of bigotry is so great I can't overcome it."

The episode was handled calmly. In a few days of quiet inquiry the two culprits—young idlers—were apprehended. Robert kept his home and continued to live in it without further threats or alarms.

Such cases as Robert's illustrate a fact too easily overlooked by most of us—that we are all at some time Victimians, that actually or potentially racial and religious prejudice threatens everyone. All of us have a direct personal stake in eliminating prejudice. We need not ask for whom the bell of bigotry tolls. It tolls for you, for me, for everyone, as long as people anywhere are treated as Victimians.

CHAPTER 3

Why We All Live in a Mental Swamp

The dictionary provides an adequate definition of prejudice: "leaning toward one side of a question from other considerations than those belonging to it; an opinion or leaning adverse to anything without just grounds or before sufficient knowledge." None of us believes that it is fair or even justifiable to form unjust judgments against whole groups of people; all of us agree that it is especially reprehensible to injure people wantonly. Why, then, is prejudice so prevalent? There is certainly no one simple answer. The reasons for group prejudice range from such innocent things as fumbling and unrealistic attempts at generalizing about whole groups of people to deliberate knavery on the part of provocateurs.

Our thinking about groups as such is crude and sloppy. We regard them with an affection or with a dislike which bears little or no relation to real merit or demerit. Someday any intelligent person taking a social-distance test, when asked whether he would admit Chinese to his country (or Catholics, Negroes, Protestants, etc.) will reply, "Some, yes, and some, no, depending upon each individual's character." Similarly the question whether he would be willing to have members of such groups as classmates or as neighbors will bring the answer, "Some, yes, and some, no, depending upon the qualities of the individual." Thus far practically every college student to whom this social-distance test has been given has furnished blanket answers which seem to be based on the shallow presumption that all members of each group deserve to be treated alike regardless of their personal qualities. The answers are doubly absurd because practically all who have been tested in American universities say that they would welcome "Americans" as roommates. Yet some say they would not accept "Jewish Americans" or "Catholic Americans" or "Negro Americans" or "Mexican Americans" as roommates. All of these are Americans! The way we use group names is in many instances highly confusing. We are all prone to speak of "the—s" when we should say "some—s."

How unwittingly we act under the influence of such stereotypes was demonstrated by the lady in this incident: Victor Chit-ai Hoo, a member of the staff of the United Nations, was invited to a meeting at 610 Fifth Avenue, New York. Dr. Hoo misunderstood the message and arrived at Room 610 of the Waldorf-Astoria Hotel where a woman opened the door, revealing a small hotel bedroom. Dr. Hoo, realizing instantly that he had made an error, started to withdraw but the woman ushered him in. She went to the rear of the room, took a bundle out of a closet, and handed it to Dr. Hoo.

He asked, "What is this, please?"

"Why, the laundry, of course," she replied.

Puzzled for a moment, Dr. Hoo bowed graciously and said, "In your country many Chinese are laundrymen, but not *all* Chinese are laundrymen."

The common practice of discussing each permanent group as though it were a distinct, complete little entity set apart creates endless mischief. By such reasoning millions of people are assumed to be as closely related as if they were members of one family, living in the same house, sharing one another's thoughts and minding one another's business. They are assumed to be fully responsible for one another even though, in reality, none of them is personally acquainted with even one per cent of the others. The fact that members of the group are keen economic competitors and that the groups are split into hostile factions on many questions is completely overlooked. In our thinking about each group, we often ignore the fact that within the group there are different social and cultural levels. We seem to be entirely unaware that there are vast ranges of difference between members of each group. We rely on false and misleading stereotypes. We judge people according to preconceived notions that may fit neatly into cartoons but have no place in a scale of values by which we live.

People do not say, "Oh, you bought a chair? It must be upholstered; chairs are upholstered." Nor would they say, "A dress? It must be cotton; dresses are made of cotton." Sane human beings do not make absurd generalizations about impersonal objects. They make generalizations, to be sure, but not unreasonable ones. But we *do* make the most outrageous generalizations about groups of people. The merits and demerits of our fellow men, the virtues, vices, and characteristics of groups embracing millions of individuals—are predicated on absurd and unwarranted generalities.

Mr. Brown, an American, had accepted the invitation of an Englishman to dine at a restaurant with five of the Englishman's friends. Seated near by were three men, obviously of Anglo-Saxon stock, who had evidently indulged overmuch in alcohol. Nothing was said about it at Brown's table. Despite the noise from the other table Brown's companions did not raise their voices. Brown was enjoying himself fully.

While dessert was being served, two people walked by, talking more loudly than necessary to hear each other.

"A couple of loud Jews," Brown remarked. "Why can't they behave like other fellows?"

His host smiled pleasantly. "You mean like those three men over there who certainly are not Jews?"

"Oh no," said Brown with irritation, "I mean like the other people here."

"You mean like us at this table?"

"Well, yes, of course," said Brown. "Why can't Jews conduct themselves the way we do?"

"Maybe Jews do," said the host, "if you must generalize. You are the only non-Jew at this table."

We inevitably draw conclusions about whole groups, of course, and not all of them are counterfeit. Certain things can rightfully be said about the culture, customs, institutions, and modes of living of various racial and religious groups. People do belong to such groups. They are influenced in some ways by their group affiliations. There *are* legitimate generalizations about groups, but to recognize whether any particular one is right or spurious, justified or unjustified, requires considerable thought and information, as well as the ability to weigh many factors in the scale of good judgment.

In Plainfield, New Jersey, a public forum was held in the auditorium of a Protestant church. A prominent author brilliantly discussed the need for world organization based on democratic principles. A question period followed, during which the speaker enunciated his views even more persuasively. As the discussion drew to a close, one listener arose. "It's all very well," he said, "for you to talk this way and most of us here certainly agree with you, but what about the Catholics? They won't go along with us or accept these ideas."

"I am a Roman Catholic," replied the speaker, "a devout Catholic. My standing in the church is excellent. I cannot assure you that all Catholics will agree with my views, but neither can you assure me that every Protestant agrees with yours."

Prejudices occasionally arise from personal experiences with members of a certain group. The dislike based on an incident involving one or several members of a group is transferred to millions of members of the group whom one has never met. Here the prejudiced person is deceived by his own "association of ideas." More often, however, a prejudice is not initiated by personal experience. It is imbibed from other prejudiced persons. Many of those most prejudiced against Jews have never met one. Nowhere in the United States are Catholics more disliked than in certain rural areas where there are no Catholics. On practically all tests of opinion among Americans the Turks have received one of the worst ratings, despite the fact that most Americans have never met a Turk and know practically nothing about Turks. The mere fact that the term "the terrible Turk" has been coined and sticks so readily in the human mind may be largely responsible for this unjustified aversion.

Some prejudices are based on historical antagonisms passed on and preserved through generations, even for many centuries. There is the story of two little children, Herman and Edith Cohen, who had associated with their Christian neighbors on the best of terms until one Sunday afternoon when they met with sudden hostility. As they approached some of the other children they were rebuffed.

"You can't play with us any more," they were told bluntly.

"Why not?" they asked in bewilderment.

"Because we learned in Sunday-school this morning that you Jews killed Jesus."

The Cohen children were appalled. They conferred for several minutes, unable to find any explanation of what had occurred. They were sure no member of their family had committed such a crime. Finally they hit upon an answer as good as any which might occur to youngsters who had never before heard this accusation. Herman approached the others and offered what he considered a plausible explanation.

"Please," he pleaded, "we didn't kill Jesus. It must have been some other Jewish children. Maybe it was the family next door."

A more informed person could have replied that crucifixion was a Roman form of execution and was never employed by Jews. But aside from details of fact one does wonder why the crucifixion story is taught by some Christian educators in a manner that stigmatizes people of today for a tragedy of nineteen centuries ago.

To trace the origins of every extraordinary bit of racial and religious prejudice would take us far afield. In one instance it may have had its roots in a mother's attempts to obtain obedience by frightening a child with "the Chinese bogeyman." In another it may have been an inferiority complex seeking compensation. It may have been the sneering tone with which parents spoke the name of a group, or something read in a storybook. Discovering how individuals absorb their various prejudices is an intricate job for psychologists. The sources of the infection are so deeply hidden that rarely can an adult recall the moment when he first acquired an aversion toward a certain group.

Once a prejudiced opinion is adopted by an individual, the prejudice perpetuates itself, blinding the bigot to everything that might weaken his prejudice and steering his attention to everything that strengthens it. A prejudiced man overlooks or ascribes to *human* conduct the misdeeds of members of his own group. Anything *praiseworthy* done by a member of the disliked group is considered the act of that *individual*. As soon, however, as something objectionable about a member of the condemned group comes to his attention, the prejudiced person extends the blame to *all* members of that group and becomes the more intolerant.

That prejudgments about groups can be more potent than reality itself is demonstrated by "serial reproduction" through such experiments as the following:

A large placard is set up in the front of a room—in this instance a drawing of a subway station, where one man is sprawled on a bench and another is reading a newspaper. The most prominent figure is a white man who holds an old-fashioned straight razor with the blade open. A Negro is also prominent in the picture. His hands are empty. The audience studies the card until they know what is on it, then the placard is put out of sight. Five or six persons who have not seen the drawing are called in, one at a time. The first to enter is told accurately what was on the card. He tells it to the second; the second to the third; the third to the fourth; and so on. Inevitably one of the five or six who has not seen the picture informs the next person that the Negro is holding the open razor. Though some details fade out, in all of the subsequent retellings the Negro with the razor remains, despite the fact that in the picture *the white man* held the razor. The actual picture evaporates and the groundless idea that a Negro is more likely to hold an open razor than a white man prevails.

A Turkish gentleman was brought to a social gathering and introduced to an elderly woman.

"They tell me you are a Turk," said the matron.

"I am," replied the Turkish citizen.

"Where's your fez?" asked the lady.

"I don't wear a fez," was the reply.

Thereupon she smiled knowingly. "You can't fool me into believing you're a Turk. You're not a Turk or you'd wear a fez."

The dictionary definition of a "fez" is "a form of felt or cloth cap, usually red and having a tassel, *formerly* worn as the national headdress of the Turks." But to one who learned in childhood that Turks wear fezzes, and who is impervious to facts, the fez remains the one essential feature of Turkish identity. Similarly when prejudiced persons meet members of some group who have none of the objectionable characteristics alleged about their group, the reaction of the prejudiced is, "You're not typical of the group. You're an exception." The hard core of prejudice remains despite the very best evidence that it is unjustified.

Prejudice makes people unwilling to meet Victimians socially, much as a preconceived dislike of Limburger cheese will keep one from tasting it. The prejudiced not only think they know all the pertinent facts but are also determined that nothing shall change their impressions. They are like the fellow who said, "I am glad that I dislike cabbage, because if I didn't dislike it I would eat cabbage and might even enjoy eating it. And it would certainly be awful for me to eat it because I hate it like poison."

The tenacious grip of prejudice on the mind and hearts of men is indicated by even the brief diagnosis we have made of its relation to the individual. But the social aspects of prejudice and its offshoot, discrimination, offer even more startling proof of the virulence and endurance of this mental blight. The very root questions that plague every practical and forward-looking person—How shall we keep children free of prejudice when their parents instill their own intolerant attitudes? How shall we teach youngsters to eschew prejudice when their teachers are often not free of prejudice? How shall we prevent the new generation from becoming infected by their environment?—these and scores of similar questions imply a tacit recognition that society itself is a breeding ground for the contagion.

When prejudice against an out-group has once rooted itself in the life of a community, social pressures make it increasingly difficult to resist it. These pressures are sometimes the most direct and primitive—harsh demands, dire threats, and brutal physical violence. A sheriff in a town in an infected area, when asked why it was impossible to persuade witnesses at a lynching to testify against the perpetrators, replied, "Because they know that anybody who takes part in a lynching would also kill an informer."

Usually, however, it is not necessary to resort to violence to force acceptance of the attitudes of a dominant in-group. The threat, even the implied threat, of excluding non-conformists from a part in community life is usually sufficient to enforce at least a passive acquiescence. Even when the prejudiced group is not numerically superior, there are often effective ways of forcing the more tolerant majority to bow to their demands. In effect, the prejudiced assert their position by saying, "Either you will respect our convictions, or we'll break up the game." The threat of non-co-operation or outright hostilities frequently preserves the remnants of prejudice against the will of the majority.

A city official was inviting seven men to discuss a certain civic project at lunch. The third man he called, a Mr. Dwight, asked who would be present. The commissioner gave the names of the six others he had in mind. One of them, Lucas, was a Victimian.

"I've never eaten at the same table with one of Lucas' people," said Dwight, "and I don't intend to."

"But Lucas is a splendid person," the commissioner protested. "Surely you have no objection to him personally."

"He's all right, but I'm not eating with him. Just count me out of this."

Recalling the incident later, the commissioner said, "If I had already called Lucas I would have stuck to my guns and left Dwight out. But I had not yet phoned Lucas, and Dwight was in a position to do much more for the project than Lucas could. I pleaded with Dwight to change his mind, but to no avail. Finally I yielded. All except Dwight would have been happy to dine with Lucas. But what happened? Five of us were outvoted, as it were, by one prejudiced person."

Kurt Lewin, who made brilliant contributions to the study of human relationships, found that "many stereotypes and dislikes are anchored not so much in the individual's personality as in groups to which the individual belongs." Because his group has acquired a relatively superior position, the individual may find it possible to disesteem or mistreat another group. These social divisions often have their origins in historical processes. In some instances it was conquest which produced dominance in one group and subservience in another. American Indians were the victims of conquest and American Negroes, too, since slavery was a form of conquest. Time of migration, economic position, and dozens of other factors have likewise created and perpetuated group inequalities on American soil.

Control of the social mechanisms makes it possible for the dominant group to stamp the disadvantaged group as inferior. The suppressed are relegated to "their place" in the social order and are said to be happiest "in their own place"—a very lowly place where humiliation, squalor, and ignorance are ostensibly the handmaidens of happiness. Adverse generalizations strengthen the impression that all of the members of a disadvantaged racial or religious group have the same objectionable traits. They are pictured as lazy, selfish, slovenly, impoverished, cowardly, rude, boisterous, avaricious, drunken, dishonest, hideous, cruel, murderous, moronic, or otherwise obnoxious. Since they are presumably so base and so inferior they ought not to expect to be treated on a plane of parity with the "superior group."

The elaboration and preservation of this fraud are readily accomplished because the channels of communication are largely controlled by members of the prestige group. Literature, art, and other media of expression are dominated by them. Laws, social customs, and community mores are determined to a great extent by those who have initial economic and political dominance. In all of these media the counterfeit concepts which differentiate the "superior" from the "inferior" groups are—by usage and reiteration—inculcated as self-evident truths.

In a thoroughly democratic society group inequalities would be unthinkable. But they do exist and make their deep impress upon us, upon our fellow Americans, and upon the world. In ten thousand subtle ways we are guided into the belief that there is a prestige group, socially superior and far more admirable than the others. By birth, faith, or color half the people of the United States cannot belong to the "superior" class.

Why is it that among the numberless nameless smokers in the cigarette advertisements there is never a colored person? Colored people use cigarettes. They buy and use all of the incredible variety of products manufactured in the United States. But advertisers always and everywhere seek to establish for their products the prestige and social acceptability which they assume will insure greater sales and increased profits. To do that they connect their wares with clearly recognizable members of the dominant prestige group, even when they themselves are members of a minority. Unwittingly, perhaps, but nevertheless in a very real sense they are helping to perpetuate racial myths.

Discrimination is the outward expression of the unwillingness of people to accord genuinely fair and equal treatment to groups other than their own. Having pointed to this primary fact some guileless individuals believe they have thrust a fatal dagger into the dragon of prejudice. That is naïveté at its worst. When have people been unwilling to accept unfair social advantages? To combat prejudice and to eliminate discrimination we need to recognize these phenomena as subtle tools for securing and maintaining superior positions for dominant groups. But we dare not assume that unjust modes of thought and codes of conduct will be abandoned because, forsooth, they are decried as instruments of special privilege! We must find better strategies. Prejudice is something of a Circe, with the deceptions of Proteus and the resilience of Anteus.

Overlooking the intricate nature of prejudice or imagining that one or two specific countermeasures is all that is needed to uproot and destroy it makes the prospect of eliminating prejudice appear simple indeed. But such thinking inevitably leads to disillusion. It is far better to know the sorry truth about prejudice, to recognize its ramifications, and to combat it with a whole barrage of counter-methods, each at the right time and in the right place. The uninformed who batter blindly against prejudice often resemble the man from the backwoods who spent a night in a hotel room trying to blow out the electric light. Prejudice is a stubborn, obdurate foe. We must not underrate its tenacity.

Were we to trace on a chart the manifestations of racial, religious, and ethnic prejudice as they wind in and out through our society we would picture something like a badly tangled skein of twine. Unwinding and untangling a heap of knotted string requires patience, persistence, and deftness; but force and short-tempered impulsiveness are likely to complicate the task. And so it is with prejudice. We must be able to move first in one direction and a moment later, perhaps, in the opposite. Undoing one tangle loosens another. Untying a knot here makes it possible to unravel something else there. Progress at one point facilitates progress at another. Some parts will never be unwound until we have first uncoiled others.

In dealing with prejudices which are woven into the lives of millions of people we must learn to resort to many intricate measures, to analyze the elements of the shifting scene accurately, to consider each move in relation not only to the immediate problem but to the total situation. Our ultimate success depends upon our fashioning weapons to accomplish as much as possible as swiftly as possible without destroying the gains already achieved.

CHAPTER 4

Beware of Quicksands

We have discussed the nature of prejudice, indicated the climate in which it flourishes, and stressed the importance of properly assessing its strength and durability. We have tried to develop a systematized understanding of our problems, an understanding essential for effective work against the multitudinous evils of prejudice.

On the road to the elimination of prejudice lie scores of pitfalls for the unwary. Too many of us, anxious to get on with the work before us, brashly assume that awareness of a bad situation is sufficient to steer us to success. It isn't. Before we can cope properly with the complex problems confronting us we must learn to recognize the ambushes. The enthusiast who rushes into a booby trap occasionally seems heroic but usually does more harm than good.

Let's examine the most common of these traps, one into which most of us readily fall. It is built on the familiar spurious generalizing we have already discussed. This is the way it works. Someone makes an outrageous, slurring remark about a racial or religious group. The statement is so obviously untrue that it irks a fair-minded person. He yields to the temptation to argue. Soon he finds himself deeply involved in a weary wrangle to disprove whatever fabrication his opponent injects into the conversation.

The bigot remarks (for example) that Victimians are lazy.

"That is not so," replies our friend. "Many of them are not lazy."

"There may be a few exceptions," says the bigot, "but most of them are lazy."

Then ensue claims and counterclaims about the extent of laziness among Victimians until the prejudiced person shifts to a new attack. "Anyhow," he says, "they're dishonest."

Sooner or later in the course of a prolonged debate of this sort new scurrilities will be injected. The person who is prejudiced against the group is not a simple, misguided person who unfortunately happens to believe just one or two unfavorable things about the group. He has a position he will stubbornly defend. Having a predilection for thinking ill of the group, he has ready a large quiver of poisoned arrows. If those prove insufficient, he can invent new canards on the spur of the moment to vindicate his antipathy. As long as the fair-minded debater handles the problem as though it were an intellectual pursuit of facts, he is at a hopeless disadvantage.

How an astute person handles a prejudiced statement is illustrated by the reaction of an Episcopal minister to a letter from a disgruntled soldier which was received by one of his parishioners some six months after V-E day. The soldier alleged that his regiment was being detained unnecessarily in service abroad but that twenty-five men had, by pulling wires, obtained their release and returned to the States. These twenty-five, according to the complainant all belonged to the same (Victimian) group.

The woman who brought the letter to the minister said, "This is obviously untrue. Army officials would certainly not be guilty of such favoritism as to single out members of one minority group and send them home while retaining all the others. Let's get the facts about this from the Army and prove to this soldier that he is wrong. Then we can publicize the story and show the world what nonsense some people believe. It will warn others against believing such rumors."

"No," said the minister, "let's not get the facts. Whatever they are, they are *irrelevant*. Even if it were true that twenty-five individuals who happened to belong to one racial or religious group did something as objectionable as this, I would still insist that their conduct be considered that of individuals and not charge it against a group of which they are an insignificant fraction."

After a thoughtful moment the woman said, "Yes, I can agree with the idea of not blaming the group. But this story is so preposterous. Why shouldn't we just explode it and get rid of it that way?"

"I'm trying to keep out of a trap," replied the minister. "How can I in the same breath furnish the facts or attempt to disprove them without implying that if twenty-five individuals really did this thing a valid accusation could properly be made against their entire group? What if there *were* twenty-five men who gained unfair advantage? What if the majority of them happen to be Italians, Swedes, Nisei, Baptists, Presbyterians, or something else? What defense would I have for the large innocent group of people who are called by the same group name as those individuals? Millions of innocent people are going to be tarred as they don't deserve to be. The only way to beat this kind of talk is to insist that it's *wrong* to connect the names of racial and religious groups with individual misdeeds. If people cannot learn *that*, there is no hope of putting a stop to intolerance. We must keep on trying to make it clear that racial and religous groups cannot be held accountable, by using group names, for objectionable things that some individuals of all groups do. Otherwise we shall be going around forever in circles. Why say anything that deepens the impression that it *does* matter to which groups offenders belong? I refuse to do that."

The temptation to try to disprove a prejudiced untruth with fact is usually great. But the impulse is almost certain to lead into a quicksand. Perhaps the following example will indicate why it is better to refrain from attempting to refute certain types of calumny.

In the autumn of 1946, when stock-market prices were falling, I received a letter from a friend in the Midwest who was troubled by a rumor. Some of his respected neighbors were saying that a nationally prominent Victimian had advised his coreligionists to sell their shares of stock in order to bring the political party then in power into disfavor. My friend asked that I obtain a denial by the man alleged to be giving that advice.

I replied that this was the first I had heard of the fairy tale, which was probably born in a barroom of my friend's city. The one way to bring it to the attention of everyone in America was for the maligned man to issue a denial. His prominence would make it certain that any interesting statement he made would appear in every newspaper in the land. Though not one editor of a decent newspaper had published the rumor itself, every journalist would rightly feel that a denial merited publication. We had a choice of having a few hundred people hear the rumor—and believe it or not as they wished—or having a hundred million people debate the matter. In the latter case a few millions would surely say, "A man who did this thing would certainly not admit it. Where there's smoke there's fire."

I advised my friend to tell his associates that if anyone mentioned this rumor to them they should ask "Who told you that?" and "What proof did he give you?" Trace the rumor, I advised, to its source or as nearly as possible to the source, but issue no public denial. "You might also suggest that the fall in stock prices may be due to some astrologer's having told his clients to sell stock. A silly rumor helps to crowd out a more sinister one."

This rumor died quietly and completely. It never reached you. Had the traduced man issued a denial, it would never have been forgotten. Each appearance of his name in the news thereafter would have awakened that nefarious rumor in some memories. He could never have lived down the denial of something which, undenied, never hurt him or his group. To this day this highly honored man has no inkling that there ever was such a rumor. That is good. He needs every minute at his disposal for the great public service he is rendering.

That an attempt to overcome vicious rumors by broadcasting both the rumors and their refutations defeats its own purpose was demonstrated by studies made of "radio rumor clinics," which were intended to curb malicious gossip hurtful to the war effort. Well-meaning persons and organizations sponsored the rumor clinics. The findings of the Office of War Information led to the decision that the "radio rumor clinics" should be discontinued. "The three programs studied," it was reported, "actually planted twenty-seven rumors for every rumor properly debunked." The conclusion was: "When you deny any specific hate rumor, you fail to spike the actual hatred which created it, but only shift that hatred to other 'facts' and other rumors . . . Hate rumors, particularly, *should never be repeated even to deny them.*"

Some people will never understand that calumnies can be canceled more successfully without mentioning them. That is, nonetheless, true. Rumors that "the British are letting the Americans and French fight this war for them" were by no means ignored. They were never repeated by British and American radio commentators, speakers, and writers. Our spokesmen used the positive technique. They gave convincing facts and figures about British men and women in the armed services, their losses and their sacrifices. That did overcome the Nazi propaganda. The positive rejoinder is known to every successful merchant who realizes that his best reply to insulting reports circulated by displeased or unreasonable customers is to keep up a stream of favorable information. A department store does not advertise, "It is being said that our beds are lumpy and uncomfortable, but that is a lie." The positive approach harps upon the virtues of the beds (or other merchandise) and makes no reference to the slurs.

Every printed denial that members of a group are swindlers and cheats can only result in besmirching their reputation, regardless of what favorable things may be said in the discussion. An argument as to whether they are benefactors and idealists will elevate their standing, regardless of what criticism is offered. *It is the frame of reference that counts.* Is the group being judged as candidates for laurels or as candidates for jail cells? Positive information sets a favorable background. Canards and their refutations invariably provide a hurtful frame of reference. You can never blot out an ugly stereotype by tugging at a few of its whiskers. It is always possible and wiser to superimpose a better and an admirable picture.

Pointing out the wrongfulness of spurious generalizations is one method of dealing with prejudiced talk. There are others. Later in this book further reasons will be given for avoiding the "disproof technique." The point here is to recognize that we are on much firmer ground when we attack prejudice at its roots—exposing the fallacy of the bigot's *kind of thinking*—than when we try to destroy a leaf here or there in the form of some prejudiced assertion.

Alfred Tennyson gave splendid advice when he said, "Cut prejudice across the grain." If you accept the premise that a man is entitled to a prejudice if he can show that some members of a certain group have a certain fault, you are trying to cut with the grain. When you cut across the grain you deny the right of anyone to condemn whole groups because of the faults that *some* of their members have. To say that Victimians are, for example, lazy is to speak an untruth. But neither can one truthfully say that "Victimians are not lazy." Cut across the grain. Say "Some are lazy and some are not."

You would not spend an hour proving that "politicians are not liars," unless you were a politician—and one lacking diplomatic sense. You'd say "Some are and some aren't and it's absurd to regard them as alike." If your opponent then said "Well, most politicians are liars," you'd say "Even if you could prove that most of them are liars, which is highly doubtful, what good can such a statement do? How would you know what each one was, unless you judged him according to *his own* character?"

The thing that is wrong about prejudiced statements is that the generalizing involved is spurious, unfair, hurtful, and unjustifiable. Cut it across the grain. Deal with it as an unfair *type* of statement rather than as a misstatement of fact.

When prejudice goes against your grain, cut it against the grain.

Maintaining good will and respect for all groups within our society requires that every one of us condemn a scoundrel and resent the activities of a malefactor without blaming the group to which he belongs. Fortunately we have made considerable progress in this direction. When a crime is committed the press of today ordinarily does not mention the criminal's religious affiliation, unless, perchance, he is a clergyman or holds office in a religious institution. It is now generally assumed by journalists that a man's religious group is to be spared unwarranted ignominy. In this area, at least, there is a genuine improvement of standards. In others, however, the record is abominable. When will newspapers cease to mention the race and ethnic grouping of persons who commit crimes? The law of the land is exactly the same for all offenders; the crime is neither more nor less heinous because the culprit is white or black, Mexican or Indian, Caucasian or Chinese. The odium cast upon other members of the criminal's race is a rank injustice. If we must have the mention of race, let's be fair. Let's say "Jim Smith, white, raped a white woman today." Give the other peoples a chance to enjoy the same sneering superiority that some white people seem to obtain from the mention of the race of non-white scoundrels.

The question of group responsibility is for many sincere men and women a most troublesome one. How, they ask, can any group refuse to accept blame for the misdeeds of an individual member of that group and at the same time take credit for the work of its more distinguished members? Isn't this a damaging inconsistency? We do not hold a university accountable when some graduate commits a crime, although universities do, in a measure, influence the ethical standards of their students. We know that no university is in a position to guarantee virtue in all of its students and alumni. Yet Harvard may well be proud of distinguished Harvard men. We would not begrudge any university a measure of pride when alumni win public acclaim. Cannot we let the same principles apply to racial and religious groups? Are they not expected to build the highest standards they can and bring the best influences to bear upon their members? Should they not hold up as examples to all members of their group the most admirable persons they can—whether of their own group or of others? Since no honest observer can deny that in our society today group reputations do exist and do color our thinking, we can hardly deny any group the right to do its utmost to make its reputation an honored one. But when a renegade appears, let only those groups who have no sinners among them cast stones at the one which includes the transgressor.

As long as people form hurtful stereotypes and harbor misconceptions we shall have to build esteem for these groups. As long as various groups are admired or despised according to group images and stereotypes, we shall have to improve the images. Those who foment hatred and wrath against racial and religious groups are on the side of mischief. Those who contribute to respect and good will for maligned groups by spotlighting admirable individuals are on the side of the angels. They are promoting good.

Why should Polish-parented children moving into a new neighborhood in the twentieth century be treated better because a century and a half ago, long before they were born, a Polish nobleman gave his life for the cause of American independence? Did they influence Pulaski or assist him? And yet the mother, who brought Pulaski to the attention of children who might be prejudiced against her children because of their Polish ancestry, acted correctly. If her children were to be judged and treated on the unwarranted basis of their ethnic origin, what could this mother do but improve esteem for her family on that very basis? And since the group had its heroes, why not display them? If folks insist on judging our worth according to the character of our great-great-uncles, we are constrained to furnish testimonials of those buried grandees.

Sincere and intelligent people are sometimes misled by the hoary statement that prejudice survives *only* because it benefits the dominant group. *If it were true* that through prejudice the majority makes a net profit at the expense of others, we would have only two means of eliminating intolerance. One would be to appeal to the conscience or to the mercy of the prejudiced. The other would be a continuous war in which the oppressed would battle by whatever means they could find against the intolerant. The first method can be used effectively only with those who are unselfish. Appeals to sympathy win only the sympathetic. The second method, combat, would in many instances be bitter and bloody. We need other methods stronger than exhortation and less destructive than warfare. We need to demonstrate to the prejudiced that they are inflicting self-injury.

The benefits of intolerance are as much an illusion as are the "benefits" of drunkenness. The blight of intolerance robs a community and all who live in it of the potential productivity of its citizenry. What happens when thirty men who could become two truck drivers, six bricklayers, two electricians, two plumbers, five carpenters, three plasterers, two painters, and eight unskilled, but dependable, laborers are deprived, because of racial and religious prejudice, of the opportunity to learn any trade and to hold regular jobs? Who profits when some of them become public charges and others drift into crime? Whose gain is it when the total earnings of these thirty men (representing what they produce) is less than that of two truck drivers?

These men and their families will live in squalor, incapable of building such homes for themselves as they might have built in a few years. The houses they would have erected for others remain unbuilt. The taxes they would have furnished are not available to improve public services. Their children become delinquent. The public pays for their crime, for their apprehension, and for maintaining them in penal institutions. Thirty street sweepers, pushing their old-fashioned brooms, cannot keep the streets as clean as two men driving electrically powered street sweepers. Thirty men with picks and shovels cannot accomplish as much as one man on a bulldozer. Using men for menial work, merely because intolerance forbids them to do more skilled and more fruitful work, is a crime against the society that must sustain the loss. The city in which they live is the poorer because of them, instead of the richer.

Those who believe that they ride in better saddles because they ride roughshod over the weak are anxious to maintain the situations which provide them with illusory gains. Appeals, based on non-existent tenderness of heart, serve only to make the intolerant more sure that they gain when they cramp others by discriminatory practices. They must be shown that the insecurity they create undermines their own security and that the injuries they cause others are hurtful to themselves.

About four years ago in an automobile factory an unauthorized strike was threatened because several Negro employees were about to be upgraded to jobs of higher classification. There was threatening talk on the part of a clique of white men who insisted that they would walk out rather than work in the same category with the Negroes or as their subordinates.

Into the factory strode one of the top officials of the United Automobile Workers. He said bluntly, "These Negroes have been paying dues to our union. They have helped to strengthen the union when we needed them. What are you proposing to do now? Drive them and other Negroes out of the union to form a pool of strike breakers on whom the employers can draw when work becomes slack and when they decide to break the union?"

The Negroes were upgraded the next day. No one walked off the job and there was no difficulty. That was a most effective way to handle an explosive situation. The dissatisfied group was shown that for what seemed to be a personal advantage—a momentary gain, at best—they were laying the groundwork for their own undoing. The old saying is as apt as it is true: "You cannot hold others down in the gutter without staying there with them."

Here and there it appears fashionable to contend that it is only the wealthy and the powerful who are really prejudiced and that the masses are intolerant only to the extent that their "masters" deliberately promote intolerance.

"Prejudice," one theorist will intone, "is purely economic. Racial and religious hatreds are manufactured and used by those in power simply to keep others poor and ignorant so that they will stay subservient."

And others will rightfully agree. "Oh yes," they will say, "there's truth to what you say. There have been instances—Nazism, for example—where social or religious hatred was used by conscience-less reactionaries to gain power for themselves and to exploit the masses."

"Now," our sage theorist will add, "what we must do is line up the masses and let them vote for laws to abolish every kind of discrimination. We need nothing but to pass laws against intolerance. If the public had its way, social and religious prejudice would be wiped out over night."

It is difficult to believe that any person who has ever raised his eyes from the pages of his musty political tract and taken a good look at the world we live in could absorb such buncombe. A glance would certainly convince him that the "public" he imagines simply doesn't exist.

There are many publics. There's the high-minded, unprejudiced public, and the mildly prejudiced public, and the public that hates one group, and the public that hates some other groups, and also a lunatic public whose members can be readily aroused to hate any out-group. To talk about "the public" or "the masses" as though they were one great herd of people, innocent of all prejudice and simply deceived by others, is infantile. Practically all people believe that prejudice against their own group is utterly wrongful, but as yet only a small segment of humanity understands that *all* racial and religious prejudice is bad. Those who grasp this truth must somehow convey it to the others. Unprejudiced folk will be found among the rich and among the poor, among the educated and the uneducated, among the great and the unknown, among those of every religion and of every race. Somehow the unprejudiced must find each other, join hands, and do a tremendous job together—perhaps the most important job on earth—before the evils of intolerance can be banished.

As Robert M. MacIver has written in *The More Perfect Union* (a book I heartily recommend), "The primary attack on discrimination should rally to the cause of national welfare and national unity. It should not uphold the banner of particular groups." In other words, the battle against intolerance should not be conducted as a war between racial and religious groups pitted against each other. Rather, this is a struggle between all those members of all groups who believe in human brotherhood genuinely applied to all against those who think otherwise. Nor is the battle against prejudice a war between certain political parties or economic groups. Anyone who imagines or pretends that the struggle against intolerance can best be won by pitting one class against another will promote class warfare and not brotherhood.

The quicksands on the road to a thoroughly democratic society are many. Our analysis of several of the quagmires shows the advisability of probing beneath surface appearances where prejudice is involved. As we examine other phases of the subject we shall see that even simple situations arise out of complex causes. To cope with the problems created by prejudice we must reckon with factors which are not always apparent.

CHAPTER 5

Dilemmas That Confront Us

You and I are seeking the best ways to cope with prejudices. We now have two major rules which will prove themselves increasingly sound as you experiment with them:

Don't treat canards and scurrilities against a racial, religious, or ethnic group as though they were factual rational accusations requiring ordinary disproof. Cut them across the grain by exposing the unfairness and the irrationality of that kind of thinking which regards groups as though they were composed of identical individuals.

Never be content with showing that the mistreatment of a Victimian group is injurious to the welfare of that group only. Spotlight at every possible opportunity the less apparent damage inflicted by prejudice and discrimination upon the *entire* public, including those who instigate, promote, or harbor the prejudices.

We shall develop other useful rules, but rules of themselves cannot provide sufficient guidance. Rules must be applied with certain understandings and reservations based upon an active awareness of the tricks prejudice plays. By now everyone knows about scapegoating, a process whereby one group is set apart in the public mind as inferior to the others. Scapegoating involves the mistreatment of that group with the sanction of the public at large. But do you know how the scapegoats are led to contribute to their own undoing, how they and their friends help the scapegoating process along? This trick of prejudice we can readily uncover by seeing how

it operated in Germany when the Nazis were deliberately under-
mining German civilization by scapegoating one religious group.

Let's suppose that in 1925 or thereabouts Adolf Hitler had told
the German people that "The Ten Commandments are valid no
longer. Women should be raped. Children ought to be killed in gas
chambers. Innocent people should be beaten, maimed, and starved
to death." What would have happened, had Hitler been so rash?
Of a certainty he would have been immediately recognized as a
madman. The Germans would have been so horrified by his barbar-
ity that he would have acquired very few followers, if any, and
Nazism would have swiftly perished. The line of civilization would
have held firmly against such a barefaced assault upon it.

But civilization in Germany was not attacked by its subverters in
a full-fledged, all-out plunge against it. Shrewdly they at first
worked to make a small crack in it; later they were able to widen
this thin line until it became broad enough to drive millions through
the breach to gruesome death, to devastate the continent. How was
that first crack made?

"It is permissible," the Nazis suggested, "to beat Jews. See, we
beat none but Jews." They acted accordingly and maltreated some
Jews. "Only Jews!" The beatings continued. "See, dear friends, all
others are safe. But to beat Jews is an Aryan duty." What did the
newspapers report of these incidents? "Jews beaten." How was the
outrage discussed everywhere? As a case of *Jews* being beaten. Who
cried most loudly "*Jews* are being beaten?" Jews.

The Nazis knew what they were about. They were cunning.
They injured more and still more Jews, until it became quite a
pastime, while non-Jews shrugged their shoulders, imagining themselves secure. If only Jews were in danger, why should Christian
Germans worry? Were the people of Germany so unusual in this?
Let the average American ask himself how alarmed he becomes
when he hears "Negroes beaten in Harlem—only Negroes." Whites
apparently being safe, how forcefully does it occur to the average
white that not Negro life, but human life, is becoming unsafe?

During November 1945 the newspapers of the world announced
"Jews being beaten in the Argentine. Jewish shops being looted.
Jewish lives endangered." Argentine newspapers and Jewish periodicals emphasized the fact that *Jews* were being injured. The impression given to everyone was that Argentina was not safe for Jews,
but safe enough for others. Might it not be in order to inquire, were

no human beings beaten in the Argentine, were no human lives endangered? Why is a Jewish-owned shop so very different from a Christian-owned shop that its Jewishness sticks out in the hour of looting? Is it because the hooligans and vandals concentrate their criminal tendencies upon Jews? They know what they are about then, the vandals. They know how they can confuse and demoralize their fellow men. But their victims, some of the press, and all of those who remain guileless and unthinking in the face of a devious plot—they do not know what they are about. They play the barbarian's game for him. They help to crack the line of civilization. They shout "Jews, Jews, Jews," or "Mexicans, Mexicans, Mexicans," or "Catholics, Catholics, Catholics." They accept the barbarian's identification of the victims as something apart from the rest of humanity, as though their blood runs a different color, as though it were possible within a mixed population to limit robbery to robbery against Jews, murder to murder of Negroes, looting to looting of one group or another. So long as it is possible to pick out a scapegoat and make the world forget that human beings, part of the human family, are being maltreated, the aggressor will win.

However much the bell ringer for bigotry may rant about the secret domination and power of the racial or religious group against whom he invokes hatred, he is aware that he is trying to frighten the gullible with a bogeyman. He would not dare to attack a truly dominant group. That would net him nothing. The lamb does not assail the tiger. But the tiger, to excuse his ravaging the lamb, may cry, "This fierce beast was about to attack me." Furthermore, as Rudyard Kipling put it, "The bleating of the kid excites the tiger." It is not strength but weakness that encourages cruelty and sadistic attack. To quote Dr. John Slawson, executive vice-president of the American Jewish Committee: "Merely evoking feelings of sympathy carries with it the concomitant impulses of aggression that far outweigh the benefits from sympathetic response."

In the *Survey Graphic* of June 1947 Thomas Sancton wrote, "It is the utter helplessness of the Negro prisoner that invites lynching. He is helpless because he is behind bars. He is helpless because of his color and race in a region which insists that it is an anti-social crime to regard a man of his color as a full human being. His helplessness itself stimulates violence."

How shall we answer the bigot who attacks a minority group? Can it be helpful to the persecuted and misprized to picture them as despised and downtrodden to even greater extent than the facts warrant? Is their status improved by insisting that they are weak, that their enemies are more numerous and powerful than their friends? Or is it by stressing the fact that they do have many friends and allies, that public sentiment is with them, rather than against them, that we build for the oppressed the kind of favorable response that assures security from their intolerant foes?

Does this mean that we should not talk about prejudice, that we must not discuss it publicly? Of course not. On the contrary, we must blast away at intolerance with every *effective* means at our command. Does it mean that we should seek to soften the fact that certain groups are disliked? In some respects, yes! In certain ways exaggerating or even advertising the unpopularity of a group worsens its plight. By crying "Behold the group that has been selected by bigots as an object of dishonor!" we may indeed injure the group.

What is it the anti-Semite wants when he smears "Down with the Jews!" on a store window? That is vandalism. No matter what he has written he has violated the law when he defaces a store window. Does the offender want to be thought of as a common, sneaking vandal? No indeed. He wants it proclaimed that someone —and he hopes that the public will think it is many persons—hates the Jews. What would be the best strategy then? Certainly it would be to apprehend him and punish him for vandalism, an offense which everyone condemns. How about advertising what he wrote on that window and publicizing it in the press? To do that would be to do exactly what the anti-Semite wants. A few people may have seen the defaced window. Many thousands would read of it in the newspapers. The more people to whom his screed is conveyed the better the hater likes it. And mark this well: some who condemn vandalism do not condemn vandalism against Jews. If you want to crack the line of civilization, then emphasize that *not vandalism* but vandalism *against Jews* has been committed.

What is murder? It is the most heinous of all offenses, something that practically everyone excoriates. What is the lynching of a Negro? It is murder plus prejudice. What does advertising a murder, not as a murder, but as the lynching of a Negro do? It leads many to shrug their shoulders and assume that the man was guilty and that it does not concern them anyhow. Juries have freed lynchers after fervent appeals to rid themselves of prejudice in reaching a verdict. Far from being unaware of their prejudice, they have been freely, openly, and unashamedly prejudiced. They do not condemn the killer more severely because he was guilty of both murder and prejudice. On the contrary, they reckon prejudice as a condoning, mitigating factor in the crime.

Prejudice, therefore, is not something which, once pointed out, arouses public wrath and indignation. Murder, robbery, or exploitation arouse the public because the crimes, as crimes, are repellent. But if prejudice has any role in the matter, it is not as something that makes the offense appear more reprehensible. On the contrary, while it makes members of the group to which the injured belongs feel more outraged, the factor of prejudice may lead others to exonerate the culprits or mitigate the extent of their villainy.

Insofar as assaults upon persons and crimes against property are concerned the laws of civilized nations require equal penalty regardless of the race or religion or social condition of the injured. When dealing with such crimes it is not to the advantage of the injured to emphasize in public discussion the group membership of the victims. Regardless of the motive of the culprit, the victim should be portrayed as a human being without any racial or religious distinction. Where, on the other hand, discrimination is directed—as in employment—against certain groups, it is impossible to deal with the matter without involving the factor of prejudice in public discussion.

The scapegoating technique consists of concentrating upon a particular group with every instrument of derision and maltreatment. The public is first made to believe that this group is highly unpopular. With this primary attack there is a parallel one based on the constant refrain "Such unpopularity must be deserved." As the reputation of the group is destroyed by canards and contumely, the growing resentment toward the group becomes the very ground for further resentment. Others are made callous toward the mistreatment of the injured group. The more the group is condemned, the more those who have circulated the scurrilities and participated in defaming and mistreating it become allies of the marauders. And since prejudices inevitably produce spurious justifications, animosity against the scapegoat becomes all the stronger because of this participation.

The incalculable brutality inflicted upon millions of Jews and the suffering of all Christian Germans as a result of Nazism have not

dispelled anti-Semitism. The Nazis did a perfect job of scapegoating.
Nora Waln reports that a German child told her, that "Hitler must
have been a Jew. He got us into the war and he lost the war." The
time to prevent that kind of warped thinking is when scapegoating
of a group is getting under way. We have already seen something
of its subtle trap. Let us examine the snares more closely.

When the public's attention is called to a murderer who has gone
unpunished, they are inevitably indignant. Tell them that young
girls are being snared by white-slavers and there is readiness to stop
that vile practice. Tell them of graft and political corruption that
has been carried on in stealth and the public will demand reform.
You need only expose certain injustices or deficiencies to the public
to arouse strong—sometimes practically unanimous—public sentiment to eradicate the evil. Pointing out the extent to which juvenile
delinquency or malfeasance has grown (to cite two examples) is a
first step in halting these scourges. Exposure has no boomerang
effect. Can the same thing be said about prejudice? Does pointing
out the extent of it have the invariable effect of marshaling the public to attack it?

The public is pretty much like the woman who was listening to
her minister's sermon. He condemned murder.

"Amen!" said the woman fervently.

He railed against gambling.

"Amen!" she repeated audibly.

He denounced smoking.

Again she pronounced a hearty "Amen!"

"And now," said the parson, "I call your attention to another sin,
gossiping about your neighbors, discussing the faults of others."

"Hmph," she muttered. "He ain't preaching any more. He's just
meddling."

Prejudice, like gossiping, is disapproved. But it is indulged in by
so many, and so sanctimoniously justified in the specific instances
where the prejudiced serve as their own judges and jury, that we
often do well to emphasize the evil effect of the offense rather than
to harp upon prejudice itself. If the accent is placed on prejudice
rather than on the malfeasant acts, we defeat the thing that we are
trying to accomplish, the rescuing of innocent victims from recurring
injuries.

When it is possible to drive at a specific goal, to obtain a definite objective, arousing public opinion is extremely valuable. To repeal a Jim Crow law, to pass a fair employment act, to eliminate a restrictive covenant or the like, warrants and in many instances necessitates the marshaling of public support for the task at hand. But simply to stir up a feeling that there is tremendous prejudice against a particular group, without offering the public something concrete to do about it, is quite useless and may even be harmful.

I am reminded of an incident told me by a Jewish gentleman, one of the most distinguished citizens of an Atlantic coast city. He has been for some years a member of the local yacht club. His nephew applied for admission to the same club and was refused. The uncle called upon the president of the club and requested an explanation. "Have you heard," he asked, "anything discreditable about my nephew?"

"No indeed," said the president, "he's one of the finest young men in town."

"That was my own impression," said the uncle. "He has a splendid record in private and public matters. I've been very proud of him. Why, then, was he excluded?"

"I'll tell you," said the president. "We've learned that no Jews are admitted to the yacht clubs of——" (He named two large cities.) "and we believe that though ours is a much smaller club, we're just as good as they are."

Prejudice smacks of snobbery. People are inclined to be as prejudiced as they think their neighbors are. If everyone would awaken tomorrow believing that everyone else welcomes Negroes into his home, an enormous amount of prejudice would vanish overnight.

A belief that prejudice is rampant is not conducive to dissipating it. It is true that a few saints may become more anxious than ever to discriminate against no one if they think there has been a great increase of prejudice. But the average person whose own group is not among the allegedly disliked becomes more cautious than ever about becoming intimate with members of the proscribed groups, lest he share their unpopularity. At the same time members of a group presumed to be disliked, fearing rebuff, often withdraw more closely into their own circle, segregate themselves, and thus do the very things that increase suspicion and prejudice.

Here, then, is Dilemma Number One: If we keep quiet about prejudice, we shall be able to do little if anything to counteract it.

If we advertise the existence of prejudice, especially against a particular group, we abet the scapegoating practice.

It is by no means impossible to solve this dilemma, so long as we are aware of it. We must simply use great care and discretion in avoiding both horns of the dilemma. We need not refrain from bringing certain matters into the open, even vigorously, especially when we have clearly defined what public action should be taken and by what concrete steps wrongs can be corrected. Crying "Wolf, wolf!" on the other hand, when we neither point squarely at the wolf nor tell those whom we alarm how to deal with him, is inadvisable.

Have you ever been asked whether you are "militant" or "conciliatory" in your approach to prejudice? There are those who would insist that you choose one of these attitudes and apply it to all situations. Insofar as they are able to reduce our thinking about intolerance to a simple process of reacting to slogans and catch phrases, these people do immense harm. Those who would persuade us to let our temperaments and emotions, rather than our reason, determine how we are to handle prejudice are certain to injure the cause they think they are serving.

"Militancy" as an ideal in combating prejudice is an absurd fetish. One might as well decide that he is going to educate his children militantly or cure cancer militantly as determine to carry on a struggle against prejudice militantly. There are times when the old fable of the contest between the sun and the wind holds true in regard to prejudice. You recall that the sun and the North Wind saw a man wearing an overcoat and they argued about which could make the man take off his coat. The North Wind blew and blew and the harder he blew the more the man tightened his coat around him and clung to it. Then the sun tried, sent his beams down hotly until the man took off the coat. It is a fine old fable with a fine moral, but it's worth remembering that there are also situations where the wind's force can do what the sun's heat cannot.

A social worker who devotes all of his time to improving group relationships became annoyed by the accusation that his organization is timorous because it is presumably not sufficiently militant. In a discussion with the accuser, the editor of a weekly journal, he pointed out that his organization had brought a prominent and militant liberal to a southern community where there has been considerable prejudice. There was a big turnout and a rip-roaring meeting. "Isn't that militant enough?" he inquired.

The editor sneered at such tactics and pointed out that segregation in the community was still continuing. One wonders by what stroke of militancy anyone could overnight terminate segregation there. One wonders also why anyone should feel that he has to prove that his organization is "militant." Is it the manner of action that is important or the results that are obtained in each instance?

There are a hundred routes by which one cannot get from New York to Chicago for every route that leads from the one place to the other. But when you tell someone who has a predilection for going East that his automobile cannot go from our largest city to our second largest that way, he may tell you that you are an obstructionist preventing his progress, and continue his journey right into the ocean. When you tell a man who has a temperamental preference for one manner of attacking intolerance that, however good his purpose, his plan is wrong, he is prone to say "You believe in doing nothing," and go his own way. The fact that you employ better methods to reach the same goal may not alter his opinion a whit.

In a suburban town the young secretary of an organization established to create better relationships between racial and religious groups discovered that a local Y.M.C.A. did not admit Negroes to membership. Although Negroes were not denied use of the facilities of the institution, it had been customary to enroll only white members. The zealous, well-intentioned but inexperienced young woman called upon officials of the Y.M.C.A. and demanded that they abandon the discriminatory practice. Finding them unwilling to do so, she threatened to picket the building. When friends warned her to be more tactful, she called them "appeasers" and insisted on being "militant."

Her threats angered the Y.M.C.A. leaders, who thereupon became entirely hostile toward her organization. In addition she lost the co-operation of many who thereafter referred to her associates as a "radical bunch that believes in strong-arm methods."

What if that young woman had analyzed the situation and asked, "What is the underlying fault in the relationship of this institution toward Negroes?" She might well have decided that there was an attitude of benevolence on a basis of charity rather than equality. Her task then would have been to change that concept of the relationship. That change could be brought about much more readily by constructive, positive steps than by arguments of a vitriolic nature. Had Negro neighbors asked permission to donate a picture of George Washington Carver or some other outstanding Negro to the Y., that gift could hardly have been refused. The picture could have been hung in an appropriate place and the effect would have been the inclusion of a Negro among those whom the institution honored. Negroes could well, with little expense, have presented athletic equipment to the institution and in other ways gained recognition as benefactors rather than beneficiaries. After such steps as these, a request for membership would have been much more likely to receive favorable reception.

It is wrong even to think about coping with prejudice in a fixed mood. Whoever adheres to a single pattern treats the mild first offender the same way he treats a hardened recalcitrant. One or the other of these is going to react disadvantageously. Strike hard at the chap who unwittingly said something offensive and he becomes embittered and his prejudice becomes entrenched and sinister. Try to appease the bigoted brute with conciliatory measures and he responds more brutally than ever. It is pathetic to see how decent folks, trying to do an honest and sincere job in destroying intolerance and in eliminating its effects, are harassed by those devoted to the mistaken idea that one must choose between treating prejudice with kid gloves in all situations or being "militant" regardless of the circumstances.

Here, then, is Dilemma Number Two, and it should not be difficult to resolve it if temperaments can yield to sound judgment.

If we treat intolerant persons mildly and regard situations involving intolerance as circumstances in which we must act unobtrusively and without vehemence or pressure, the practices of intolerance may go on undisturbed and we may fail to make any impression at all. If we attack mildly intolerant persons vehemently, denouncing them publicly and arousing their wrath, their intolerant attitudes will be confirmed, thwarting future attempts to win them over.

The solution of this problem is almost obvious, provided we do not make a fetish of "militancy" or of "gentleness." There is no inherent virtue in any temperamental attitude where dealing with prejudice is concerned. A blast in the newspaper may serve best in one situation and be utterly useless in another. *In counteracting intolerance we should be as soft-spoken and as conciliatory or as harsh and as vociferous as each particular situation requires.*

These two things must be done in all instances:

1. Figure out all the possible courses of action.
2. Choose the one that is most likely to obtain the best result.

To fly into action without thinking out *all* the possible ways of handling the problem is an egregious blunder. The fellow with a strong *emotional* preference for *one type* of action is a nuisance and a handicap.

The choices are often very difficult to make because it is generally not entirely right or entirely wrong to do one thing or another. But that only makes it the more necessary to rely upon judgment rather than impulse. One must never use a sword or a feather because of a predisposition to weapons or fluff.

A prejudice shared by many people, especially by the dominant element of a locality or region, tends to unite them into a we-group (or in-group). The sense of solidarity makes the prejudice seem quite sacred and ennobling. The desire for conformity is not weakened but strengthened when persons outside of the locale become denunciatory. Abuse heaped upon the residents of an area by outsiders, because of the defense mechanisms that are stimulated, is certain to intensify their prejudice.

When Senator Theodore Bilbo campaigned for re-election in 1946 he made frequent reference to statements denouncing him and his bigotry by persons, organizations, and journals outside of his state. In effect he told the citizens of Mississippi that they were being castigated and maligned for having chosen him as their senator in previous elections. He as much as asked "Who is going to elect the senators of Mississippi, the citizens of Mississippi or New York?" On a platform of white supremacy and anti-Negro sentiment he won the election.

Following the reelection of Senator Theodore Bilbo in November 1946, the New York *World Telegram* published an editorial captioned "Outside Interference Backfires." It read in part:

> *Voters in Mississippi and Nebraska and the Argentine*
> *may not seem to have much in common, but they do share*
> *a resentment against outside interference in their politics.*
> *Nothing has helped Senator Bilbo more in his efforts to stay*
> *in office than the strident attacks of persons not eligible to*

vote in Mississippi and not represented by the Senator. His record provided talking points against him, but none with the sure-fire appeal in his behalf of the issue of outside interference.

Here, then, is Dilemma Number Three:

The prejudices of the majority in some localities are deeply entrenched. Resulting injustices to minority groups seem likely to continue indefinitely. Yet the expression of adverse criticisms by outsiders is likely to evoke a jingoistic sense of local pride that strengthens the hands of the prejudiced.

Where there is a clear-cut victory to be won or lost at the polls and only those within a prescribed area can vote, outside friends of those who suffer discrimination or ill treatment will refrain from injecting themselves directly into the situation. They will give whatever assistance they can to local citizens combating intolerance, against whom none can raise the cry of "outside interference!" Moreover, it is possible to express helpful opinions in such situations in kindly tone, rather than in a holier-than-thou-art blast. When the nation as a whole can be brought into the situation, as in the case of a federal anti-lynching law, thus outweighing the voting strength of the recalcitrant, other tactics may prove more effective.

We dare never forget when opposing intolerance that *who* says something makes a great difference. One spokesman within a group is often better than a score on the outside. Rabbis are not so persuasive with Catholics as are priests; Jews are less influenced by priests than by rabbis; where Protestants are concerned ministers carry much more weight than either priests or rabbis. To say that it does not matter *who* issues an appeal or advances an argument is to deny the truth of the obvious. Many a contest for public opinion has been lost because unacceptable spokesmen for a cause drowned out voices of esteemed citizens trying to say the very same things. The endorsement of suspect persons is rightly called "the kiss of death."

By now it should be evident that dealing with prejudice is not a job for a man swinging an ax, who pays little attention to where and upon whom each blow falls. Some situations do require strong, vigorous strokes. In many cases a scalpel making delicate incisions along a very fine line does a much better job. Before leaping into action against a single bigot or against an army of bigots, every proposal of how to proceed should be carefully weighed. *Immediate action is rarely necessary. Wise action is always necessary.*

In the spring of 1944 a young Jewish woman asked me whether her husband, then stationed at an army camp abroad, had acted properly when another soldier in the canteen had blurted out some anti-Semitic insults. Her husband had said nothing during the tirade nor had he done anything about it. He wrote, however, that he had been "burned up, being so far away from home fighting Hitlerism and getting a dose of it in my own camp."

"Shouldn't he have spoken up?" she asked. "I'm surprised he didn't hit the fellow and shut him up."

"On the little information you've furnished," I replied, "I don't know what he should have done. Can a doctor say what a man ought to do for a pain in the abdomen, without knowing anything more than that he has a pain in the region of his stomach? You don't expect a doctor to prescribe the same remedy for all abdominal pains."

"That's all he wrote me about it," the troubled wife replied. "But don't you think he should have done something?"

"Probably yes, but perhaps no," I told her. "Suppose the fellow was drunk and disorderly, disgusting everyone there and arousing their antagonism? He may have been an Exhibit A of the folly of intolerance. Or what if some highly respected Christian buddies expressed their indignation then and there? They could have handled the matter more persuasively because they would not be on the defensive. If the remarks were addressed to your husband, making it appear that he was a coward in accepting the insult, it would have been his duty to stop the tirade, even if it required use of his fists to do so. An insult is one thing and a challenge is another. Highly abusive language may be tantamount to a challenge. In an army camp honor will not survive the constant toleration of abuse without fighting back. In a courtroom, on the other hand, the first to resort to physical violence, no matter what has been said or how it has been said, is subject to severe penalty. Only in extreme cases is it advisable to precipitate a brawl to punish intolerant remarks. In some places it is necessary to avoid striking the first blow, no matter how hot the exchange of words."

I told the young wife an incident I heard from a USO worker. In a barracks for a month a slender nineteen-year-old lad, Harry, had been jeered at and derided daily by a bully five years older and far huskier. Every taunt was a barbed reminder that Harry was a Victimian. Harry argued with the tormentor a number of times and begged him to desist. But the taunting continued whenever Steve was in a mood to badger Harry. The humiliation became increasingly painful.

One day Harry was standing near the barracks stoop when Steve approached and greeted him with a volley of profane invectives. Unable to control his rage, Harry stepped up to Steve with clenched fists. "There's no use arguing with you any more," he blurted. "I know you can knock hell out of me but I'd rather be beaten to a pulp than take this lying down any more."

Steve looked down at Harry and began to roll up his sleeves. "So you want to fight?" he laughed. "Well, you all heard this. I didn't start it; now did I?"

A crowd gathered as the two squared off, while Steve relished the prospect of battering the little fellow. Some were yelling, "Ah, no, Steve," but Steve moved in.

Before the first blow could be struck another soldier, three inches taller than Steve, stepped into the fight. Rolling up his sleeves, he stood facing Steve.

"Get out of this," the bully whined. "It isn't your fight. I never said anything against you."

"Oh yes, it's my fight," said the young giant. "Five weeks now I've been on the bunk next to you, listening to your stinking line, waiting to see how long you'd keep it up. I'm fed up with seeing a poor little guy who never hurt you or me or anyone around here abused by your dirty tongue just because he didn't pick the same kind of grandfather you and I did. You bet this is my fight. Get away, Harry. I'm taking over."

When Steve lay flat on the ground, he blubbered that he meant no harm and promised under threat of a worse drubbing to stop tormenting Harry.

It is possible that Harry might have handled the matter better than he did. Perhaps he should have reported it to his commanding officer long before this crisis. I don't know whether that would have been the right step because I never saw Steve or Harry or their commanding officer. Was the latter capable of handling the problem? Was he someone who would have bungled it? Probably the chaplain would have been the person to consult. For all I know Harry did talk to a chaplain without securing results. Without knowing the people involved I cannot say what other possibilities may have existed. But if this was the final resort remaining to him, Harry was right in offering to take a beating as a protest. It may have been the *best* thing to do in this instance. And in every instance the proper question is not "What is a good thing to do?" but "What is the *best* thing and the best way to do it?" Often something can be said in favor of, and something against, every course that might be proposed. If there is only a moment in which to arrive at a decision, a cool, calm head, calculating all of the factors in the situation and choosing the most effective course, is the most valuable asset.

What to do in each instance depends on the total picture. Who else is present? What kind of person is the culprit? How do the others feel toward him? How offensive has he been? Is this a first offense or a continuous practice? Is he a person who will, even if unrebuked, regret tomorrow what he is saying now? Or is he a hardened offender? Does the atmosphere or occasion call for restraint or is it advisable to speak up loudly?

Whether you are trying to figure out how to deal with the whole wide problem of prejudice or whether you are coping with a single instance you should examine the matter from various angles. You can never find the right answers unless you ask all the appropriate questions. Keep on examining, searching, and comparing pros and cons. Always keep in mind not only the obvious effects of a proposed course, the results that anyone can readily see, but think also of the submerged effects that are equally and sometimes even more important. It is the *total* result that counts.

PART TWO

The Daily Grind of Prejudice

CHAPTER 1

The Constant Factor

A few years ago a telephone company employing thousands of switchboard operators had no Victimians on its staff. An official was asked why the company refused to engage any Victimian girls.

"Their arms are not long enough to operate a switchboard," was his compact and complacent reply.

Though that company no longer asks the race or religion of girls seeking positions as switchboard operators and now employs many who would formerly have been barred, the incident is illuminating. The executive who offered that unreasonable reason for excluding certain applicants knew as surely as you do that every group has long-armed and short-armed people. Those girls were being excluded because of prejudice, and for the official any trumped-up excuse, however ridiculous, was sufficient justification for a discriminatory practice of which he approved.

There is no need for me to protest here against such discriminatory practices. You realize that all types of racial and religious discrimination under which individuals suffer unfair treatment are socially destructive. Nor would I say that any of these practices is more inimical or less inimical than another to personal and public welfare. The whole fabric of prejudice is composed of these small threads woven together. All of them are important and until all have been broken we shall never be entirely free of discrimination. So long as any group suffers one form of discrimination, it will be all the more vulnerable to other types. Prejudice is indivisible.

There is, however, another aspect to be considered. Even though we understand that prejudice is basically a single entity, experience in combating discrimination has shown that it is often necessary to assign relative importance to individual problems and to classes of problems. Unless we are able accurately to evaluate the situations which face us, we cannot direct our efforts to the points at which they are most needed and where they will accomplish the greatest good.

Prejudice which culminates in physical attack is the most shocking type. Like all incidents involving brutal assault, it receives a great deal of attention and invariably arouses much more general response than do the injuries resulting from the incessant but less spectacular discriminatory practices. Yet the effects of these unfair practices against Victimians are incomparably more destructive than the sum of all the harangues, vandalism, pummeling, and black-jacking to which members of minority groups are subjected in the United States. The Indian, confined to a reservation, would be better off if he received a few punches annually but was granted full rights as a human being. The man who had the qualities to make an excellent surgeon, but instead spends his life in a butcher shop solely because of anti-Jewish quotas, has been injured economically, socially, and psychically immeasurably more than he could have been by anything less than a paralyzing beating. The woman who must live in a wretched, squalid black ghetto only because she is a Negro, when for the same rental she could otherwise occupy a pleasant, sunlit apartment, suffers more harm than from listening to twenty tirades against her race.

In spite of the revulsion it arouses, physical violence is hardly the most damaging aspect of prejudice. The most seriously injured victim of intolerance is not necessarily the one who has been reviled by bigots or buffeted by a gang of bullies. The most criminal injuries are inflicted on Victimians who daily travel a thornier path, whose hourly lot is much harder, whose opportunities for a happy and satisfying life are sharply reduced because prejudice has clamped a yoke on their necks—has, indeed, determined their fate and their status before their birth. These people have not sinned and yet they are punished constantly. Their maltreatment is all the worse because it is so unobtrusively inflicted. What recourse have they? When oppression is the sum of the innumerable contributions of an entire society, who can single out the persecutor and bring him to trial?

Where *does* this vague and creeping evil arise? On what level *does* discrimination against racial and religious groups begin? The answer is not difficult to find. It begins on the level of personal companionship. But when we have located the source of the infection, we have not cured it. Indeed, we have only encountered another problem—perhaps one of the most difficult we shall meet. We say that prejudice begins on the level at which personal companions are chosen. We know that prejudice must be attacked at its roots. Are we, then, to question the right of every man to choose his personal friends, and to choose them by whatever criteria he prefers?

It is obvious that in any community those who belong to the dominant group commanding social prestige tend to monopolize for themselves the best residential districts, the best jobs, the best schools, the best of everything which goes to make up the good life. In its broadest sense this "social discrimination" is at the root of every exclusion that restricts the opportunities of human beings on the basis of creed or color. To share *fully* in the advantages of any society the individual must be unhampered by social barriers. "Social discrimination" erects scores of such barriers—in clubs, resorts, or any grouping in which social intercourse is a primary factor.

For the most part these restrictions apply on the level of social intimacy. Many a man employs people in his business whom he would unhesitatingly bar from his club. Students are enrolled at colleges where some—or even all—of the fraternities will discriminate against them. In the generally accepted sense, social discrimination does not preclude working together, learning together, living in the same neighborhood, enjoying the same rights before the law, and in many other ways enjoying most of the privileges of membership in the society. While it is entirely true that social discrimination is the soil in which the vicious forms of racial and religious discrimination flourish, it is not in itself the most reprehensible form. The strangling kinds of persecution which grow out of it often may be controlled or entirely eliminated even though we cannot reach to their deepest roots. We should be thankful, perhaps, that this is true, for we face no more baffling problem than the removal of social discrimination.

The situation is baffling because it involves so many loyalties, rights, and duties among its obvious injustices. Children from many diverse groups will play freely together—in fact, will often be encouraged by their elders to participate wholeheartedly in general group activities. But as they enter their teens, young persons frequently discover to their dismay a growing aloofness on the part of those with whom they have previously associated. By the time they have reached marriageable age discrimination has become a decisive force. Parents, loyal to their own faiths and conscious of their social origins, carefully guide their children into a more or less exclusive membership in their own group. Quite naturally they strive to perpetuate their own faith and to preserve their own national and social entity. They are motivated by perfectly real loyalties to their religious and social groups and by a natural and laudable concern for the happiness of their children. To blot out all dividing lines between racial and religious groups obviously is not only impossible; it is proposed only by those who have little group loyalty and few religious or cultural ties. Social discrimination is compounded of snobbery, selfishness, and many other unlovely qualities. It is also sometimes the reverse of a coin on whose obverse is stamped "to your own group be true."

Certainly a church or synagogue cannot be denied the right to conduct clubs and camps for its own young people, although social segregation is thereby promoted. But how can people in good conscience insist that they be barred from no club because of race or religion unless they also insist that their own clubs be opened immediately to all otherwise eligible without regard to race or religion? If the basis of membership in a seminary, house of worship, men's or women's club of a religious institution is adherence to a certain faith, obviously no one of another faith can cry "social discrimination" and demand membership without accepting that faith. And so long as cultural differences between groups remain, it will be difficult to deny that there is a certain amount of added ease and relaxation in being "among one's own kind."

A Negro teacher was asked by a white friend to send her children to an interracial camp.

"I appreciate," replied the mother, "your friendly attitude. I hope the camp will be a great success. But I feel that my children are under such tension all year round, being among white children, that I'd like them to spend the summer where they will feel a complete and unquestioned acceptance."

Psychiatrists have all too many cases of people who would have been far happier as confident members of their own groups than they were after attempting vainly to leap social barriers or clinging desperately to the fringes of groups where they were grudgingly accepted. Whether or not we wish it to be so, a social discrimination is the hardest of all barriers to overcome psychically as well as physically. Frankly, I do not know how to end all unwholesome aspects of social discrimination without infringing upon the rights which any group and any individual should be free to exercise. All of us live with some problems that are never solved; we struggle along and do the best we can without a final solution. Social discrimination is like that. I know that social discrimination does considerable injury but I have yet to see a ready-made answer that can be helpfully applied in all of the thousands of instances wherein social discrimination operates.

Where *public* accommodations are concerned, in all places open to the general public, racial and religious discriminations are totally out of place. Where *private* institutions are concerned, where sociability is restricted to guests who assume the right to one another's personal companionship, blanket rulings do not fit so well. It is on the border line between public and private that we run into great difficulties.

Will people continue to form social cliques and clubs with racial and religious lines playing quite a large part in determining membership? Yes, for a very long time. Will that be fatal to democracy and brotherhood in the United States? Not necessarily. Not if we make sufficient gains in eradicating the types of discrimination which do not involve intimacy.

Given adequate opportunity to learn, to work, to enjoy all public facilities, and with a chance to live in whatever homes they can afford, men and women will build satisfactory lives socially even if some social discrimination remains. There is so much work to be done to secure the clear-cut rights of housing, schooling, employment, and educational opportunity that we shall do well to concentrate the available man power to attain well-defined objectives which do not involve intimate social relationships. We are primarily concerned here about necessities of the good life. Some of the luxuries will remain unobtainable until the necessities are secured.

We need not wait for the millennium, when all social discriminations will have disappeared, in order to get rid of discriminatory practices which destroy the very basis of democratic life. The process of eliminating these flagrant violations of the rights of the individual goes on constantly. Civil-rights legislation will help immensely, but voluntary action can be taken any day by anyone who prefers fair practices.

Some years ago the chief executive officer of one of the largest department stores in the United States was asked why his firm did not employ Jews.

He was quite puzzled. "Don't we?" he asked in genuine surprise.

"No," he was told. "There are no Jewish employees in your entire establishment."

He called in the personnel manager and others, all of whom confirmed the fact that they did not employ Jews.

"When I came here twenty years ago," said one man, "I found no Jewish employees. So I assumed that it was a policy and engaged none."

Others answered similarly.

"You mean," said the head of the firm, "that all of you simply took the matter for granted and thus established a precedent you have all followed?"

"Well," murmured one of the men, "you didn't say anything against it."

The chief executive drew a deep breath. "I was entirely unaware of this," he said truthfully. "I never gave it a thought. But I'm telling you now. There is to be no discrimination in hiring our employees from now on. For every job we need the best person available."

Since the public has until recently been quite unaware of the extent to which practices of this sort have been wreaking inestimable damage, open discussion is undoubtedly in order. But let it not be on the ground that one or another racial or religious group is being mistreated. Appeals for sympathy or for kindness toward any group will bring more boomerang than improvement. Nor will chips on anybody's shoulder benefit the injured. This is *everyone's* problem. Everyone is paying a heavy price for discriminatory practices. When an aviation company turns away excellent aviators—former fliers of Uncle Sam—because their skins are the wrong color or they don't worship in the right church, and when the company's officials put into the pilots' seats men less competent but with a more correct ancestry, the lives of all passengers are endangered. Can you afford the kind of squeamishness and fastidiousness about creed and color which gives all of us poorer merchandise, worse service, and even risks lives? Ask your friends who lose when should-be clerks are made executive heads and should-be executives are turned into delivery boys?

The workingman and the employer are both injured by discriminatory practices. What they mean to business has been well stated by Eric Johnston, former chairman of the United States Chamber of Commerce:

> *The withholding of jobs and business opportunities from some people does not make more jobs and business opportunities for others. Such a policy merely tends to drag down the whole economic level. Perpetuating poverty for some merely guarantees stagnation for all. True economic progress demands that the whole nation move forward at the same time. It demands that all artificial barriers erected by ignorance and intolerance be removed. To put it in the simplest terms, we are all in business together. Intolerance is a species of boycott and any business or job boycott is a cancer in the economic body of the nation. I repeat, intolerance is destructive; prejudice produces no wealth; discrimination is a fool's economy.*

Leaders of labor are similarly concerned about the evil effects of racial and religious discrimination. Speaking as president of the Congress of Industrial Organizations, Philip Murray had this to say on the subject:

"The policy of the CIO toward the question of discrimination is clear and unequivocal. In our constitution we declare that the object of the CIO is to organize workers 'regardless of race, creed, color, or nationality, and to unite them for common action into labor unions for their mutual aid and protection.'"

The question before us is not "How loudly can we wail and fume about the poor mistreated Victimians?" That only prolongs a discussion that goes round and round in circles without helping matters. The issue is whether the American public—every one of us—can afford to deny human beings the right to become as useful as possible to society. Anyone cramped, thwarted, and handicapped by discriminatory practices because of intolerance resembles good soil on which nothing is permitted to grow but weeds. Surely no one profits from that in ours or in any nation. The price of prejudice is unbearably high.

CHAPTER 2

Discrimination in Employment

Harry Brown was a genial, hard-working Negro who for six years had been the porter of an apartment house in Mount Vernon, New York. Three incompetent superintendents came and went. Harry cheerfully did his own work and much of theirs. There was nothing a superintendent of an apartment house needed to do that Harry could not do better than any of the three. How well Harry could have used the comfortable basement apartment assigned to the superintendent of that building! Harry well deserved the much higher salary which the superintendent's job paid.

The third superintendent quit. Harry asked for the job but another white man was brought in. The cost of living was going up. Harry asked for a few more dollars weekly and was refused. To the regret of every tenant of the apartment house, Harry took a position as a porter elsewhere where he could earn a bit more. The tenants were sad and sympathetic. But did they do anything about it? No. Did anyone risk unpopularity by urging the landlord to give Harry the job of superintendent and have him move into that basement apartment? The few who might have been willing waited for someone else to make the proposal. Once more it happened, as it happens a thousand times daily, that many people directly suffered the consequences of discrimination against one person. In this case the effects were abundantly clear to those who were forced to put up with inadequate service when excellent help was available.

To distribute jobs among people on the basis of their own personal character and ability is plain ordinary fairness. Hence the term *"fair employment"* (in contradistinction to discriminatory hiring). In March 1944 William Hard wrote: "I do not want to give a Negro anything just because he is a Negro. All I want to give him is everything he can prove he can get as a man." Apply that idea to employment and it means never mind a man's creed or color; never mind where he was born; never mind the irrelevancies and give the fellow a chance to show what he can do. If he has what it takes to do the job right, let him work at it.

The practice of fair employment is best when done voluntarily, simply because it's accepted as the right thing to do. But unfortunately, as everyone knows, indispensable qualifications for obtaining many a job today are race, creed, ethnic origin, et cetera. In some cases the labor union or the manufacturer or merchant who discriminates, admits it. More often a dodge or a pretext is offered without admitting that rejection of an applicant has been based upon racial or religious discrimination.

The story is told of a young Chinese-American who had completed a course in a welding school. With a diploma testifying to his skill, he answered numerous advertisements for welders, but invariably was turned away as soon as his race became known to the potential employer. He became increasingly discouraged. Early one morning he applied at a newly constructed factory where there were evidently many jobs and few applicants. The employment agent looked at his credentials and asked some technical questions to which the young man gave answers indubitably correct.

Finally the manager asked, "Are you married?"

"No," said the lad.

The agent heaved a sigh of relief. "We prefer married men here."

The next morning the Chinese-American welder put in another appearance.

"Weren't you here yesterday?" asked the employment manager.

"Yes."

"And what did I tell you?"

"You told me you wanted only married men."

"That disqualifies you, doesn't it?"

"No," was the happy answer. "I got married yesterday."

"Oh, I see," said the other, taken aback. Recovering, he added, "I'm sorry, I made a mistake. This particular job requires single men."

No one of sound mind would advocate a law requiring an employer to hire, or a labor union to accept the membership of, a person solely because that person is a Victimian. But there is an increasing demand that no one shall be denied employment merely because of race, creed, or color. That distinction should be clearly grasped. It is a tremendously important one in every phase of legislative action against discrimination. No member of any group is going to receive anything more on account of *fair employment practice acts* than is made available to all persons; namely, opportunity to be considered for a job on a *fair* basis. Any law that establishes fair practice is a device for granting *equal rights* to all. Inevitably some will be found who do not need its protection as much as others do.

A fair employment practice act and the machinery needed to enforce it are generally designated as FEPC or FEP. In the United States the first experience in attempting to prohibit discrimination in employment-by-government effort was under the aegis of a federal Fair Employment Practice Committee during World War II. Its authority was derived from an executive order issued June 25, 1941, by President Roosevelt. This committee went out of existence June 28, 1946, because Congress refused to appropriate funds to continue it. Since then efforts made to establish a permanent national FEPC by congressional action have been blocked by parliamentary maneuvers and by filibuster. There are, however, several states in which FEPC laws have been enacted, and so long as a federal act is blocked, efforts should be redoubled to secure FEPC laws in states where a recalcitrant minority cannot defeat its proponents. The first states to adopt FEPC laws with adequate enforcement provisions are New York, New Jersey, Massachusetts, Connecticut, Washington, Oregon, New Mexico, and Rhode Island.

The working of the laws in the states in which they have been adopted with due *procedure* for *enforcement* clearly demonstrates that FEPC can operate successfully through a state commission or even through a municipal agency. In fact, the best *brief* description of an FEPC law and how it works, which I have seen, appeared in a brochure issued by the Fair Employment Practice Commission of the city of Minneapolis. I quote part of it:

> *Freedom of enterprise is a basic right which Americans hold dear. The opportunity for full use of every worker's highest skills, without discrimination because of race, creed,*

color, national origin, or ancestry, is as important to the welfare of the community as it is to the freedom of the individual.

To secure these rights and to safeguard the community welfare, Minneapolis adopted a Fair Employment Practice Ordinance on February 5, 1947. Chicago and Milwaukee had previously adopted similar ordinances, but Minneapolis was the first city in the country to establish a commission to administer the law. A second commission has now been established by the city of Philadelphia.

Five Minneapolis citizens serve as members of the commission without pay. An office has been established in the City Hall, and an executive director has been employed to investigate and adjust complaints. The commission has been successful in solving most of the problems involved in individual complaints that have been brought before it. The existence of the ordinance and of the commission, furthermore, has focused the attention of major employers and union leaders on their employment policies. This has resulted in extensive correction of discriminatory practices and has opened the gates of employment opportunity to many workers who previously had found them closed.

If any individual believes he has been discriminated against in hiring, promotion, wage payments, or in other terms or conditions of employment, he may file a complaint with the commission. The executive director then discusses the problem with the person against whom the complaint was made. If he is unable to secure immediate adjustment, he presents the case to the members of the commission.

The commission arranges a private meeting with the parties concerned. Together they try to work out a fair employment policy and to overcome whatever barriers may stand in its way. If these meetings fail, the commission may hold a public hearing in which both parties would be invited to state their case. During the first eighteen months of its operation, *the commission did not find a public hearing necessary.*

If the commission is unable to effect compliance with the ordinance by the foregoing methods, it is required to recommend the case to the City Attorney for prosecution. A *person found by the court to have violated the ordinance is guilty of a misdemeanor. He may be fined up to $100 or imprisoned up to ninety days.* During the first eighteen months after the adoption of the ordinance, no cases were taken to court in Minneapolis. All complaints were adjusted by the commission.

Some employers are willing to follow a fair employment policy but are afraid their customers or employees may not like it. The commission is prepared to deal with any complaints which an employer may receive as a result of following such a policy. The members and director of the commission are ready to confer with any customer or employee to explain the importance to him and to the community of eliminating practices of discrimination.

The Minneapolis FEP Ordinance differs from similar laws enacted by the eight states in that such state statutes require the commission to issue cease and desist orders after the public hearing instead of referring the matter to the city attorney for prosecution, as provided under the city ordinance. If the order of a state commission is not obeyed, the case is referred to a *civil* court for a judicial order compelling the respondent to obey the Commission. Obviously a refusal to obey the court's order subjects the respondent to punishment for contempt. Criminal punishment, in the form of a fine or imprisonment, is only provided in the State FEPC statutes in cases of *willful* interference with or obstruction of the Commission or its agents in the performance of their duties. And in such cases, punishment could only result after conviction at a formal criminal trial with all the safeguards that our legal system provides for the protection of persons accused of crime.

Every FEPC body engages in programs of both private and public education. Invariably discussion and conciliation are paramount. In more than three years of operation New York's FEPC law had not resulted in even one appeal to the courts by the commission or by anyone else. All cases were handled privately. This last fact is resented by those who believe that progress is best achieved by punching as many noses as possible. If FEPC is to become nationally accepted, the less it uses its bludgeon, the better.

A typical case from the records of the New York State Commission Against Discrimination (SCAD) is that of a Negro boy who applied along with two white boys as ushers in a large theater. The white boys were hired but the Negro was told that Negroes were employed only as porters. The Fair Employment Commissioner investigating the case found that the Negro was well qualified in character and experience. Conferences were held. The commission directed that the Negro be engaged. As in all cases, there was a subsequent checkup. It was found that the boy was still employed and that other Negroes were also employed as ushers by the theater.

Another example of SCAD's functioning was told to me by Commissioner Caroline K. Simon of the New York Commission:

A woman answered an advertisement for a seamstress and was interviewed by the owner of a dressmaking establishment. The job was refused her and she attributed the refusal to discrimination. She appealed to SCAD.

A member of SCAD's staff called on the employer, who readily admitted that he had practiced discrimination.

Almost in tears he said, "I came to this country to escape Nazi persecution. No one could hate intolerance more than I do. I was a dress manufacturer in Germany and so I opened a little shop here. My first employee was a woman. It did not matter to me that she was not Jewish. When I needed more seamstresses she brought in a few of her friends. Now I have six very capable workers. All of them threaten to quit if I hired anyone who is not of their own nationality."

The seamstresses were called together and the representative of SCAD explained to them that their insistence on discrimination in employment was not only morally wrong but that in New York State it was also illegal.

Not only was the complainant in this case hired but there was no difficulty when another seamstress of another ethnic group was engaged. It is hardly necessary to add that the seamstresses got along very amiably with those whom they would have excluded.

New York's Fair Employment Practice Act became law on July 1, 1945. In an article in *Harper's Magazine* (October 1947) Irwin Ross wrote: "Two years of State FEPCs have done more to end job discrimination than fifty years of private agitation, good-will conferences, educational campaigning . . . and you see the results every time you encounter a Negro usher in a theater, a Negro desk clerk in a hotel, a Negro salesgirl in the lingerie department of your favorite store."

The greatest gains from the FEPC laws everywhere have been the voluntary alterations of hiring practices of many employers. In states having such commissions thousands of business firms and employment agencies have removed questions about race and religion from their application blanks, either to conform with the law or immediately upon being notified that they were violating the law. No one acquainted with the operation of the acts would say that compliance is perfect or even nearly so. Subtle evasions will continue as long as there are intolerant people. But FEPC has worked without the appearance of any of the objectionable conditions that the voluble enemies of FEPC had threatened were inevitable. The success of the acts has had the splendid effect of proclaiming "Equality of employment opportunity is not something a few fanatics want. It is the will of the people of this state." Let's hope that before long a federal FEPC will make it possible to say "This is the will of the people of the United States."

FEPC legislation turns the balance in favor of those who are opposed to discriminatory practices. In *All Manner of Men* Malcolm Ross, recording the successes and the failures of the federal wartime FEPC of which he was chairman, says: "Unless there is a prod from government an employer who is apathetic toward hiring minority workers can easily turn down a union suggestion that he do so. By the same token, a union which wishes to discriminate will not find much opposition from the employer."

The American Friends Service Committee issued a report on the unsuccessful strike of Philadelphia Rapid Transit employees who subjected their fellow Philadelphians to hardships and inconvenience because eight well-deserving Negroes had been upgraded. In part the report said:

> *The real answer to fair opportunity for the Negroes in America is not only a permanent FEPC, but an enlightened public opinion to support it . . . Men cannot long stick to the guns of prejudice if they are made uncertain of their moral ground, if every respectable citizen evinces contempt for the ignorance and bigotry they betray. Men striving to justify themselves in an unjustifiable situation can be made to retreat with shamed faces much faster by fellow citizens who let them know they are ashamed of them than they can*

by all the armed soldiers and prisons in the country. Can the FEPC expect that kind of support from your community?

The standards established in law have been reflected in the normal employment practices of many employers. A New Haven firm during the war sought to induce its employees to accept Negro workers as fellow employees. It mimeographed a notice, of which this is the first paragraph:

> *If a man is discriminated against because of ignorance, he can study, acquire knowledge, and overcome the handicap; if he is discriminated against because of poverty, he can work, acquire wealth, and overcome the handicap; if he is discriminated against because he is unclean, he can wash, acquire habits of cleanliness, and overcome the handicap; but if the discrimination is based on color, he cannot change that.*

The second paragraph appealed to the patriotism of the workers on the ground that "millions of American boys of all races, colors, and creeds are now fighting shoulder to shoulder . . ."

The third paragraph urged "willingness to employ those who are best qualified for employment opportunities."

In this instance patriotism and appreciation for Negro service on the battlefields did the trick. The white workers accepted Negroes with a friendliness much greater than the company had anticipated. These tactics are not, of course, invariably effective. Even during the war in some instances every argument failed. You can make progress by appealing to conscience and decency provided those to whom the appeal is made have a conscience and a moral sense. Experience proves that unfortunately sometimes both are absent.

What about the self-interest of those who want to monopolize jobs for those who belong to their own race, creed, and national origin? Whatever may be their regard for their own racial, religious, or ethnic group, they are also concerned about their own interests as taxpayers, workers, customers, parents, et cetera. In any of these spheres denial of employment opportunity operates to their disadvantage. It is always better to stress these concrete disadvantages than to plead for charitable sympathy for any group. People can be shown that when they ride in a car, tune in on a radio, or use a washing machine it does not matter who built these machines, provided it was those who could make them most ably and efficiently. They do not ask when they ride in an elevator whether the men who made it or installed it were white or black, of one faith or another, of one national origin or another. It requires no profound understanding of either philosophy or economics to understand that it is safer to use an elevator inspected by a person thoroughly informed about elevators than to risk one's life in a machine inspected by men chosen according to race or religion.

We have stressed in this chapter the legal phases of securing fair employment free of group discrimination. Little has been said at this point about educational methods because the building of attitudes against all forms of discrimination is discussed at length elsewhere. But it is appropriate to point out here that no law can be devised which will keep the prejudiced from refusing their patronage to a Victimian physician, architect, barber, tailor, cab driver, accountant, lawyer, or other self-employed person. Nor can any law assure the right to be hired on job levels where unique personality or other intangible factors enter and where refusal can be placed on spurious but plausible grounds. Despite FEPC laws, if prejudice persists, the level of Victimian occupational opportunity may be frozen at a point where Victimians get somewhat better jobs but are still excluded from highly desirable types of work.

While FEPC is a needed helpful advance we should not forget that it has come upon the heels of education for liberalism. It is a device whereby those who have not caught up with the liberal trend may be brought into line with public sentiment. It would be wrong to assume that from here on laws combined with the educational programs of FEPC agencies will assure maximal economic opportunity on all levels of work. Without in any way disparaging FEPC it is well to recognize that there are highly important areas of income-earning activity where FEPC can have no direct influence.

In brief, then, what can we do about employment discrimination?

1. We can rid ourselves of the notion that excluding people of any racial, religious, or ethnic group from opportunities of employment assures us and "our kind" a better livelihood. The opposite is true.

2. We can express our readiness to welcome those excluded by discriminatory practices as fellow workers in our own establishments.

3. We can provide for all who obtain employment in our own offices, stores, plants, or wherever we work, the same congenial, friendly atmosphere that people of our race, creed, and ethnic origin enjoy.

4. We can actively express our approval of the upgrading of workers on the basis of merit, regardless of their race or creed.

5. We can insist that emphasis be placed on the only relevant question, "How well can that person do that job?"

6. We can patronize stores which do not exclude from their sales force qualified members of any minority group.

7. We can advocate FEPC laws and support legislators and administrators who do.

8. We can demolish the asinine argument that FEPC is a communist idea by pointing out that one way to defeat communism is to assure fair employment practices and remove some of the injustices to which communists point in order to stir discontent and turmoil. As Elmer A. Carter, a commissioner of New York SCAD, has rightfully said, "The freedom of America from the blight of communism lies in the attainment of equal opportunity for all, which is the keystone of our concept of government."

Apparently because of the composition of the United States Senate and the opportunity for any determined minority to employ the filibuster it will be extremely difficult to secure a national FEPC. This should lead to an even greater determination to secure FEPC legislation in states where none exists and in fostering sentiment throughout the nation for fair practices in employment.

Discrimination in Education

You could hardly have found a man more loyal to his Alma Mater than Bill L. He had a thriving private medical practice and was also physician for the city's principal factory. He was on the local school board and an active civic worker. Yet he managed four or five times every year to visit the college a hundred miles away. He had gone to games, participated in conferences, and attended annual reunions. He contributed in the various school drives and helped to raise funds every time he was asked. He "pepped up" the local chapter of the alumni whenever it threatened to become moribund. You couldn't spend much time with Dr. L. and not hear praise of "Dear Old C————."

It was natural that Fred L., the doctor's son, would want to be a physician. His aptitudes were quite apparent. Fred was highly intelligent and a diligent student. His character was impeccable. With leadership and athletic abilities, he established a good record in extracurricular activities. At high school graduation he ranked among the high honor students.

Dr. L. was well aware that the limited accommodations of medical colleges made it exceedingly difficult to obtain admissions. But undergraduate schools were not so overcrowded.

"We'll worry," Dr. L. told Fred, "about your getting into medical college when you're getting on with your pre-med. Just make as good a record in your undergraduate work as you've made in high school. If you do the best you can during these next few years at

C——" (the doctor named his own college) "they'll probably admit you to the medical school."

Fred and his father always assumed that Fred was going to C—— College. In view of the fact that several local boys had been admitted with high school records undoubtedly poorer than Fred's and in view of Dr. L.'s many services to his college, it is difficult to believe that Fred was not admitted even as a freshman. Everyone in the doctor's city who knows about this says "It's almost incredible." They can explain Fred's rejection only by referring to "the quota system—only so many Jews admitted."

I had not seen Dr. L. for several years when I heard about Fred's rejection. A mutual friend told me about it.

"It was a nightmare for Bill and his wife. They got word late that Fred was not admitted. Bill isn't one to put pressure on anyone. He made an inquiry to be sure there had been no clerical error. Then he told Fred to apply to other colleges. The summer was going by and all they received was 'too late' until finally a college in Iowa admitted the boy. It's done something to the entire family. Bill suddenly became a tired-out old man. That grand smile of his that encouraged so many patients and helped so many people over a rough spot is gone."

What happened to Fred L. has happened to many young men and women. As Victimians they were not admitted into colleges where otherwise they would have been most welcome. Because of this, members of certain racial, religious, and ethnic groups view with considerable trepidation the prospect of obtaining college admission for a son or daughter whose academic record is highly creditable.

Speaking privately and off the record, officers of colleges defend the policy of limiting the number of students accepted from each minority group. They say they want a highly diversified student body, drawn from all parts of the country, a cross-section of the American population. They allege that it is not prejudice on their part, but merely a desire to maintain a balanced, well-proportioned clientele that enmeshes their schools in quota systems. In *some* instances this may be entirely true.

Publicly, however, college authorities are embarrassed to confess discriminating on the basis of race and religion. They deny, ignore, or rationalize practices which are so manifestly contrary to demo-cratic ideals. Certainly no American educator of standing would want to go openly on record as opposed to this statement made by Thomas E. Dewey as governor of New York State:

"Education, and particularly higher education, is quest for the truth; baseless distinctions have no place in that quest. Education controls the opportunity for professional careers; careers should depend only upon ability to serve. Education flourishes in the controversy of divergent groups, in conflicting ideas and ideals; intellectual inbreeding has always proved disastrous."

Dr. Edward J. Sparling, president of Roosevelt College, has stated the problem bluntly and unequivocally: "A quota system poisons and warps social, political, and moral attitudes and creates serious guidance problems among minority groups."

The President's Commission on Higher Education (appointed by President Truman on July 13, 1946) has indicated how very serious the problem of discrimination has become. The commission declared: "To the extent that intolerant attitudes against members of minority groups are given support by our educational institutions, the fabric of our democratic life is endangered." And yet the commission recognized that "complete correction of the difficulties cannot take place immediately or suddenly. Such deep-seated problems require time and education for their eradication. They require patience and mutual forbearance."

Limiting the number of Victimian admissions into each institution of higher learning parallels the less clandestine practice of maintaining separate schools for white and for Negro students. Segregation cannot be concealed and therefore cannot be denied. Yet the advocates of segregation and many who condone it quibble or resort to downright untruth when they defend *separate* educational facilities for Negroes and for whites with claims that *equal* facilities are furnished.

On January 12, 1948, the Supreme Court of the United States ordered the state of Oklahoma to provide immediately for the education of a Negro student who desired and was fully qualified for law training and who had been refused admission to the University of Oklahoma Law School because of her race. The Court ruled that Ada Lois Sipuel Fisher should be given facilities for law training equal to those provided by the state of Oklahoma for white students. Thereupon the Oklahoma State Regents for Higher Education promptly announced the establishment of a Negro School of Law as a branch of Langston Negro University.

"I don't see," said Roscoe Dunjee, editor of *The Black Dispatch,* of Oklahoma City, "how the Regents can give us a school next Monday which is equal in faculty and facilities to the forty-year-old tradition of the Oklahoma Law School."

Rather than abandon even a particle of the fetish of segregation, Southern states are setting up regional professional colleges for Negro students. To those who do not entertain racial superiority beliefs, this seems a fantastically wasteful step. To those who fear that one race would contaminate the other, the maintenance of separate institutions appears to be the only proper procedure. There is an unbridgeable gap between these two views which only a process of education will close, although court rulings may hasten the day when prejudice will yield to understanding.

An incident such as the following indicates some progress in the right direction. At Cornell University a new candidate for the football team who excelled in throwing passes was told in pre-season practice to direct the ball to a Negro star of the team.

"I can't play football with him," drawled the white recruit. "I'm from Texas and I've been brought up differently."

"Oh, just throw it at him," said the coach, "and he'll catch it. Then when he throws it back at you, you wouldn't want us to think you can't catch it; so grab it."

Soon the Negro and the white player were exchanging passes. Several days later it was apparent that they made an excellent passing team. They were working well together and both were obviously enjoying a rapidly developing companionship.

"You're getting along nicely together," remarked the coach to the Texan.

"Yeh," replied the white player. "You know, that fellow's getting whiter and whiter every day."

The preferable way to terminate discrimination in our schools of higher learning would be by voluntary action on the part of those institutions. But voluntary action has been very slow. In fact, discrimination has been increasing in a number of colleges and universities since 1920. Therefore, while favoring voluntary action, the President's Commission recommended that educators themselves support the passage of state laws designed to remove arbitrary discriminatory practices in admission of students.

It is noteworthy that New York State, which already had a fair employment practice law in operation, was the first to adopt a fair educational practice law. The adoption of that law was accompanied by provisions for the establishment of a New York state university to provide increased facilities for higher education. The New York Legislature which passed the anti-discrimination law took cognizance of the fact that without new college facilities 80,000 to 100,000 students in New York State would be unable to find college accommodations by 1958. In this connection some candid lines in the 1947 report of the President of Colgate University are pertinent: "Last September the 350 freshmen we admitted were chosen from some 2,200 applicants. When a commodity is in short supply relative to accumulated demand, provision for old customers—and for such new markets as one has marked for special cultivation—naturally comes first. New customers, converging in large numbers on established centers of supply, can expect only fractional satisfaction, whether they belong to majority or minority groups. In doing what it can in all good faith for their accommodation, a college of limited size inevitably risks the charge of employing a double set of standards." The inability of Colgate University to provide accommodations for more than a small fraction of the applicants has, of course, been a typical situation confronting other institutions of higher learning.

Since the number of applicants for college training increases more rapidly than the college facilities to meet their needs, the problem of discrimination in higher educational institutions becomes more acute. As the pressure increases, disproportionately larger numbers of well-qualified minority group students are turned away. Society is the loser when young men and women of marked ability and great promise are the victims of unfair preferences. Unless our universities are influenced by moral persuasion or compelled by law to accept candidates for degrees solely on the basis of their individual merit, this trend toward educational discrimination will continue and its effects upon our national life will be increasingly pernicious.

Students of the Law College at the University of Arkansas used strategy to terminate segregation in that branch of the university. A legal decision compelled the university to provide *equal* facilities for qualified Negro law students. Thereupon a Negro student was admitted under an arrangement that maintained racial segregation. Separate classes were provided for the one Negro pupil. White students then applied for admission to the Negro's classes. They pointed out that in the Negro's classes there were fewer pupils and hence greater attention on the part of instructors and more intensive instruction. Consequently white students were admitted to the Negro's classes. Segregation, having been made farcical, could not be continued. Since then Negro students have also been admitted to the Medical College of the University.

An honest and determined desire on the part of college, university, and professional school admissions officials to disregard the race, religion, and ethnic origin of applicants would do more than anything else to eliminate such discrimination. The removal from application blanks of questions which reveal creed, color, and ethnic origin is a step in that direction. The expansion of accommodations will likewise tend to lessen discriminatory practices. Laws forbidding discrimination should hasten the process of democratization of our institutions of higher learning. All of these measures will operate to best advantage in those states which do not practice racial segregation. Where segregation is not only condoned but required, a long, uphill struggle of even more perplexing difficulties is inevitable.

> *Segregation of the races in educational institutions legally requires the maintenance of a double school system. In most states this greatly increases the total cost and difficulty in making equivalent education accessible to all. A double system thus means an almost certain lessening of educational opportunity and a lowering for all of the quality of education. The more advanced in the field of endeavor, the more wasteful and futile become attempts to justify a double system. It is a tragic paradox that the communities and the states which are generally least able to afford this dual system of education strive to maintain it by virtue of their laws and traditions. (From the report of the President's Commission on Higher Education.)*

Co-ordinated voluntary elimination of quota systems on the part of a large number of schools of higher learning is likewise desirable. But in the opinion of the President's Commission on Higher Education "There has been too much tardiness and timidity. It now seems clear that many institutions will change their policies only under legal compulsion." However the change may be effected, it is essential that it may be made soon.

To quote the report again:

> When colleges admit all qualified students—when scholar-
> ship, ability, and other defensible standards are made the
> basis of admission rather than race, color, creed, sex, national
> origin, or ancestry—then a democratic solution will have
> been reached. When our colleges and universities are being
> vigorously administered in ways which promote equal op-
> portunity for all qualified students, the local communities
> and the community of the nation cannot help but follow
> such leadership in other areas of our national life.

In the progress toward greater democracy our schools of higher
learning should certainly be in the vanguard. If they set a bad example, our hope of achieving genuine democracy will remain an
idle dream.

What you can do to diminish discrimination in schools of higher
learning depends upon your attitude toward this type of unequal
treatment. The mere recognition of the need for equality of opportunity based solely on criteria of the individual fitness of those
seeking higher education and your readiness to speak up for fair
educational practices will be a helpful contribution. If you can
address yourself to school officials with whom you have some
influence (such as the officials of your own Alma Mater) you may
aid in persuading them to eliminate discriminatory practices.

The likelihood is, however, that each institution of higher learning
will be much more willing to let down the bars against Victimians
when other colleges and universities admit them freely. Otherwise
each fears that if it acts unilaterally it will obtain not only its share
of Victimians but also a great many who should be absorbed by
other institutions, thus creating an imbalance in its own student
body. Under these circumstances it is apparent that you should
encourage the passage of a fair educational practice law in your
own state if none exists.

Before attempting to promote a fair educational practice law in
your state, study the text of the New York State law or the one
enacted by the Massachusetts legislature in August 1949. Familiarity
with these laws will enable you to discuss this type of law to better
advantage. Any librarian can obtain copies for you.

That law provides that aggrieved persons may file complaints with
the educational commissioner. If, on investigation, the commissioner

finds that the complaint is justified, he will seek to gain admittance for the complainant to the college or university which has refused to admit him. If the school continues to refuse admission, the commissioner will file his report with the Board of Regents. The Board of Regents may order a public hearing where witnesses and records may be subpoenaed. If, after this hearing, the board confirms the finding of the commissioner and the educational institution still refuses to comply, the board may obtain an enforcing order from the State Supreme Court. Refusal to comply with the court's order would bring contempt proceedings.

Institutions supervised or controlled by religious organizations are exempt from the provisions of the New York State Fair Educational Practice Law with respect to the religious basis for selection, although they are subject to the law as to race, color, and national origin. At the time of the law's adoption one hundred and twenty-six institutions of higher learning became subject to its regulations. Since New York is the first state in the United States wherein government authority has been applied to eliminate racial and religious discrimination in schools of higher learning, the results obtained by the administration of this law will be closely observed. The intent of the New York law is obviously excellent, but its actual effects will depend upon the regulations, policies, and procedures employed in its enforcement.

If you live in a state which has not yet adopted a fair *employment* practice act, you will be well advised to work for the passage of one before making any attempt to secure a fair *educational* practice law. To make more and more people aware of the harm done to the nation by discriminatory practices of both types is desirable everywhere at all times.

When you are drawn into a discussion of whether or not laws should be adopted to end discrimination in schools of higher learning, someone is likely to inject the old teaser, "You can't legislate morality," or "You can't legislate civil rights." I was surprised to find that during a week's institute on the community, the subject of an evening's session was "Can we legislate civil rights?" I was told by several people who were present that the speaker for the negative came off better than the speaker for the affirmative, although the affirmative speaker (as well as his opponent) spoke very ably. The result could hardly be otherwise. Anyone attempting to prove that careful auto driving can be legislated is defeated in advance. Of a certainty you cannot, by legislation, turn incompetent and reckless drivers into competent, careful drivers. Road laws are not adopted to "legislate safety." Using the word "legislating" in that way can only create confusion. We can and do by legislation lessen the extent of dangerous driving. It can hardly be denied that we have fewer collisions and fatalities than would be the case if there were no speed limits and other safety regulations.

A proper question would be, "Can the amount of racial and religious discrimination in college admissions (or in employment, et cetera) be lessened by well-conceived laws?" The answer is, "Yes." To the question, "Can civil rights be legislated?" or, "Can morality be legislated?" the proper answer is, "Rephrase the question. As it stands now, it resembles the slogan of those who opposed woman's suffrage with 'Woman's place is in the home.'" Such incongruous phrases have hampered many a good movement. "Can civil rights be legislated?" merely keeps people from thinking clearly on the subject and disposes them toward a belief that the arm of the law is somehow being misdirected. Don't answer the question. Challenge the use of the phrase.

What you can do about discrimination in education can be summarized as follows:

1. Drive home to everyone you can influence the baneful effects of closing academic doors because of unfair discrimination.

2. Try to persuade college and university officials to stop practicing discrimination against racial and religious groups in admissions to their institutions.

3. Urge the elimination of questions concerning the race, religion, and ethnic origin on the application blanks of institutions of learning. These are not indices of merit. Numerous other questions provide the information that should matter.

4. In states where neither fair employment nor fair educational practice laws operate give priority to the enactment of fair employment practice laws. Concentrate first on achieving fair employment opportunity.

5. Where fair employment practice laws are in effect work toward passage of state fair educational practice laws.

Be sure to study the wordings and the workings of fair educational practice laws in force elsewhere.

6. Where separate schooling is provided for pupils of different races, get all the facts. With patience but persistence insist on genuinely equal schooling. You will inevitably awaken an increasing number of the misinformed to the fact that segregation and equality are incompatible.

CHAPTER 4

Discrimination in Public Accommodations

For Negro Americans, Washington is not just the nation's capital. It is the point at which all public transportation into the South becomes "Jim Crow." If he stops in Washington, a Negro may dine like other men in the Union Station, but as soon as he steps out into the capital he leaves such democratic practices behind. With very few exceptions he is refused service at downtown restaurants, he may not attend a downtown movie or play, and he has to go into the poorer section of the city to find a night's lodging. The Negro who decides to settle in the District must find a home in an overcrowded, substandard area. He must often take a job below the level of his ability. He must send his children to inferior public schools set aside for Negroes and entrust his family's health to medical agencies which give inferior service. In addition, he must endure the countless daily humiliations that the system of segregation imposes upon the one third of Washington that is Negro.

The shamefulness and absurdity of Washington's treatment of Negro Americans is highlighted by the presence of many dark-skinned foreign visitors. Capital custom not only humiliates colored citizens but is a source of considerable embarrassment to these visitors. White residents, because they are the dominant group, share in both the humiliation and the embarrassment. Foreign officials are often mistaken for American Negroes and refused food, lodging, and entertainment. However, once it is established that they are not Americans, they are accommodated.

THE DAILY GRIND OF PREJUDICE 83

This description of conditions in Washington was not written by an agitator attempting to discredit our nation or to cause internal dissension by exaggerating the plight of the American Negro in our national capital. It is a carefully considered statement made in 1947 by the highly responsible citizens selected by the President of the United States to serve as the President's Committee on Civil Rights. Having pondered the matter, they concluded, "This is the situation that exists in the District of Columbia. The Committee feels most deeply that it is intolerable."

The abolition of segregation in places of public accommodation in Washington is not a local issue. It is a national one. Washington is our nation's capital. Your congressmen and mine administer its affairs. It should reflect the most enlightened social and moral outlook of our entire country. In the eyes of the world you and I are responsible for this sorry state of social backwardness in the District of Columbia. All of us, in every section of our country, have an urgent duty to bring pressure upon our federal legislators to rectify this situation insofar as they possibly can.

In a world where the white race is outnumbered two to one, Americans can ill afford to give communist propagandists the enormous advantage of being able to point to the systematic, deliberate mistreatment of colored people in the national capital or anywhere else in the United States. True, Moscow is inhabited almost entirely by whites, but there is no segregation along racial lines. Within the Soviet sphere there are no Jim Crow laws. As the champion of liberalism and democracy, we are the target of propaganda. Such flagrantly discriminatory conditions in public accommodations as those admitted in the report of the President's Committee and in *A Report of the National Committee on Segregation in the Nation's Capital* do us inestimable damage everywhere in the world.

You may ask, "Just what do we mean when we use the term 'public accommodations'?" The exact definition of the term has occasionally caused difficulties. It obviously includes any establishment to which the public at large has access and where even a stranger may come and be served. On the other hand, an establishment whose services are provided only for its own limited, well-defined clientele is not a place of public accommodation. For example, a restaurant, a barbershop, or a bookstore conducted by a corporation solely for its employees is a private, not a public, accommodation. A social club may have a *private* swimming pool, whose use is restricted to its members and their friends. But a swimming pool that draws its patronage from the public at large is a *public* facility. Whether it is privately or publicly *owned* is, of course, immaterial.

From time to time individuals have attempted to avoid the clear intention of the law by misusing the distinction made above. The owner of a public swimming pool, having been penalized for barring Victimians, made a "club" out of his enterprise. Any white person who came, even for the first time, was instantly made a "member" of the "club," in return for paying the price of admission. "Membership" was automatically refused to any person who was not white. But, unlike the membership of a genuine club, the "members" of this one had no interest in it whatsoever beyond using the swimming pool. Flimsy ruses of this sort are sometimes used to exclude unwanted groups. Fortunately they cannot for long circumvent the law when determined effort is made to enforce it.

All of us are apt to think of discrimination against Negroes as though it were the whole story, to the neglect of similar mistreatment of other dark-skinned peoples. In addition to 13,000,000 Negroes, there are in the United States some 3,000,000 persons of Mexican derivation, approximately 350,000 Indians, about 80,000 Chinese, more than 125,000 Japanese, as well as members of other races. And for every individual and family for whom the road to normal happiness is blocked by unfeeling prejudice, the problem is a grievous one, regardless of whether their particular situation is shared by many or a few.

A revealing sidelight on discrimination in places of public accommodation is furnished by a report of the Governor's Inter-racial Commission on the Mexican in Minnesota. This painstaking report was prepared, attractively printed, and widely distributed, thanks to the conscientious concern of Governor Luther W. Youngdahl and the citizens of Minnesota for the five thousand Mexicans permanently resident in St. Paul and Minneapolis, as well as for the thousands of others imported annually from Mexico during the harvest season. The report points out that "The Mexicans who come into Minnesota even for only a season are part of a cultural chain stretching down to Texas across the Rio Grande and deep into Mexico. In their letters and their visits they record the treatment they experience in Minnesota. For good or evil they are ambassadors for Minnesota." "The United States" may be appropriately substituted for "Minnesota" in the last sentence.

The report indicates that Minnesota offers far superior treatment to these Spanish Americans than they receive in the Southwest. It frankly admits, however, that "In the rural areas there are some cases reported where Mexicans have been refused service in restaurants. They encounter signs reading, 'No Mexicans May Eat Here.' The basis of opposition seems to be a point of hygiene."

That "point of hygiene" is in no way explained. It is left dangling. But let us assume that it does mean something. Let us assume that a Mexican laborer looking for a place to eat in some sparsely settled area where the restaurants are all closed to him *is* dirty—as dirty as any other man doing the same sort of work. Is he, then, a pariah? He is healthy and free of disease. He is even literate, for otherwise he could hardly be expected to read the "No Mexicans" signs he encounters. ("No Mexicans," not even the President of Mexico!) Given access to the restaurant's washroom, he would be, from the standpoint of cleanliness, indistinguishable from the other patrons of the restaurant. But he isn't permitted inside to wash. He is excluded because he is dirty. What should our Mexican "ambassador" do then? Throw his hat in the air and cry, *"Viva los Estados Unidos"?*

Minnesota law for years has forbidden such signs, has prohibited that type of discrimination. If Minnesota's unprejudiced citizens cared enough, every such sign would be buried in a refuse dump. Yet an official report to the governor concedes that some restaurants still display signs reading, "No Mexicans May Eat Here."

Orientals, even those born in this country and therefore citizens, as well as Negroes, are unwelcome in restaurants and hotels in many localities. For them the shadow of a too-dark skin falls across the doors of many of our places of public accommodation from east to west and north to south. By pointing up national conditions of discrimination along these lines I am in no way condoning the discriminatory situation in the South. I am, instead, pointing out that the liberal who wants to work most effectively (rather than display his own superiority) works at home. There is plenty to be done close at hand. Rifle shots at nearby targets will accomplish more than shotgun blasts fired far away.

Someone has said, "The lynchings take place in the South and the protest meetings are held in the North." Sadly enough, the excellent editorials of liberal Southern editors do not get so much national publicity as the more intemperate fulminations of excited Northerners, who have the same advantage as a little dog on one side of an iron fence barking at a much larger dog on the other side. As a Northerner who does not regard tact, discretion, and honest diplomacy as vices, I prefer to leave it to far-sighted Southerners, as idealistic as any of us, to provide the techniques and specific measures for eliminating Jim Crow laws and customs. *All* I ask is, "Abolish Jim Crowism completely—every vestige of it, by whatever stages will do it best."

The wisest of Southerners who have the welfare of their Negro neighbors at heart do not ask Northern friends to be silent about the mistreatment of Negroes in the South. They even advise others to exert the pressure of friendly criticism. But they are averse to blatant, abusive attacks upon the South which arouse resentment and resistance because they are couched in intemperate anger-provoking terms.

To my mind the most important game of the 1947 football season was played at Durham, North Carolina, on November 23. It was the third annual Piedmont Tobacco Bowl program and was staged at the Durham Athletic Park. There were only 3,000 people on hand, which, as football crowds go, would make this game seem a third-rate affair. Yet newspapers throughout the nation wrote it up and it will live in history when much more touted games will have been forgotten. It was the first football game played in the South between a team of Negroes and a team of whites. And the crowd that witnessed the event was not segregated.

The weather was terrible. But the Vulpine Athletic Club of Philadelphia, the whites, and the Willow Tree Athletic Team of Washington, D.C., the Negroes, playing on a muddy field during a steady rain, proved that sportsmanship can weather intolerance. The final score was certainly unintended but is perhaps symbolic—6 to 6.

There is no such thing as the "Solid South"—or any "solid" community, for that matter. There are liberal and enlightened people everywhere and they *can* meet on common ground anywhere and at any time. They are making progress. The Freedom Train rightly bypassed the few Southern cities which insisted on segregation. But most Southern cities eased their restrictions, realizing that the refusal to allow whites and Negroes to view together the historical documents of their mutual heritage would make a mockery of the occasion. The people who are making these advances possible in their own communities need help and encouragement. They can well dispense with the kind of abuse which only provides ammunition for bigots.

Turning our attention away now from legalized segregation, let us consider the more subtle forms of segregation employed in the North. The results are just as real. It is just as unpleasant in the North to walk a mile past many restaurants to find a place where you will be allowed to eat. It may be worse to enter a restaurant and be told "No service." It is small consolation to know that there is no legal segregation if people of your race are made to sit for hours, while whites get immediate service and until finally you receive rude attention from a glowering waiter who does his best to make you wish you had never entered.

The mere passage of civil rights statutes does not usher in Utopia. Since 1885 Illinois has had a law specifically mentioning inns, restaurants, eating houses, hotels, soda fountains, soda drink parlors, taverns, roadhouses, barbershops, department stores, clothing stores, hat stores, shoe stores, bathrooms, restrooms, theaters, skating rinks, concerts, cafés, bicycle rinks, and fifteen other categories, as well as other places of public accommodation, as places wherein "all persons . . . shall be entitled to full and equal enjoyment of accommodations, advantages, facilities, and privileges . . . Any person violating these provisions except for reasons applicable alike to all persons of every race and color, may be required for every offense to pay a sum not less than twenty-five dollars nor more than five hundred dollars to the aggrieved person." This basic law has been strengthened by subsequent statutes, requiring various officials to enforce the law.

The Illinois laws—I use them only by way of example—are sufficiently stringent and specific to make it *seem unlikely* that they would be violated to any considerable extent. Yet you need only look into the lobbies and restaurants of the best hotels in Chicago to convince yourself that the law is pretty much of a dead letter.

The same is true in scores of other cities, where laws on the subject are more breached than observed.

There are several reasons for non-enforcement. People as a rule do not want to go where they are not welcome. Members of some groups have a silent boycott against restaurants where the proprietors have let it be known they would rather none of the group entered. They do not want to give their patronage to those who accept it grudgingly. If, however, discriminatory practices are to be terminated, Victimians will have to forego their pride and for the sake of the larger principle assert their legal rights.

A second reason why accommodations are denied to Victimians is that it is often easy to evade the law without furnishing proof satisfactory to a court of law that discrimination was being practiced. The waiter was very busy or there were no more rooms available or the particular person seeking accommodations did not make his wish clear or he was discourteous and unruly. There are plenty of pretexts difficult to overcome, since the burden of proof is upon the complainants. The problems involved in pressing such charges and the notoriety incurred make the average citizen reluctant to be the guinea pig, especially since he knows that even if he wins his isolated case the discriminatory practices may continue after payment of penalty. Yet to get enforcement of the present laws charges have to be brought and suits have to be filed and penalties inflicted. A system by which a state commission would handle discrimination in public accommodations as fair employment practices are handled by a state commission would be preferable to the present arrangements. In 1949 New Jersey blazed the trail by amending its law against discrimination in employment to give its established commission jurisdiction over charges of discrimination in places of public accommodations and also in educational institutions.

It is possible, however, to secure enforcement of existing laws. By a series of civil suits the Vanguard League of Columbus, Ohio, formed for the express purpose of obtaining admission for Negroes to the local theaters (in compliance with the Ohio Civil Rights Law), obtained their goal. First there were friendly discussions with the theater owners. The results were zero. Then large numbers of league members went to the theaters and were refused admission. They brought their complaints into the office of a city official, where many Negroes had come previously as individuals and had received scant attention. But now a campaign was organized. As many as eight suits were brought in a single day against two theater owners. Finally the league was invited by the attorney for the theater interests to a conference, something that would not have occurred in the case of individuals taking cases to court. On June 27, 1941, the theater owners agreed, in exchange for the dropping of these suits, to obey the Civil Rights Law. There has been practically no cause for complaint on the part of Negroes since then and no complaints by the operators that any of the white patrons have objected to sharing the theaters with Negroes. There have been no reports of racial friction or of decline in business.

Economic considerations can frequently be used to rout local bigotry. This happened when a national organization planned a meeting of its district workers in a Southern city. Both white and Negro members of the professional staff were to attend the conference. It was necessary that the sessions be held where Negroes would be welcome. The only suitable place proved to be the Negro university in the convention city. Very good accommodations were available there. The arrangers of the conference were predominantly liberals who swiftly overrode any objections to their plan and issued the invitations. The organization agreed to pay the university five dollars per day for each person's room and food. Those invited were so informed. Among the replies were some from white workers whose hearts were bleeding. How gladly they would take lodging and meals at the Negro university, but, since they worked and lived in Southern communities, they dared not admit that they had spent nights under any but lily-white roofs. Oh no! It was impossible. Despite their own lofty sentiments they had to yield to the archaic concepts of some of their constituents.

The arrangements committee could have replied, "You will have to come as directed and room where you are told." That would have given the complainants opportunity to appeal to their prejudiced neighbors and stir up trouble. Instead, the guests were informed that only five dollars per day could be allowed to each of them for room and board during the conference. If they could manage to follow their own noble inclinations—and disregard possible objections from the misguided—the university quarters would be available for that amount. Stopping in town would be perfectly all right. It would be well to figure, however, on four dollars per diem for a hotel room, about three dollars more for each day's meals, and bus fare each way to the university would be another dollar. With tips at the hotel and other incidentals it would probably mean a difference of three or four dollars each day. The decision on how to proceed (with this information in mind) was left to each person.

Without a single exception, everyone attending the conference decided to stop at the Negro university, where they received more than ten dollars' worth of accommodations per day. The sessions were very successful. There were no unfavorable repercussions whatever, and none of the white professional workers will go about the rest of their lives saying, "So sorry. I would have liked to have shown my own liberal spirit. Some of my best friends are Negroes. But you know what public opinion is in the South!" Hypocrisy often yields to monetary considerations. When it can be tactfully and judiciously employed, an argument that bears the dollar sign is as potent in dispelling bigotry as it is in other matters.

The story I like best in reference to discrimination in eating places is one I have obtained third hand. I have been assured that it actually happened, but I am not certain of the details. A football squad was gathered at the bar of a New Jersey tavern. One member of the team was a Negro. In compliance with New Jersey law the bartender served them all. But when he had cleared away the glasses of the others, he lifted the glass from which the Negro had drunk and smashed it on the floor. (There is no law in effect or under contemplation that would enjoin the breaking of a glass.)

The football players were a cool-headed lot. "Just like that!" said one of them. "Just like we sometimes do when we want to toast a guy."

They ordered another round of drinks, and again everyone was served. When the glasses were drained, the captain called for a toast. "Here's to our jolly bartender! Great guy, isn't he?"

They drank, and then in gleeful chorus crashed the glasses on the floor. The bartender's remonstrances were utterly futile under the raillery of his guests.

"Let's have another drink," the boys decided, and again they were all served. When they had finished, the captain said, "Want us to break these or are you going to take them all?"

There were no glasses broken this time. Once more bigotry yielded to economics.

Responsible Negro leadership believes that the greatest progress in securing the rights of accommodation in public places can be secured by non-violent, good-will direct action. Violent action is ruled out because the minority generally gets the worst of it when violence flares. Even minor violence, such as brushing past the ticket taker and swarming into a theater, leads readily to major violence, such as race riots. Non-violence is therefore the rule of the Congress of Racial Equality (CORE). This organization has found that where the entire pattern of a community's restaurant is discriminatory, as in Washington, D.C., a change in one place is not likely to occur unless some similar places—preferably all—change. Even if pressure campaigns compel just one restaurant to accept Negro patronage it will slip back into the pattern of the other restaurants soon after pressure is removed. But there are localities where the discriminatory pattern is not complete and where the removal of restrictions in a few strategic eating places is decidedly helpful. To accomplish this change CORE has developed some highly interesting techniques. One instance has been described by Mary White Ovington in *The Walls Came Tumbling Down* (Harcourt, Brace and Company, 1947).

This occurred in a restaurant which discriminated against colored people:

> *The manager was approached and asked to serve Negroes. When argument failed, direct action began. Some twenty young people of both races went into the restaurant together and asked for service. The Negroes were told they could not be served. They remained in their seats and the white companions with them refused to take the food offered them. Other white and colored came in, stood in line, and were refused counter service. So Core members remained for hours, some talking, some quietly reading, all behaving with the utmost decorum. The manager called in the police, who refused to make an arrest since there was no disturbance. Hours went on. Other diners, interested in the outcome, remained in their seats. At length a woman not in Core left her place to invite a colored girl standing in line to sit at her table. The room broke into applause, and the manager gave the order to serve the colored. The restaurant continues to serve Negroes and has not lost trade. "What are you?" an inquiring policeman asked. "Communists?"*

*"No, Christians." Once a man is won over by these methods,
Core finds, he becomes a friend and is won over for good.*

Direct action, coupled not with rancor or abuse, but with good
will as firm as it is cordial, offers considerable help in the difficult
job of turning civil rights laws, bearing upon public accommodations, into enforced statutes. But as Nathaniel L. Goldstein, attorney
general of New York State, reported on January 11, 1948, in reference to several hundred complaints of discrimination in hotels,
resorts, restaurants, and other places of public accommodation,
"The problem of eliminating racial and religious discrimination in
the hotel and resort field, as knotty a problem in human relations
as any confronting public officials, is susceptible to solution by
informational and educational tactics without recourse to the firm
legal powers which can be utilized in willful instances." The soft
silk glove covering a hand of iron can be used nowhere to greater
effect than in eliminating discriminatory practices.

On the whole the members of the colored races suffer far more
exclusion from places of public accommodation than do any white
persons. In part this is because of a greater amount of social discrimination against them and in part to the fact that they are more
readily identifiable. But Jews, both native and foreign born, as well
as foreign-born members of some other groups who are readily welcomed in commercial establishments, are denied accommodations
in resort hotels which should be classified as places of public accommodation. Here an anomalous situation exists. There are states
where it is permissible to discriminate on the basis of race or creed,
but advertising such discrimination is legally forbidden.

In Maine a law reads: "No material shall be published directly
or indirectly . . . which tends to or does discriminate against any
religious sect, creed, class, denomination, or nationality in the full
enjoyment of accommodations and privileges offered to the general
public; neither may anyone incite to such violation." A penalty is
provided. And yet, "nothing in this section shall be construed to
prohibit the mailing of a private communication in writing, sent in
response to a specific written inquiry." Note that this statute does
not forbid advertising *racial* discrimination. The degrees and kinds
of discrimination that are forbidden or permitted are many.

Surely it is not sufficient to forbid publicizing discrimination
while permitting the actual practice to continue. Yet it was gratify-

ing to find, after the passage of a statute in New Hampshire, similar to the Maine law cited above, that many objectionable signs disappeared along the roadways. Even a small step in the right direction should be welcomed, especially since it is likely to be followed by other desirable steps.

What can you do about discrimination in places of public accommodation? If you happen to be the owner of an establishment where discrimination is practiced, stop it. That is the first move. But it is only the first. Your responsibility doesn't end with your own business. If your establishment discriminates, presumably others in your locality do the same. Bring the matter up in your trade group, your businessmen's association, or hotel managers' association, or whatever organization can institute a change. Your help is needed wherever your influence is felt.

But the elimination of discrimination is not a one-man job. It is not a job for whites, or for Negroes alone. This is an interracial job, or an interreligious job, a job for members of the group that discriminates, in co-operation with members of the group that is discriminated against. It requires organization to investigate the possibilities to decide what to do and how to do it, to co-ordinate the efforts of all groups. The experience of others should not be overlooked by each new group going into action. Whether a statute needs to be passed or a present one amended or efforts need to be made to secure conformity with the law, line up with others who are similarly interested in order to get the job done as quickly and as easily as possible. Above all be prepared to stand up for your beliefs. If, for example, four or five white persons are going out to dine and someone suggests inviting a Negro and one of the others says he will not go along if a Negro is invited, don't kowtow to prejudice. Let that fellow count himself out. All too often the exponent of Jim Crow has it his way, even where there are no Jim Crow laws.

You should know what legislation can do to end discrimination in places of public accommodation in your own state and city. Is there a law covering your locality forbidding discrimination in places of public accommodation? The efforts of many well-intentioned people are made ineffective simply because they are ill directed or uninformed. A pamphlet in the Minnesota laws sums up the situation nicely: "Much discrimination and segregation are successfully practiced due to lack of knowledge on the part of American citizens, and to their negligence about taking advantage of existing laws. We must learn not only to fully use the perfectly good state civil rights statutes and fair employment practice legislation, but to exert our full strength in getting similar laws passed in the remaining states."

CHAPTER 5

Discrimination in Housing

A Negro and a white man had undergone operations to restore their sight. During their convalescence the Negro faced the ordeal of waiting to learn the outcome of surgery with such cheerful courage that the nurses suggested he spend some of his time with a wealthy, socially elite white man who was grumbling in fear and hopelessness. The Negro's soft, pleasant voice and his optimistic, religious outlook were tonic to the white man who, unaware of the difference of race, developed a great liking for his companion. But there was no doubt of his own parochial preference for "the right class of people." The Negro skillfully avoided any deception but provided for the other man badly needed reassurances during the waiting period. At last the bandages were removed from the Negro's eyes. He was able to see dimly, but to see, with excellent prospect of further improvement. He paid his last visit to the other man, whose bandages were to be removed the following day.

"Write out your name and address for me," requested the white man as they parted. A moment later a piece of paper was put into his hand. It was blank.

"Don't tell him who I am," the Negro told the hospital staff. "Some people's opinion of a man changes completely when they find out he lives in Harlem."

Who consigned this Negro to Harlem? Who forces him to stay there as long as he makes New York City his home? Who condemns millions of the well deserving to live in squalid discomfort, no matter what their personal virtues and abilities may be?

It is easy to find individuals and organizations upon whose shoulders the blame can be placed. We might point to the realtors and hold them responsible. A brochure issued in 1943 by a national association of real estate dealers warned its members against instigating "a blight" by selling to undesirable applicants. Four examples of objectionable prospective buyers are mentioned. Three of the types listed were "a bootlegger, a madam who has a number of call girls on her string, and a gangster who wants a screen for his activities by living in a better neighborhood." Their refusal to sell to such disreputable characters entitles the realtors to our respect. People who have invested their funds in a neighborhood should not suffer loss by reason of vicious intruders. But there was a fourth example: "a colored man of means who was giving his children a college education and thought they were entitled to live in a good neighborhood."

According to the description this Negro was not criminal, or vicious, or disorderly; he was not shiftless or even poor. He was a man of means who sent his children to college. Yet the bulletin of the national organization of fifteen thousand realtors stigmatizes him along with bootleggers, prostitutes, and gangsters as someone who would contaminate a residential district. How dare this father and his well-educated children expect "to live in a *good* neighborhood"! Presumably he and his brood belong in a bad one along with the bootleggers, gamblers, and prostitutes.

Where shall this well-to-do Negro, who apparently has no fault other than the color of his skin, live with his college-bred family? He is to remain in—or squeeze into—the Negro area, a frightfully overcrowded ghetto in the most run-down section of town. As described by Herman H. Long and Charles S. Johnson in *People vs. Property*, the Negro areas "tend to be located in the oldest part of the city, where the first housing was erected, and thus they contain the oldest and most obsolete dwellings. . . . They tend to exhibit the greatest municipal neglect, not only because the dwellings and surrounding facilities are hardest to keep in repair but because the residents themselves have the least to say about the services provided." In these areas there is the least fire protection, the least enforcement of health and sanitary codes. Garbage disposal is at its poorest; street repairs are neglected. The police are indifferent to the growth of crime in the area. The inhabitants are powerless against the whole downhill trend.

Discriminatory practice in housing is not confined to Negroes. It is practiced against many kinds of Victimians, including Orientals. Mrs. William Yee, a Chinese war bride, met her husband, then a sergeant in the Fourteenth Service Group, at the Red Cross center at Kunming. She and the other Chinese war brides had heard a great deal about American democracy. But when they arrived in the United States they found that they could reside nowhere except within the confinement of a metropolitan Chinatown. Said Mrs. Yee plaintively, "They say Chinese don't want to spread out. We want to spread out but people here don't let us."

The unfair treatment accorded to colored people and to Orientals extends also to Indians as well as to a number of other groups. In a brief submitted to the United States Supreme Court against restrictive covenants the American Indian Citizens' League pointed out: "This entire continent was once the property of the American Indians. Occupation and use was unrestricted and both the aboriginal owners and the European immigrants found ample room. . . . The White people . . . continually asked for a larger and still larger space until there is no longer any room for us."

The practices of real estate groups have undoubtedly contributed to the growth of discrimination. But the shameful fact that we have built tight walls around certain neighborhoods (to the injury of more than twenty-five million Americans) cannot be explained simply on the grounds of realtors' prejudices. Real estate operators are merely the agents who transact property deals. Financial institutions, with whose funds houses are usually built or bought, have also developed restrictive policies. How deeply these policies have penetrated is well illustrated by instructions given by our federal government's financing agency, the Federal Housing Administration.

The Federal Housing Administration in guaranteeing mortgages has followed the practice of respecting local racial patterns instituted by an earlier government agency, the Home Owners' Loan Corporation. The FHA *Underwriting Manual of 1947* reads: "If a neighborhood is to retain stability, it is necessary that properties shall continue to be occupied by the same social and racial classes." Valuators are advised in the *Manual* that deeds should include "Prohibition of the occupancy of properties except by the race for which they are intended." In response to public pressure the Federal Housing Administration eliminated these strictures. But the removal of such provisions from the written code does not necessarily alter the practices of FHA appraisers, who consider the mingling of racial groups an unacceptable risk.

The ultimate cause of residential discrimination lies not with some restricted group such as the realtors or financial groups. It is the result of anachronistic public opinion. Realtors and financial institutions are the on-stage parties whose transactions enforce residential restrictions. They can rightly plead that they are merely responsive to the prods and tugs of hosts of citizens cheering them on from the wings off stage. To negotiate a lease, a sale, or a mortgage loan for a member of a rejected group would in many localities bring down the wrath of the community against the dealer or the bank. In some instances it might result in disastrous loss of clientele. The ultimate culprits are those countless homeowners and tenants who insist on excluding from their neighborhoods any and every member of a Victimian group, and the even greater body of citizens who thoughtlessly acquiesce in the practice.

Denouncing restrictive covenants, the Most Reverend Bernard J. Sheil, Auxiliary Bishop of Chicago, quoted Father George H. Dunne, who wrote in his article, "The Sin of Segregation": "The sophistry and hypocrisy of those who defend residential segregation by appealing to their right to maintain a proper standard of morals, of cleanliness, or of beauty surrounding their homes is made manifest by the undoubted fact that these same people, for the most part, would prefer a white neighbor who violated all of their standards to a Negro neighbor who more than measured up to their most stringent demands."

Attempts to enforce segregation by overt schemes is an innovation of some fifty years ago. As long as the Negro population was concentrated in the South with only tiny trickles above the Mason and Dixon line and as long as Negroes lacked economic strength, the segregation of Negro homes was unplanned and automatic. They and the "Orientals" lived in the alleys back of the homes in which they served as domestics. But the migration of Negroes into Northern industrial centers, the moving of the Chinese and Japanese out of the alleyways on the West coast, and the drifting of Mexicans, Italians, Jews, and members of other minority groups from the colonies where they clustered as immigrants, brought resolute attempts to preserve certain urban areas as precincts into which entry would be permanently denied to whole groups of people. In the name of "urban redevelopment" and "housing reform" zoning ordinances were passed in many localities between 1900 and 1917 to exclude some racial groups from certain neighborhoods. This scheme received a setback when in 1917 the Supreme Court invalidated a Louisville ordinance forbidding Negroes from moving into any block occupied by a white majority. Cities were not permitted to "zone people out" in that fashion. But as Charles Abrams says in *Race Bias in Housing*, "A civil right may be nullified by indifference as by decree. . . . Subterfuge will be resorted to or other means found for defeating the law's purposes." The subterfuge in this case has been the restrictive covenant.

A real estate covenant is a recognized device for protecting oneself and one's neighbors by mutual assurances that none of the covenanters will sell his property for uses (such as a glue factory or a tannery) which would decrease the value of the neighborhood for residential purposes. A restrictive covenant against a race or other group is an agreement written into each deed by a large portion of the property holders in a certain neighborhood in which each of them declares that he will not transfer the property to or permit occupancy by a member of the proscribed group. In most instances exemption is made permitting servants to reside there.

In 1910 covenants against selling for Negro occupancy were introduced in St. Louis. Not until 1927 were they used in Chicago. They are now very abundant in those cities as well as in New York, Detroit, Los Angeles, San Francisco, and many others. It is probably not true, although frequently alleged, that 80 per cent of Chicago's residential property is restricted by racial covenants— we have only estimates—but even if 40 per cent is nearer the correct figure it is a shameful state of affairs, especially since the covenants are so placed as to hem in the Black Belt from all contiguous desirable homes and to prevent the compressed mass of its inhabitants from expanding beyond arbitrarily fixed boundaries. And the increase in covenanted areas is only one aspect of the situation. In many areas of Chicago and other cities no covenants are needed since "gentlemen's agreements" between real estate brokers, bankers, neighbors, and all who are in a position to prevent Negro entry into an area assure airtight exclusion even though there is no formal, documented agreement among the property owners.

How did the restrictive covenants come into being? Sometimes by the agitation of a few of the residents of a neighborhood who

arranged meetings (usually in a school or a church) and warned
the other neighbors of the great "peril of invasion" confronting
them. Sometimes a land development company inserted a restrictive
covenant in all the deeds it issued. Most often a neighborhood
improvement association which had been serving some good purposes undertook to get more than three fourths of the property
owners to adopt restrictive covenants. The association then became
the guardian of the covenants and used whatever powers it could
to prevent infraction. In Chicago one of the most vocal and powerful neighborhood groups has proudly issued annual reports of its
accomplishments. Like similar associations, this one fought attempts
to pass state legislation nullifying restrictive covenants and brought
successful lawsuits to prevent sales of covenanted property to
Negroes.

Although racial restrictive covenants are private agreements
between individuals, they had, until recently, the strength of law,
since they could be enforced in the courts. Anyone violating the
covenant in his deed could be forced to desist from a sale not in
conformity with it. Negro organizations went to great pains to
annul a covenant here and there by proving that the signatures
were incorrect or that the covenant had been defaulted by earlier
infraction and the like. But in the main the covenants worked like
a yoke around the neck of the Negro settlements. However, a decision rendered May 3, 1948, by the Supreme Court of the United
States began a new era in regard to these covenants. The Supreme
Court declared that no law courts can enforce restrictive covenants
barring people because of creed or color from acquiring property
or leases. (Private property rights are by no means unlimited. They
are subject, for example, to forced sale when needed for public
thoroughfare.) In this instance property owners in effect have been
told that the courts will not help them violate the Fourteenth
Amendment via the path of restrictive covenants.

Obviously this decision of the Supreme Court will make it easier
for members of proscribed groups to get into neighborhoods from
which they were previously barred by restrictive covenants. If someone sells or rents to them no policeman or sheriff will turn them out.
But that does not solve the problem by any means. We are only at
the beginning of a new struggle. We dare not forget the sounds of
shooting, the smell of stench bombs, the crackle of burning timber,
and memories of men killed at spots where Negroes dared to move

across the color line. There have been large-scale riots, such as occurred in Detroit when Negroes moved into a public housing
project, and individual instances of isolated Negro residents firmly
standing their ground during successive nights of terror. Stoning,
housewrecking, arson, and even murder have to be risked—and no
doubt will be risked—and suffered—by Negroes taking a desperate
stand for the simple right to live somewhere other than in a rat-
hole.

Personal attributes should determine fitness to live in a neighborhood. These include morality, integrity, cleanliness, aesthetic tastes,
courtesy, and consideration for the happiness of neighbors. In comparison with these characteristics of the good neighbor, the race,
ethnic origin, and religious affiliation of a family are immaterial.
Some people profess to believe that when a hundred-dollar-a-month
house is offered for rental a shabbily dressed, ignorant non-white
earning less than thirty dollars a week will move into it unless all
non-whites are kept out. That is sheer nonsense. Non-whites with
education, culture, character, personal charm, and income comparable to those of white people who can afford the same accommodations will be the tenants.

Well-meaning people will occasionally point out that according to
a poll taken among real estate dealers "the Negro does take good
care of property if it is in good repair when he obtains it." The
favorable verdict on that question was 70 per cent against 30 per
cent who voted adversely. But here again even the stanchest defender of the Negroes' rights falls into the old trap of generalization. Do Negroes take good care of property? Some do. Some don't.
By what canon of good sense does a blanket judgment presumably
about all Negroes tell a landlord anything about a particular applicant? Regardless of his race or creed a tenant may be clean or filthy.
Does anyone rent to all whites or refuse to rent to all whites on the
basis of a judgment of the whole group?

The whole sorry spectacle of racial discrimination revolves
around the fear of losing social status by living on a street with
members of a race which is regarded as "inferior." It is very much
like women smoking cigarettes. Any woman who did so a generation ago lost the respect of her acquaintances. Now that so many
women smoke cigarettes, no woman need have the slightest fear of
public disapproval for doing so. Segregation is similarly rooted in

style. People become accustomed to the proximity of members of other races quickly. The struggle does not come after a mixed neighborhood has been established. The hostility occurs beforehand and in the process of changing. It is anxiety and fear and the fantastic, pernicious ideas of the prejudiced which create the trouble. People of various races and religions who have been living for a while in the same neighborhood or apartment house get along as well as—and no better than—they would with members of their own race.

Many a white man or woman living happily in a non-segregated housing project is subjected to the sympathy of oversolicitous friends who are quite aghast. "I hear you have Negroes in the same building! It's awful, but of course there's such a housing shortage." The answer is very different than the one expected. "Yes, there are Negroes in our building. They're lovely people. We are glad to have them near us. Our neighbors are considerate and congenial. They are big-hearted, free of miserable little spites and prejudices. A mixed neighborhood is a pleasant, cheerful place and I'm happy to be living in one." Such sentiments as these are common among the occupants of mixed-housing projects. There are, of course, people who are dissatisfied. There are also people who are dissatisfied in segregated housing projects.

There is no more vicious aspect of prejudice than housing discrimination. Every legal method of eradicating it should be employed, especially where public housing is involved. But even more necessary is a campaign of education among both Victimians and non-Victimians. In that campaign remember these six things:

1. *The best time to influence others on the subject is before a crisis arises.* Before an acute problem is presented, facts can be offered in a calm, orderly, and open-minded fashion. Don't wait to discuss conditions with friends until after it has been discovered that a Victimian is moving into your neighborhood. After feelings are aroused it is always more difficult to explain that racial restrictions are injurious to all concerned and should therefore be abrogated.

2. *It is not too late to take up the cudgels in favor of Victimians even after a controversy has been precipitated.* I recall that nearly twenty years ago in a previously lily-white section of White Plains, New York, a Negro doctor and his family bought a home. There was

an immediate outcry, and pressure would have driven the doctor out had not the minister of the Community Church and the rabbi of the Jewish Community Center fought valiantly in his behalf in the court of public opinion. The doctor still resides in the house he bought. In another part of White Plains there is a delightful place, called Parkway Gardens, an unsegregated development of individual homes where forty-two middle-class white families and eight middle-class Negro families are enjoying right now the friendliness of kindly neighbors who do not intrude upon each other or encourage undesired social relations. They find life in an attractive environment much more pleasant, affable, and congenial than any narrow-minded bigot ever finds any spot on earth. There are unsegregated government housing projects likewise reporting great success.

3. *Organized resistance is essential wherever organized effort is made to evict new tenants or homeowners whose only disqualification is their race or religion.*

An excerpt from an article by Helena Huntington Smith, "Do You Know Your Neighbors?" which appeared in the February 1948 issue of *Woman's Home Companion,* illustrated the value of community protests in defending residential rights:

> In a modest pleasant residential district of San Francisco two Filipino families and a Chinese family were threatened with eviction because they were not white. One of the Filipino men had served twenty-seven years in the United States Navy and was a veteran of two world wars. The Chinese was also a veteran. The second Filipino had worked in a navy yard all through the last war. But it didn't make any difference. There was a restrictive covenant which said that "only members of the white race are allowed to reside in this district, except as servants" and some white neighbors proposed to start enforcing it.
>
> But other white neighbors flew to arms under the banner of fair play and freedom for all; the San Francisco Council for Civic Unity jumped into the race; newspapers aired it; and the would-be evictors received such a barrage of indignant letters and phone calls from fair-minded citizens of San Francisco that they backed down and withdrew their suit. A similar attempt to evict a Jewish family in a subur-

*ban area of Washington similarly brought angry response
from the public and was dropped.*

In Detroit, in the Ferndale district of Chicago and elsewhere,
attempts to keep Negroes out of public housing projects, although
backed by rioting, failed because of the determination of spirited
white citizens who organized so that the effort to drive out these
tenants should not succeed.

4. *In discussing residential restrictions against members of minority groups beware of stereotyping.* Insist upon judging people on
their individual characteristics. Refuse to accept the classifications of
race and creed. While some white Americans on the West coast
used every foul means at their disposal to drive out their Japanese
neighbors at the beginning of World War II and practically con-
fiscated their property, other white Americans within the same
Western states protected and tended the farms of expelled Japanese, welcomed them back at the end of the war, and assisted in their
rehabilitation. In Suffield, Connecticut, when the home of Mr. and
Mrs. Alonzo Wayne, an elderly Negro couple, burned to the ground,
the white neighbors did not rejoice that a Negro family had been
removed from the neighborhood. Instead, they raised $3,500 and
recruited volunteers to build a six-room, story-and-a-half structure
on the foundations of the old house. They even insured it against
fire. Mr. Wayne, a former professional baseball player, said, "There's
a lot of good people in the world." Those good people are the
nucleus for a movement which will eventually stop the vile practice of penning people in overcrowded areas and depriving them
of the right to live elsewhere.

5. *Make homeowners and renters aware that neighbors are best
protected by agreements which call for standards of maintenance.*
Emphasis upon those factors which are truly essential to a good
neighborhood should be made as explicit as possible, with the understanding that *any* family meeting these legitimate requirements
shall be welcome.

6. *Legislators need both education and public support.* The pattern of the past, however much "equal treatment" has been assured,
is a sorry one of cruel injustices, of unnecessary deprivations and
degradations, and of social evils as costly as wars. During the next
ten years one third of the nation will need to be rehoused. These

years will tell whether the United States is really to fulfill its promises for a democratic way of life or whether members of various races, religions, and national origins will continue to view one another suspiciously because of deep social cleavages fostered by segregation. Since much of the financing of housing will be done by our federal government, Congress can to a considerable extent determine the outcome.

You and your friends *can* influence your congressmen to declare themselves in favor of equitable treatment in housing for all of our citizenry. Write to them and get like-minded citizens to do the same, stressing the need for ending housing discrimination. Remember that you are not asking for any individual anything that person does not merit. You are requesting that the well deserving shall not be shunted into miserable quarters because of their racial, religious, or ethnic origin. You are doing your part in making a decision which will certainly be one of the most critical tests our democracy has ever faced.

PART THREE

Guises and Disguises of the Enemy

CHAPTER 1

Hate Organizations

Suppose the morning's mail has brought you a letter from an organization you have never heard of. This letter asks you to contribute to a movement to defend Americanism and to maintain freedom. Communism is denounced and the American way of life praised. This much sounds fine. But with the letter is some printed or mimeographed literature whose screaming headlines urge you to "WAKE UP" to the enormous perils confronting you and your dear ones. There are sly insinuations about a racial or religious group of other Americans. Recognizing the typical appeal of a hate organization, you know that your welfare and that of your fellow countrymen is not threatened by those whom this organization denounces, but by the very people who taint the mail and the air with such poisonous propaganda. What can you do about it?

The likelihood is that you can do very little, if anything, of a direct nature. You may comfort yourself with the knowledge that thousands of crackpots in the United States have ranted orally and in writing against racial and religious groups, without emerging beyond the stage of annoyance and without shaking the pillars of our nation. Their howls have usually subsided like the barking of so many dogs, without any consequence. Of the hundreds of hate organizations that were active between 1938 and 1942, many of which are mentioned in Roy Carlson's *Under Cover*, all but a very few have gone out of existence.

However, to return to the letter on your desk. You aren't satisfied to know that in all probability this organization is a picayune scheme for picking the pockets of the gullible. You want some specific information about the organization. You want to know if there is anything you can do. Then write to one of the organizations interested in the promotion of better human relations. Be guided by what advice you receive from this source. *Don't* make the mistake of thinking that you—or you and a few of your friends—should handle this situation in your own way. Any action to be taken will depend upon the size, scope, nature, and plans of the hate organization. That information is not available to the average citizen except through agencies which investigate hate promoters. These agencies have the facilities for gathering and correlating the facts. They have experience in handling these poison purveyors. You can best help them—and yourself—by following their advice.

Before you tackle one of these hate organizations in your community, you will, of course, need to know the history of that particular group. You'll need to know more. If you are to function effectively, you will have to be able to recognize the common characteristics of these groups—the hoary tricks and sleazy techniques which they so consistently use. Your local community agency will give you that information, high lighting those aspects bearing on the immediate problem. They will usually try to give you some historical background so that you can get a perspective on the problem.

In the first place (they will probably tell you) very few hate organizations in the United States have ever attained any lasting national importance. There have been a few—the Native American Party and the American Protective Association (APA), for example. But they are dead and gone. You needn't worry about them. They mushroomed to importance by exploiting temporary conditions and they shriveled into oblivion as those conditions were corrected.

Only one of these lawless hate organizations, the Ku Klux Klan, has survived. It is by all odds the most despicable organization ever spawned in this country. It has perpetrated more flogging, torture, arson, and murder than any other organization that ever polluted our national life. All the vile deeds of all other organizations together will not match the Klan's in number or depravity. Unlike the others, the Klan is not yet dead. Here and there it still writhes. It will have to be watched for years, perhaps for generations, lest it again become the menace it once was.

The Klan was and is the prototype of all hate organizations in this country. We need not concern ourselves with the others, but we should understand the techniques and history of this monstrous growth. It requires considerable examination.

The first Ku Klux Klan was a nightmarish aftermath of the Civil War. Its chief purpose was to prevent the emergence of the Negro from the squalor and degradation bequeathed by slavery. Taking the cross as their symbol, Klansmen formed secret bands whose activities were dictated by rogues bearing fantastic titles. With that perverted psychology which led them to burn crosses, they prated of honor and patriotism while profaning both. Prowling at night, they lashed, tortured, and killed thousands of unoffending citizens. Nor were the ex-slaves the Klan's only victims. White native Protestants who opposed the Klan met the same gruesome fate as did the terrorized Negroes. In 1872 a Committee of the House of Representatives branded the Klan as "a fearful conspiracy against society" which "had demoralized society and held men silent by the terror of its acts and its power for evil." The Klan reached the height of its infamy in the late 1870s. Finally, however, the reign of arson and murder by which Klan leaders held parts of the South in subjection was broken by federal military forces.

In 1915 an attempt was made to revive the awesome name. William Joseph Simmons invited thirty-four citizens of Georgia to sign an application for a charter of the Knights of the Ku Klux Klan, which was granted on December 4 of that year. But organizational efforts were not startlingly successful. In four years fewer than four thousand members were enrolled. In 1920, however, Simmons signed a contract with two streamline promoters, Edward Y. Clarke and Elizabeth Tyler, who (to quote Max Lerner) "saw the limitless possibilities for making money out of an organization that combined secrecy, fanfare, white supremacy, religious hatreds, and sadism."

In December of 1921 the New York *World* in a series of well-substantiated articles revealed the hypocrisy and villainy of the Klan. The investigators announced that the Klan had built an "invisible empire," with congressmen, mayors, judges, and policemen giving fealty to the Klan against the interests of the public. Surely if exposure is an unfailing way and always the best way to defeat hate organizations the Klan should have rapidly declined. Not at all! "Far from hindering the Ku Klux Klan's growth, the revelations before a congressional investigating committee and the exposés in some leading newspapers only hugely stimulated inflow of its members."

(Gustavus Myers, *History of Bigotry in the United States.*) Prior to these public revelations the Klan recruiters had bragged and blustered of its might. Now they could display proof—in fact, it was displayed for them—that the Ku Klux Klan was a mighty and terrible organization. Publishing pictures of Klansmen in full regalia in every newspaper was a splendid service to the Klan recruiters. Droves of hesitant persons were stampeded into joining the Klan, which now buttressed its usual inducements with the fear that it would not be safe to be on the outside.

On the heels of the 1921 exposure the Klan grew fabulously. In 1922 enrollment of new members was 1,200,000. The rate of increase rose in 1923 and 1924. By the end of 1924 more than five millions had joined.

The Klan of the 1920s came into utter disrepute and began to recede because of internal dissension and quarrels within the Klan. In 1923 Simmons was ousted from the post of Imperial Wizard by H. W. Evans, who succeeded him in office. Thereafter Simmons went about forming competing hate organizations and creating quarrels within the Klan. In Pennsylvania the Klan in 1928 brought suit against five former Klan officials, suing them for one hundred thousand dollars and seeking to deprive them of the privileges of operating in its name. The five, in turn, made startling revelations of corruption. Other disclosures were made by D. C. Stephenson who had been convicted of murder and who divulged the felonies of the Indiana Klan, which he had headed. Coming from a Kleagle, this was highly damaging to Klan prestige. The hooded order dwindled to a few thousand members but did not disappear entirely.

In 1946 an attempt was made to revive the Klan to its former power and ominous fame. In scores of places flaming crosses, parades of white-robed men, and well-advertised initiation ceremonies served notice that large-scale recruiting had begun. This time, however, the Klan organizers found upon the scene numerous organizations and alert public officials prepared to deal with the threat calmly, not frantically. Georgia, which has been the national barometer of Klan strength and activity, had in Governor Ellis G. Arnall a progressive statesman who met the Klan challenge squarely. The Georgia charter of the Klan was revoked and other state charters were similarly canceled. Radio commentators and journalists told scornfully of the Klan's past crimes. The Federal Bureau of Investigation and the Civil Rights Division of the Justice Department moved swiftly to punish each new violation of federal laws. Far from exaggerating the strength of the revived Klan and picturing the organization as omnipotent, molders of public opinion scorned and derided it. The term "invisible empire" was in the discard. Drew Pearson said he would speak on Stone Mountain, which the Klan regards as its sacred mountain, and despite threats of Klansmen that to do so might cost his life, Drew Pearson spoke there and came away uninjured. Protestant clergymen and organizations, both national and Southern, denounced the Klan. There was no cowering before it this time, and none of the awesome tributes to its malevolent power which the Klan had previously turned to its advantage. Arrayed against the Klan were well-informed writers, speakers, and government officials who pictured the Klan for what it has always been—an aggregation of foolish men, headed by contemptible hoodlums. Not the least of the factors resulting in the total failure of the Klan leaders to rebuild the organization in 1946 and 1947 was the keen regret of hundreds of thousands of decent men that they had signed a Klan membership card in the 1920s.

A prophecy that new attempts will be made to revive the Klan is warranted. Schemers are likely to try to capitalize upon the myths, the ceremonies, the methods, and the name burned by fiery crosses into American memory. The counteroffensive of 1946 and 1947 should never be forgotten, for it provides a pattern for dealing with this scourge hereafter. One thing was made particularly clear—the advisability of placing on the statute books of all states which do not yet contain such provisions a law similar to the one invoked against the Klan in New York. No single weapon has been more effective in halting the Klan than the 1923 statute of New York State which requires every corporation and association, other than labor unions, fraternities, benevolent societies, et cetera, having more than twenty members and requiring an oath as a condition of membership, to file with the state a sworn copy of its constitution, by-laws, rules, regulations, and oath, together with a roster of all members and officers. All persons who become members of, retain membership in, or attend meetings of such an organization with knowledge that it has not complied with the law are liable to prosecution. This law, adopted in a heyday of the Klan, was upheld by the Supreme Court in 1928 in a decision which included a denunciation of the Klan. To require disclosure of officers and membership is an effective fumigant against Ku Klux Klan mentality and ambitions.

The Klan is the model for most hate organizations in this country. The rancor-rousing outfits you may encounter will usually be puny imitations hopefully contrived by some petty racketeer. Like others of his ilk, the hate organizer figures on making a living by preying on others. He is a fraud, and he knows it. He is "selling" something to the public—or to the part of it susceptible to his exhortations. He is working his little racket consciously and deliberately. Usually he is purveying some sort of "protection," simply because he has found it the most salable commodity he can offer. His concoction is carefully prepared—just as carefully compounded as a showman's snake oil. He is offering protection against a menace. There is always at least one menace—one or several social or religious groups which must be curbed to save our hearths, our homes, our children, our country. He has nothing constructive to offer—no talk of building schools, improving health facilities, providing housing. He only presents his menace.

How does he pick a menace? Let's watch a couple of inventive organizers as they develop one.

NICK: *What people are scared of now is communism. These aliens are all commies, of course.*

DOC: *Oh, sure. We got to use that angle. That pulls in rich guys afraid of losing their dough.*

NICK: *Sure. And let's not forget prices are too high.*

DOC: *Right! The aliens are cleaning up fortunes. People are sore about that.*

NICK: *You bet they are. High cost of living is a swell tag to tie on to the dirty aliens. And those rats don't pay income tax while everybody else does.*

DOC: *Now you're getting on to the line. Everybody feels they're eaten up by taxes and here the lousy aliens are cheating on their returns. Tax evaders, that's what they are.*

NICK: *Let's see what we got now? Communism, high prices, taxes—how about high divorce rate? All these broken homes—you know where that's taking this country to.*

DOC: *No. That's out. You can't tag everything on them. You got to be reasonable. But we can bring in this Marshall Plan, spending all this money on Europe. There's one for the book. I tell you, Nick, it makes people sore to think*

*of putting all our money down the drain. They're driving
this country into bankruptcy.*

NICK: *Fine! Lots of people are against this foreign-aid business. That gives us four good lines and that's enough.
We're fighting communism, higher prices, unfair taxes,
and foreign aid. We'll pin them all on the lousy aliens.*

DOC: *Now what we need is a good name for the organization
and enough dough to get started.*

NICK: *How about the Order of Native American Defenders?*

DOC: *That's not big enough. Sounds like small fry. How
about the National Confederation of Native Americans?*

NICK: *I like that word "Defenders."*

DOC: *Then let's make it the National Confederation of Native Defenders of America.*

NICK: *O.K. Now all we got to do is to scare the pants off
enough guys and we'll be sitting on top of the earth.*

Ridiculous? No. Just simplified. Anyone who has been acquainted
with professional hate mongers knows that the process of organizing
a hate organization is as false, as callous, as scandalous as that brief
dialogue indicates. But that alone is not sufficient. Scheming is not
half enough. The organizer desperately needs—must have—the help
of people like yourself if he is to score a sufficient success.

No hate organization can make headway unless there is some
worry or fear which can be directed against its quarry. The scare
may be a fear of social readjustment. ("Do you want your daughter
to marry a Victimian?") Or a political tocsin. ("The Victimians are
in control of Washington.") An economic plot may be alleged.
("Victimians are back of all these strikes.") Or fear of war, fear of
corruption of morals, fear of alien domination, or fear of losing
status may be the wedge on which the hate monger may hammer.
He may appeal to greed, as when Japanese-Americans were compelled to sell their homes and farms for a pittance after Pearl Harbor; but here, too, fear was introduced by alleging Japanese
treachery.

But whatever appeal the hate monger may choose to use, he must
be able to arouse response in the public. He can picture the horror,
the chaos, the destruction which his menace is about to wreak on
the country. With arms semaphoring and sweat pouring down his
face he can picture the utter desolation of the good, the pure, the

unsuspecting American. He can offer himself heroically to save you from this catastrophe. But unless he can scare you—really scare you so that you are willing to swallow his vicious concoction—he is licked. If you don't respond to his inciting screams, he is just a mountebank flailing the air. *You have to react* or the hate monger is a deflated bag of wind. The snake-oil artist can describe scores of horrible physical conditions which his nostrum is guaranteed to cure, but only the man who thinks he has the symptoms ever buys a bottle. If you can't be scared, the hate artist can't win.

The petty hate monger is usually so incompetent, so inept, that he contributes most of the elements necessary for his own undoing. One lout who had decided to build an organization for the propagation of animosity hired a hall, announced a meeting, sent invitations to his friends and distributed handbills. The gathering was scheduled for eight o'clock on a Sunday evening. An acquaintance of his who regarded his plans askance argued with him a week before the meeting. "You'll get into trouble," he warned, and prophesied various possible catastrophes.

The hate promoter was worried by the dire prospects pictured to him but was lured by hopes of renown and of monetary gain. He refused to cancel the meeting.

"Very well, then," said the acquaintance, who had a plan to stop the meeting anyhow, "I'll meet you in your room at six o'clock that evening. I'll bring along a good dinner. Let's just the two of us eat heartily and enjoy ourselves before the meeting."

The evening arrived and the dinner was brought. The basket contained two quarts of whisky. Later in the evening fifty people assembled, but the speaker never arrived. He was sleeping off the effects of alcoholic indulgence.

A West coast crackpot who had gone into the business of selling bigotry advertised his venture in several disreputable sheets. Three dollars for a subscription for his monthly periodical came from a New York member of the religious group against whom this fanatic was raging. With the three-dollar check the New Yorker sent a note asking the entrepreneur how the young organization was faring.

"Wonderful," came the reply. "I already have six other subscribers in New York and before long we'll have a big branch there. You might talk to these other people about setting it up. Here are their names and addresses."

The recipient of the list of six names did look up each of them.

He found that five of the six were, like himself, members of the group excoriated by the new hate outfit. They, too, were propelled by morbid curiosity to read all the villainies written about their group. Few people are so intensely interested in a new hate organization as are those whose security it threatens.

It is needless self-torture to assume that each time a new exponent of racial or religious bigotry appears on the scene the career of Tom Watson, Theodore Bilbo, or Adolf Hitler is likely to be re-enacted. The average professional hate agitator in the United States has remained a wretched, miserable failure without power or influence. Despite the pompous high-sounding names hate organizations assume, each is more likely to become a dud than a monster, for that has certainly been the case in the past. Invariably a hate organization thrives on fear and strives to create an impression of tremendous influence and strength. Scorn, contempt, ridicule, and jeers cripple a hate organization. Awe and panic accelerate its growth. A hate organization thrives on the terror of its prospective victims.

Most hate organizations defeat themselves. It would be a mistake, however, to assume that *all* of them fade away because of the stupidity of the organizers. An occasional operator presents serious problems because he is shrewd, cunning, and convincing. Some have been as adroit in winning admirers as any successful swindler.

In 1945 an ex-senator of the United States had visions of a third political party which would have as its nucleus the most rabid nativist elements of the country—those sweet souls who believe that America is their own private property because their immigrant ancestors arrived a generation or two earlier than the immigrant ancestors of others. Isolationism, intolerance, and selfish ambitions were the major creeds of the American Nationalist party, but these were dressed up in the glowing phrases and noble sentiments typical, as we have seen, of every hate organization. The ex-senator's wealth, his excellent connections with men of affairs throughout the country, and his political sagacity were huge assets. Since this was to be no little sapling but a giant oak dominating the American scene, the ex-senator set about raising millions of dollars to support it.

He engaged a highly experienced fund raiser who, in turn, hired a number of solicitors. They were armed with letters, signed by the ex-senator, asking important personages in various cities for contributions and for introductions to other men of wealth and influence.

The purposes of the American Nationalist party were so laudably presented that almost anyone with a dollar to spare could happily contribute to it. In fact, it required considerable knowledge of unstated but covertly understood objectives fully to understand whither the American Nationalist party actually would lead its followers.

The fund raisers had an almost foolproof plan for garnering large contributions. They avoided chambers of commerce or other bodies which would investigate before giving approval. Instead, they called exclusively upon men of large affairs who could hardly refuse to see an emissary of the ex-senator. These bigwigs were shown photostats of checks for large amounts contributed by others whose judgment they highly respected. It seemed for a while that this scheme of fund raising might endow the new organization handsomely and that it would soon show a roster of many outstanding citizens.

There were weak spots, however. There always are. One of the organization's solicitors talked too freely. He revealed that the chief fund raiser was getting 50 per cent of the money raised and that his share was divided with his solicitors. Any organization that will pay 50 per cent of the funds it raises to get the funds is a racket, as any businessman knows. There is something shady when such an arrangement is necessary. Moreover, one day in Cleveland a discredited rabble-rouser, for whom no man of integrity would have anything but contempt, was discovered to be working, under a false name, as a fund raiser for the American Nationalist party. The Scripps-Howard newspapers got wind of these facts and a staff writer investigated. The resulting articles blasted the new movement out of existence. Better-business bureaus warned their membership against making contributions. The easy money dried up. Another hate organization died a-borning. And this was no back-alley organization; it was one that might have gained large membership and immense power.

To deflate organizations of this sort requires the most careful analysis of the membership, methods, backers, et cetera, of the movement. Because of the necessity for a vast amount of accurate, up-to-date information and because of the delicacy of the work involved, handling such organizations is a job for well-equipped national agencies with the facilities to do it properly, using effective methods. When, for example, it has been determined that the organization has used the names of distinguished citizens without authorization, the public announcement of that fact by the persons concerned can be done so that it is a telling blow to the organization. When respectable men and women have been enrolled without understanding the true nature of the organization, facts—and nothing but honest facts—will usually assure their public withdrawal. Many such correct and effective techniques for coping with hate organizations have been perfected. All of them depend upon complete and careful observation. Once accurate information is available one of the following procedures can be applied:

> 1. *If the organization is making no headway, let it languish.*
>
> 2. *If an organization's leaders are guilty of heinous or criminal plans, reveal them to the public, as was done when some of the Columbians were brought to trial.*
>
> 3. *If it is gaining strength through the favor of misguided persons who can be enlightened, present the facts to them.*

Why hate promoters create organizations is easy to see. They claim that they are motivated by religious, patriotic, and other highly laudable incentives. According to their own testimony their sole purpose is to save the nation from a group allegedly injuring the citizenry. It requires little analysis of their methods and activities, however, to see that what they actually want is fame, fortune, and power. The best-known rabble-rouser of the last several years is a moneygrubber who rarely misses an opportunity to extract every obtainable dollar from his dupes. His organizations have no boards of directors. None but he and his wife examine receipts and expenditures. He is a fast liver, a reckless spender, accounting to no one for funds received and spent. And he always cadges his audiences by pleading that he is financially hard-pressed.

Why people join hate organizations is a much more complicated matter. Psychologists who analyze the hate membership find that frustration, greed, fear, envy, ignorance, aggression, emotional insecurity, and other forms of psychic maladjustment play a large role in the thought processes of those who form the hate mob. No general formula provides an adequate explanation of the delusions of these neurotics. Re-education and complete readjustment would be needed to save each embittered victim from his aberrations. Most of the habitual joiners of hate organizations are within the lunatic fringe. Dowdy, middle-aged, or elderly misfits, they are beyond influence of mass therapy. Prejudice has twisted their minds to such an extent that only perverse ideas penetrate wherever their phobias are involved. These derelicts, however, are a relatively small fragment of the American public. No hate organization whose membership is limited to the lunatic fringe can make much progress or do more than minimal harm.

For a hate organization to expand considerably and to become a potent force it must intrigue a great many average citizens and win the allegiance of normal, decent citizens. It is at this point that the plans of hate organizers can be wrecked by continuous mass education.

The hate organizers must have scapegoats and exciting reasons for whipping the scapegoats. Eliminating repulsive group stereotypes or replacing them with favorable stereotypes lessens the possibility of finding convenient scapegoats. The allegations by which crowds can be incited against scapegoats can likewise be nullified. Though this requires alertness on the part of those upon whom the public depends for correct information on vital issues, it can be and has been done.

In 1906 the San Francisco school board decided that oriental students were to be segregated. This measure, isolating ninety-three Japanese pupils (in a school population of 25,000) was a political maneuver, to divert attention from sundry felonies of the mayor of San Francisco for which he was subsequently convicted. The agitators directed public attention to a weak, inoffensive group because weakness is in itself exploitable. By hard-hitting propaganda as well as by legal enactment they ruined the good relationships which had previously existed. Had the public been properly informed, an artifice of this kind would never have been possible. What has been done to Orientals by hate racketeers in the United States could not be done to British Americans, to Methodist Americans, to French Americans (of whom there are very few), or to any group strong in numbers *or strongly entrenched in popular favor*. I cannot too often repeat the warning that making a group appear weaker or more hated than it actually is, is an incitement to sadism. For every sympathizer gained by the defensive propaganda of ill-advised apologists ten harpies are stimulated to attack it and a dozen average people are inclined to despise it.

Group standings do change. They change tremendously. Some of the most respected groups in our country today were at one time hated and reviled. The Society of Friends (Quakers), who received a Nobel Peace Prize in 1947, were a century and a half ago the most disparaged and abused religious group in America. They won the excellent status they hold today by outstanding service to the needy, persecuted, and oppressed of *all* races and creeds. The Friends entered into no debates with their maligners. (This you can verify at the public library by reading the literary works of Friends from the writings of George Fox on.) They were too busy with good deeds to waste time on argumentative defense.

Despite the humiliations and injustices to which the Negroes are still subjected, no other group in the United States has made so great a proportionate gain during the past several decades. True, the distances to be traveled toward decent respect and treatment have been far greater to traverse than for any other group. These gains are the more remarkable because there were very few Negroes among journalists, legislators, business executives, and others who greatly influence popular opinion. The self-restraint and the genuine poise of Negroes under the lash of derision and abuse have brought consistent gains in public favor. A *Fortune* poll in October 1947 contained one very good question, "Do you think any of these groups should be getting a better break in this country than they are now?" Thirty-four per cent responding replied that Negroes deserve a better break. For no other group did even 10 per cent recommend a better break. Anyone but a hopeless bigot must admire the American Negro for enormous fortitude and loyalty to country. They have accepted adversity with dogged patience and inexhaustible good humor.

The Irish, noted for handsome men and beautiful women, now reckoned among America's finest, were not so regarded fifty years ago. The vile epithets and obnoxious adjectives applied in daily conversation to the Irish at the turn of the century have been forgotten. It has not been solely because of their increase in numbers and the improvement in their economic status that the Irish have won the respect and approval of their neighbors. Other groups who have grown as rapidly and made equal economic advance have not secured the same gains in public esteem. Cheerful, good-natured response to criticism common among the Irish ("Now, now, there, my boy, take it easy!") has won a more desirable reputation than back-bristling, hot-headed retort at the slightest provocation. ("How dare you say anything against us, you rat?") Americans admire the man who is not easily frightened or intimidated. They have learned to respect the Irish for those qualities.

The picture is not always one of steady improvement. Unfortunately the popular image of some groups—and their status—far from improving, has unquestionably worsened in the United States during the past century or even during the last few decades.

As long as group stereotypes play a part in the mental processes of the average mind, racial and religious groups need respect and even admiration. A good reputation cannot be acquired in a day or in a year. What people already think about a group when a hate campaign is launched against it cannot be speedily altered in their favor. Least of all can the needed improvement of reputation be made under fire. The time to build a favorable position in public esteem is now—always is *now*. Otherwise the hate monger will find plenty of tinder into which to hurl his firebrands.

In recent years there has been a tendency in some quarters to assume that the growth of hate organizations is an inevitable by-product of economic crisis. People otherwise well informed will sometimes tell you that though it may be possible to control and defeat the hate vendors during a cycle of prosperity, they are certain to make giant strides in times of crisis. These economic theorists usually take a very philosophic attitude toward the matter, sometimes verging on the defeatist. "We have to expect these things," they seem to say, "and prepare to endure them as best we may."

The idea that hate organizations necessarily increase their hold in bad times is nonsense. List the years of greatest prosperity in the United States and the years of financial collapse and then jot beside these the hate organizations which flourished in each year. You will find that hard times have not been marked by clashes between racial and religious groups to more marked extent than the good times. Our country had a panic in 1907 but no outburst of group hatred. What about 1924? Business flourished and yet bigotry was rampant. How about 1931 and 1932? Economic disaster for all; intolerance at low ebb. It was the advent of Adolf Hitler to power in 1933 which unleashed tidal waves of anti-Semitism in the United States. That *political* event sprouted more hate organizations than an economic crisis in this country ever did. The American crop of agitators were satellites, imitators, and dupes of the Nazis.

Germany embraced Nazism while several of her neighbor nations, as financially crippled as Germany, were spotlessly free of intolerance. Even under the heel of Germany, totally prostrate economically, the Danes, the Dutch, and the Norwegians—to mention only a few—totally rejected anti-Semitic propaganda. Yet economic determinists continue to spin their theories of how to combat intolerance as though racial and religious animosities wax and wane with the economic tides. Easy enough if you call attention to only a scattered fact here and there. Why overlook the fact that the worst anti-Catholic organizations in the United States thrived when there was practically no anti-Semitic agitation? (Shades of that filthy sheet, *The Menace!*) In the late 1930s and early 40s anti-Semitic propaganda was worse than at any other time, but Catholics were not similarly abused. *It is readily verifiable on the record that the index of business in the United States is not a reliable thermometer of passions against racial and religious groups here.*

It is true that keen economic competition can set members of different groups against one another when jobs are scarce. But it also does that in good times. Common economic interests frequently weld together individuals from many diverse groups. In a free economy Protestant, Catholic, and Jewish industrialists may be expected to favor legislation favorable to industry. Protestant, Catholic, and Jewish laborers join together in opposition to anti-labor legislation. Where one racial or religious group is trying to exclude another from education and occupations or from residential districts, it is not the economic system that is at fault but the stupidity and the ignorance of the intolerant. As long as there are people sufficiently warped to yield to the blandishments of intolerance, monetary lures —openly displayed or slyly suggested—will sometimes make them dupes of the hate mongers. Yet that is not inevitable. Living under this same system of ours, where half-wits swallow vicious rumors against innocent groups, there are millions of fine, intelligent men and women whom no hate monger can ever influence.

It is imperative for a thousand reasons to prevent the recurrence of hard times. But it is wrong to assume that an economic recession will undo good group relations built up during good times. That defeatist attitude has no basis in fact. The history of our nation indicates the opposite. Friendly feelings between groups, once established, make it far easier successfully to counteract tensions that arise for whatever reason. Hate organizations will make little or no headway if constant effort is maintained to create respect and good will toward all groups, if we use proper countermeasures against these opportunistic organizations, and if we provide a stream of corrective information that crowds out the fantastic theories of hate mongers.

To prevent the blaming of innocent groups for the things that frighten or disturb other people, explain to them the real causes underlying their hardships and their anxieties. To explode fictitious issues, present the true issues clearly. In a nation of ignorant illiterates it may well be possible to make great numbers accept the most outrageous fabrications. In medieval times bubonic plague was blamed on a religious group, accused of poisoning the wells. There were scores of bloody massacres because of this canard. But what fool would attempt to launch a campaign in the United States to blame influenza and infantile paralysis on a racial or religious group? Some fantastic explanations of dire events will undoubtedly be accepted among the ignorant, but these can be short-circuited by correct information which usually requires no reference whatsoever to the maligned group. We now have radio, press, and other media of mass communication with which to defeat the witch doctors of today. Give the people light and they will find their way without tumbling into pitfalls of group hatred. Investments in inter-group understanding and in educating the public concerning the genuine causes of economic, social, and other problems should be made at all times. If hard times come, despite all our efforts to avoid them, let the nation be so immunized against hate organizations that no demagogue will ever be able to capitalize on distress.

What can you as an individual do about hate organizations? First of all you can keep your wits about you when you find one of these would-be pickpockets trying to work his barefaced, bigoted frauds. You can remember that these petty connivers never amount to anything unless they are helped to success. You can prevent your friends from becoming alarmed and jittery about some despicable little band of haters, no matter how sonorous and sinister the title they may have assumed. Those names, convenient fictions used to impress the gullible, may be changed overnight. "The National Confederation of Something" usually lacks even one substantial unit. Don't be alarmed by a hobgoblin. If you want to know what the organization is, go to your local agency or write to a national one. They will give you the information you need and tell you what you can do.

Any intelligent member of any racial or religious group *can* do something to keep disruptive, divisive organizations from getting a toe hold in his town. That something is to help make your community the kind of place where people of all racial and religious groups live together companionably and work together constantly for their mutual welfare. If one set of people won't welcome you or work with you, others will. Find them. Join them.

Far more dangerous to its own citizenry than a hate outfit a hundred miles away (or even on one of its sidewalks) is any bad neighborhood situation causing annoyance and friction. People jammed into busses become discourteous toward one another. Forced to live in squalor, they become frustrated, and although frustration does not always lead to group hatreds it well may. To undo the harm done by hate organizations, to prevent them from exploiting the fear and misery on which they can thrive, work for better housing, eliminate discriminatory employment, improve the schools, get better transportation, and labor continuously for inter-group amity. Above all, don't let attention shift from hate-breeding *conditions* in your own vicinity to dramatic reports of the activities of a handful of hate-filled morons in Atlanta or Los Angeles or some other distant spot.

People of all kinds, everywhere, are happiest and friendliest when striving together. There is much to be done in your town that will require the co-operative efforts of all groups. Do it. People who are long accustomed to standing together and working together are the mightiest obstacle that can ever be set in the path of a hate organization.

CHAPTER 2

Rabble-Rousers

On April 1, 1946, a well-known demagogue, whom we shall call "Little Kodfish," addressed an audience of two hundred persons in St. Louis. These two hundred were run-of-the-mill bigots, most of them somewhat on the lunatic side. Few of them had any more personal influence than a month-old baby. There was nothing the Kodfish might say which these soured, frustrated folk had not heard repeatedly. It should have been a tepid affair with as little consequence as two hundred infants shaking their rattles.

However, it was April 1, and evidently the spirit of the day descended both upon the bigots and some of their opponents. Thirty-five veterans marched into the hall where the Kodfish was scheduled to speak, denounced him, and appealed to the audience to leave. Not one person left. Instead, when the Kodfish entered he was greeted with increased enthusiasm. He had assumed a hero's role.

Commenting on this incident, the St. Louis *Star-Times* wrote: "One may well wonder if any good can come from the kind of tactics employed against Mr. ——. He characteristically made the most of the situation to present himself as a man who is so feared that he must contend with such intrusions, and so courageous and devoted to his cause that he refuses to be silenced or intimidated. The seeming inspiration which he gets from such show of opposition suggests that he might be less effective if more generally ignored."

After considerable publicity occasioned by the veterans' fiasco in St. Louis, the Kodfish announced that he would call a national convention of his satellites there in May. Still greater clamor followed. Attempts were made to prevent him from engaging the Municipal Auditorium. Defenders of freedom of speech debated with those who believed that the visitor's utterances constituted an unjustifiable abuse of that right. Even after this valuable publicity the convention drew less than two hundred. But those who demonstrated against him scuffled with the police. Again there were arrests, with still greater publicity. Did the Kodfish avoid St. Louis as a result of this open hostility? Far from it. Although he rarely visits the same city more than once or twice a year, he announced a return engagement in St. Louis for June—his third within four months.

A large part of St. Louis's police force had to be mustered at the Municipal Auditorium the night of this third meeting. For a time the most prominent and dramatic figure in St. Louis was Little Kodfish. There are a great many clergymen and other St. Louis speakers who, without press notices, regularly attract far larger audiences than two hundred. No visiting speaker drawing so small and so nondescript an audience would merit even a stick of newspaper space. But the Kodfish obtained columns of publicity, press photographs, and large headlines as a gift—the contribution of a small noisy faction among the many who sincerely abhor rabble-rousers. This little group of excited opponents honestly supposed they were courageously facing a menace and warning an apathetic public of a present danger. Actually they provided the fanfare which the Kodfish desperately needed to dramatize his meeting.

Some notable persons, including men of influence, wealth, and high station, have publicly vented malice against racial and religious groups. Their utterances are of serious consequence because they are given respectful hearing by many who admire these men. They are not pygmies such as Little Kodfish. When one of them speaks on the radio or is welcomed on respectable platforms he should never be regarded, classified, or treated in the same way as the professional hate monger whose stanchest followers are among the lunatic fringe. For the respected or respectable preacher or sponsor of bigotry, exposure is the correct antidote. Such men must be held publicly accountable until they either recant or lose their ill-deserved standing with the public. The responsible person who makes irresponsible statements or covertly promotes intolerance must be unmasked and convicted in the court of public opinion.

But Little Kodfish is of another ilk. He is a despicable, disreputable rabble-rouser who makes his living by peddling intolerance. He has no standing and little influence. He cannot profitably be called to account. He craves notoriety and capitalizes gleefully on his nuisance value. He realizes that the average person has little desire to hear an unknown ranter. There is so much else we need to do or would like to do that an unheralded speaker is no attraction. This makes things very difficult for any rabble-rouser. But if he can somehow contrive to goad someone into screaming his name from the housetops, he will get increasingly large audiences. Who could resist going to hear Adolf Hitler if that most publicized of all scoundrels should return to earth?

Unless a rabble-rouser can influence those who come to hear him and can pollute their thinking, there is no reason to bother about him. If he *is* a convincing demagogue, it is even more foolish to rescue him from obscurity by doing a publicity job for each of his meetings. As a rule, his chief desire is to garner as much cash as he can. He generally holds one or at most a few meetings in each city where he has hired a hall. The handful of dowdy dupes who will come to hear a rabble-rouser are short of funds. At the first session the fervent appeals at collection time and the purchase of "literature" extract almost the entire amount the suckers can spare. The vein of coins being thin, a second digging will leave too little to warrant additional meetings. So the rabble-rouser moves on to fleece others in another spot. If he stays in one town long you may be sure he does not have a hope for success elsewhere. The history of demagoguery in the United States shows that most rabble-rousers have sooner or later gone out of business—largely because rabble-rousing has proved unprofitable.

But because the rabble-rouser is a tangible, visible demonstration of prejudice, he becomes a problem—the more so since the inexperienced and excitable too often feel both compelled to handle him and competent to do so.

What to do when the rabble-rouser comes to town is a question that has elicited a host of dissimilar and contradictory recommendations. There is hardly a situation for which the well intentioned have developed so many and such varied counterattacks. Many of them are merely spur-of-the-moment techniques resulting largely in the satisfaction of a need for some sort of action. Some are ineffectual but relatively harmless. Others—many of which have been thoroughly tested in action—are now recognized as dangerous boomerangs. Among the methods still advocated are the following:

1. *Bar the rabble-rouser from publicly owned halls and auditoriums.*

2. *Invade his meeting and break it up; keep him from talking.*

3. *Picket the meeting and demonstrate at the door.*

4. *Hand out to those who enter the meeting pamphlets or leaflets denouncing the rabble-rouser.*

5. *Hold a pro-democracy meeting at the same time the rabble-rouser's meeting is in session.*

6. *Ignore him completely.*

A moment's reflection reveals that the first five suggestions have one thing in common: they are based on the assumption that the rabble-rouser is a menace (which he is) and that the public should therefore be alerted to the evil he does. But fire in a theater is also a menace, and yet the person who screams "Fire!" is far from helpful. A crackpot disseminating virulence to a tawdry crew of similarly minded bigots does not constitute the kind of danger to a hundred thousand or more residents of a city that warrants screaming the alarm in the streets. The rabble-rouser is like a tiny speck of fire that flickers out faster when the breath of multitudes does not fan it into a blaze. No rabble-rouser has gone out of business because he drew a torrent of angry clamor. Many who would still be plying their nefarious trade have closed shop because they could not arouse sufficient attention. "Say *anything* about me," says the rabble-rouser, "provided you say it loud enough."

The argument that because a rabble-rouser is a threat to public welfare he must be held up to public scorn is deceptive. Like a Broadway performer, the hate-mongering orator depends on publicity to draw a crowd. The well-meaning person who exerts every effort to denounce such a scallawag in every medium of public information is actually providing cheap and effective advertising which the rabble-rouser himself could never secure. Let him blow his own tin horn. Why should decent citizens provide the wind for it?

Another argument presented by those who make the arrival of a rabble-rouser an occasion for vociferous opposition is that the hate peddler, his followers, and the general public should be shown that more people can be summoned to demonstrate against him than he can muster to applaud him. Even the most impressive array of strength, however, proves nothing to anybody. If it did, we would have the amusing—and alarming—spectacle in America of finding at the door of every controversial speaker a swarm of opponents waving garish banners. That might be well enough if the issues of the day were best determined by street brawls, for it has usually happened that if bitterly opposing factions are brought together there is a resulting melee. Though most people recognize the futility of these counterdemonstrations, unfortunately there are extremists who do not like law and order. Some enjoy the excitement of a fracas, others are glad to be arrested in the hope that they may be able to pose as martyrs. All of them are hindrances to those who want clarification of complex issues rather than personal gratification.

What actually happens when this technique of mass opposition is applied is clearly shown by another page taken from the adventures of the same Little Kodfish whose career we've already looked at. In Boston on July 13, 1947, he spoke in the morning at a church to an audience of less than forty people. Such a weak showing must certainly have pained the Kodfish and disappointed his followers. That afternoon he was scheduled to hold a meeting in Old Town Hall where, had the event gone unpublicized, his followers would certainly have been lost in a sea of empty seats. In this instance, however, the Kodfish had the help of enthusiastic alarm criers. A group of leftists, including officials of the Communist party of Massachusetts, arranged a counterdemonstration for the afternoon occasion. The hall was packed with leftists, fellow travelers, silly young people, and downright fools. They kept up a clamor that prevented the Kodfish from being heard. The police sided with the Kodfish, since it was the opposition that was out of order. It was not they but the Kodfish who had rented the hall. The Kodfish enjoyed it immensely. He hugged an American flag for the benefit of press photographers and cheered the crowd on with "Louder, you dopes!" The net result of this whole misbegotten adventure was that the Kodfish got a hundred thousand dollars of free publicity throughout the nation.

A million people in Boston had indicated unmistakably that they did not like the Kodfish. They had shown their antipathy in a way that frustrated and defeated him by ignoring him entirely. But thanks to the leather-lunged children of bedlam, Boston and the nation were given a graphic and exciting demonstration of the communist vs. fascist technique. This time a rabble-rouser was the exponent of freedom of speech. The next time it will be communists who are the victims of strong-arm suppression. Both extremes thrive in an atmosphere of disorder for they know that these tactics will in time entirely destroy freedom of speech; riots and disorders will spread until genuine democracy will be forced to give way to a well-organized, ruthless, despotic faction.

You cannot educate the public by massing crowds at a rabble-rouser's meeting any more than you can end illiteracy by demonstrating at the doors of illiterates. To pass out at his door handbills denouncing the demagogue to the persons who enter his hall is like standing at the door of a synagogue and handing anti-Semitic literature to the worshipers. Any and all counteractivities at or near a rabble-rouser's meeting place invite violence which can only redound to the benefit of the organizer of the meeting.

Still other groups of those who insist upon counterdemonstrations —but are willing to hold them at some small distance from the rabble-rouser's quarters—contend that by so doing they are taking advantage of aroused public interest in the problem of intolerance. They hope to use the incident to unite alarmed liberals and to instruct the public in the basic tenets of better human relationships. Their hopes are illusory. An examination of instances in which a rabble-rouser's meeting was used to spark a pro-democracy gathering clearly indicates that the two gatherings became firmly linked in the public mind with the hate monger assuming the more important role. Even when the public had previously been concerned about fair employment practice laws, better housing for disadvantaged groups, the cementing of friendly relations between social groups or other real problems, the double bill of Mr. Rabble-Rouser at Corner A and his opponents at Corner B effectively shifted attention to the rabble-rouser and crowded the constructive job out of public attention.

"Should he be permitted to speak?" "What's that man like anyhow?" and "What can we do about him?" became the questions of the day. They were privately and publicly debated by individuals and by groups. Almost invariably the discussion sooner or later was aired in the press—to the great benefit of the rabble-rouser while important matters of community concern were forgotten. The single dominant issue became, "What about this man and what should be done about him and his kind?"

No one will ever undo whatever evil a rabble-rouser does. Publicity about him merely distracts the attention of the better elements from the important tasks in which they might profitably be employed and sends them off on a fruitless chase after a bothersome weasel, which (or whom) it is impossible to capture or shoot. The struggle against hatred, poverty, ignorance, and greed is a colossal one which requires the co-operation of every available person. To make good people believe that great gains can be achieved by barking at rabble-rousers is altogether mischievous.

Advocates of the "Let's-tangle-with-that-rat-at-his-own-door" policy sometimes attempt to justify their actions by arguing that, no matter what is done, some misguided dupes are certain to attend a rabble-rouser's meeting and be swayed by his demagoguery. It is alleged that the presence of more sensible people will exert a restraining influence. The fallacy here is that the fire-eaters who are demanding an on-the-scene demonstration will be joined by hoodlums and undependable people. Time and again experience has shown that those who go to harry a rabble-rouser or demonstrate at his door are not subject to discipline. At best they are certainly not models of thoughtfulness and decorum. Usually they are dissuaded from disorderly conduct only when the police outnumber them. When they find a large enough crowd presumably on their side they become more reckless and more vehement. Not only are they prepared for violence; if necessary they will provoke it. Violence is the rabble-rouser's game. If there are going to be stupid disorders, no self-respecting organization or individual should have the slightest connection with them. Don't be on the scene of a likely riot. Your presence only makes it more difficult for the police to handle the crowd and quell the disturbance. Let those who insist on trying by direct countermeasures to offset a rabble-rouser's meeting go it alone and take the consequences alone.

Those who believe that the ill effects of an objectionable speaker can be overcome only by centering public attention on him, denounce all other measures to accomplish that same purpose as cowardice and "hush-hush." Either you rage against the hate peddler as loudly as you can, or else you are said to be "ignoring him" and his views. Either-or classifications of this sort usually clarify nothing. They are often deliberate attempts to obscure the facts. This particular one has sowed an infinite amount of confusion in the minds of genuine liberals.

I have been in close touch with hundreds of persons who are greatly concerned about the rabble-rousers. Those who have spent the greatest amount of time and energy investigating their activities and formulating techniques for defeating them have been the least noisy about it. It takes only one evening of a man's life to go to a rabble-rouser's meeting, carry a signboard, shout lustily, and attract press notice. Even if such activity were desirable, it would still be a small sacrifice for so great a cause. The thousands of patient workers who have contributed most to the permanent eradication of bigotry have given infinitely more. Most of them have never participated in the shenanigans which so delight the "activists."

If reason and common sense alone were not enough to demonstrate the futility of the counterdemonstration techniques, the unrelieved succession of failures resulting from their application should furnish the final proof. Actual case records showing the name of each rabble-rouser, the date of each meeting, countermeasures taken, the effect upon the public and upon the career of the rabble-rouser have been kept. They leave no doubt whatsoever that the more intensively each appearance of a rabble-rouser is advertised in a community, the more he profits by it. For the hate monger who has neither wit nor merit to acquire fame, notoriety is a welcome substitute. An unknown rabble-rouser is a weak little worm. Why should any man of good will lend him a ladder onto a front page of a decent newspaper?

Is there no alternative between publicizing each rabble-rouser and ignoring him? There most certainly is. In September 1946 an article I had written, "Checkmate for Rabble-rousers," appeared in *Commentary*. It described a method, quite new then, which was called "the silent treatment." That title had disadvantages which later became apparent, and the following year I suggested in a number of periodicals that it be replaced by "Quarantine Treatment." In October 1946 the National Community Relations Advisory Council, whose constitutent bodies are the Jewish community relations agencies, recommended that this technique of dealing with rabble-rousers be tried during an experimental period. Having proved effective in actual practice, the Quarantine Treatment of rabble-rousers was adopted December 17, 1947.

Quarantine Treatment is a method designed to prevent the rabble-rouser from becoming a serious public menace by depriving him of the publicity he needs to increase his audience. It employs a dual technique: legal recourse, where warranted, and persuasion offering concrete information to persons or agencies (such as newspapers, hotels, et cetera) likely unwittingly to abet the rabble-rouser.

The advocates of Quarantine Treatment realize that a capable rabble-rouser might eventually enroll a substantial number of followers. Under favorable circumstances he might even attain considerable political power or influence. But they are also aware that thousands of rabble-rousers throughout history have lived and died without achieving any greater recognition or influence than a singing waiter in a third-rate night club. Few of them have ever realized as great a financial return as they would have gotten through honest work. Few of them have either the personality or the brains to make a success in their sordid careers.

Since they are buncombe artists and political confidence men, rabble-rousers desperately need to acquire some sort of sham glamor to impress their victims. They cannot claim the distinctions that others attain by winning high office or by other genuine achievement. Their records are always such that *intelligent* people, when fully informed about them, recognize them for the petty racketeers they are. But it is possible for even the worst scamp, once he gets the public eye, to press-agent himself into favor with a multitude of dupes. That has actually been done by a number of unsavory but skillful political adventurers. To thwart the rabble-rouser's ambitions it is necessary, therefore, to acquaint persons in influential positions with the true facts about the hate peddler, *and to do it in such a way that he will not become a glamorous figure in the eyes of his potential followers.* That can be done and has been done. The technique is a simple one available to anyone who will take the trouble to use it. It can be stated in a sentence: *Don't use the newspapers, the radio, or other public media; instead, write letters, use the telephone, make personal visits.* The latter method is not the easier one. It is far more exacting and laborious than scandal crying. It is the best method for obtaining a lasting beneficial effect.

Here is a typical instance of what has been happening in many cities during the past several years:

It becomes known to those who read the bulletins of rabble-rouser B or through a spoken announcement he has made elsewhere that on October umpteenth B will speak in Middletown. Now B knows very well that if he runs a tiny advertisement in the newspaper announcing his meeting, he will seem like small fry. Even the active bigots won't come out to cheer a nonentity. If, on the other hand, he takes a full-page ad or even a half-page, more will come, but not enough more to pay for the price of that advertisement. Paid advertising in newspapers is not a profitable operation for him. But B has a list, a sucker list of the lunatic-fringe boobs who read hate literature instead of comic books. He can depend on them. They receive invitations by direct mail and provide a shabby but ardent audience. But the boob audience alone is insufficient. To draw a profitable house, B knows it is essential that he get free press notice and as big a one as possible.

B has ways of getting newspaper space. He has done it before. One of his friends calls on the editor. He has great news. B is coming to enlighten Middletown.

"Under whose auspices?" asks the editor.

B's admirer was afraid of that one. In the past it has been possible to hornswoggle some unsuspecting organization into letting B use their platform. But something seems to have gone wrong this time. No respectable organization has been willing to present him under their auspices. B's friend has tried hard to get a good organization to do so, but, thanks to Quarantine Treatment, the program chairmen, officers of clubs, ministers, educators, and others have been acquainted with B's career. They know what he says when he gets an audience.

Although B's spokesman winces, he has an answer for the editor. "He's talking for the 'Native Loyal Sons of America,' a great organization."

"Never heard of it," says the editor.

"B's president of it. We're saving the world from communism."

"Well," replies the editor, "just leave those four pages you've written. I'll see about giving it space."

When the visitor has gone, the editor calls in a member of his staff.

"Find out something about this man and his organization," he says. "A man who speaks in Middletown without the auspices of any accredited organization is probably not worth a line of type. But see who this chap is."

Accurate, honest, convincing information is readily available to the reporter. It doesn't take long to have the answer for the editor. "He's a phony. Just another guy who wants free advertising but doesn't rate it." Quarantine Treatment, if you please.

B has other ways of handling his little shakedown trick. He may try the disguise system. He needs a hall for his meeting. If he wants to use a publicly owned auditorium open to all who request it, without sponsorship, he should receive permission without any objection whatsoever. That goes for *everyone*. That is what freedom of speech is. Where community tax money has provided a platform for everyone (those whom we dislike as well as those we like), a place where *all* may speak, the officials who rent that hall have no right to censorship. If it is a shrine or a courtroom or an auditorium reserved by a university for genuinely educational purposes, or any place where only certain well-defined types of meetings may be held, the authorities have the responsibility of choosing between sheep and goats. But nobody can rightfully be refused the use of a publicly supported hall whose use does not imply endorsement by anyone. If what the rabble-rouser says warrants arresting him for breach of peace or the like, he should be arrested. But let there be no mistake about freedom of speech in *advance* of the speech.

The use of a privately owned hall is entirely different from use of publicly owned auditoriums. No one need let anyone speak in a room he himself owns or controls. No one is duty bound to lend his soapbox to anyone else.

Suppose B's advocate asks a hotel manager for a hotel meeting room for "The Defenders of Militant America."

"Who are to be the speakers?" asks the manager.

B's friend names a few local persons of whom few outside their own family circles have ever heard. The manager becomes suspicious and asks for references from people who have his respect. Finally he postpones decision.

One of three things happens then. The manager makes inquiries and learns that, although it is not known to the public at large, "The Defenders of Militant Americans" is one of B's organizations. It is a paper thing created, built, and established three months ago by the very simple process of inventing the name. The manager obviously won't do business with a fly-by-night outfit of that sort.

Or, having been informed about B (Quarantine Treatment), the manager simply refuses to rent the space for the occasion. He does not court trouble by letting people of unsavory or questionable reputation use his hotel as a meeting spot.

The third thing that may happen is that the manager rents the hall and discovers only a day or two before the meeting that the organization is a fake and that B is to speak. He is justified in canceling on the ground of false pretense. For B there is nothing to be gained in even protesting the cancellation, since it is a private matter involving no publicity.

These are all constant and annoying difficulties for B. They can, however, be obviated by unwise opponents. Suppose that B has been successful in hiring a hall in a low-grade hotel where the proprietor does not care if Satan himself speaks on his premises. It is, of course, quite possible to notify the press and promise them a riot at the meeting. B will like that; it is sure-fire publicity. It is also possible to send a strong-arm squad around to "persuade" the recalcitrant proprietor. If he is a bigot whom persuasion will not influence, pressure is likely to end in his giving B the hall rent free. No one should ever *demand* that anyone refuse the use of his premises to a rabble-rouser. You can only furnish information and leave the decision to those who own the auditorium. That is all. The decision is entirely within the province of the owners. The giving of correct information concerning someone who had concealed the truth about himself is thoroughly legitimate. Coercion of any kind, on the other hand, is utterly improper.

Someone should always be on hand to record what a rabble-rouser says. There should also be present someone well acquainted with the laws and their interpretation. An arrest likely to result in an acquittal or in an insignificant penalty should never be made. Rabble-rousers do, however, sometimes commit illegal offenses. These crimes should not be overlooked. In New York City on October 6, 1945, three anti-Semitic rabble-rousers at a street meeting distributed a piece of literature so vile and repulsive that it warranted legal action, which was brought. One of the men received a year's sentence and the others terms of six months. The convictions had important results. In all likelihood they are in large measure responsible for the fact that very few such meetings have since then been attempted in the New York area.

The five-to-four Supreme Court decision of May 16, 1949, in the Terminiello case does not diminish the power of the police to deal with agitators who incite *their audiences* to commit a breach of the peace. The disturbance in Chicago was not begun by Terminiello's followers or by people sympathetic to him. Had no hostile crowd come to the scene to protest, there would have been no public disorder. The fracas was precipitated by the counter-demonstrators.

The majority of the Supreme Court members were unwilling to punish a speaker for angering people who *object* to what he says. Were a man penalized whenever a hostile crowd came to express vociferous opposition to him, every unpopular speaker and many a liberal speaker would soon be silenced. The police would automatically find it necessary to side with those who intruded with enough force upon a meeting. But when an agitator urges *those who are sympathetic to him* to perpetrate violence or commit a breach of the peace, he can be—and should be—arrested and penalized. Be sure in such an instance to record *exactly* what he said, have witnesses who can reliably report the manner in which he said it, and get copies of the literature he distributes.

While it is far better to deal quietly with individual rabble-rousers, there are times when publicity is useful. The widespread dissemination of information which exposes the time-worn frauds of *all rabble-rousers* helps to defeat *each* of them. We very properly can warn the public of the poses, the tricks, and the motives of rabble-rousers just as the public is warned of pickpockets. But such information should apply to all rabble-rousers rather than to any particular one. To single one out is only to glamorize him and to make it more profitable for him to ply his trade. It is far better to educate about rabble-rousing than to work up a lather about one, two, or ten specific rabble-rousers.

We are learning how to handle these hate-peddling nuisances. A number of good articles about rabble-rousers have been published, notably, "American Fuehrer in Dress Rehearsal," by James Rorty in the December 1945 *Commentary*. In *Overcoming Anti-Semitism* (Harper & Brothers, 1943) I devoted some twenty pages to describing and analyzing this type of pest. Many others have written and spoken well on the subject. It is encouraging to every sincere liberal that many people now react with disgust to the speech of even the most clever rabble-rouser.

The rabble-rouser will remain for a long time an annoyance no doubt. So will the common house fly. Both *can* do great damage. But there are ways of controlling both. No one should become so disturbed about the danger to health which flies present that he falls out of a window trying to reach one fly with a swatter. Something like that applies to rabble-rousers too.

CHAPTER 3

Hate Writers

There are people who, merely by prodding their own dank imaginations, discover alarming things about racial or religious groups they dislike. Sometimes these distorted little people suffer obscure compulsions to display the creations of their warped minds for the admiration of others less fearfully imaginative. Usually the diatribes and the snide innuendoes that stem from animus are distributed only to those unfortunate enough to enjoy the correspondence of these haters. Now and then one of these malicious creatures achieves a greater sense of release by somehow getting a few hundred or a few thousand copies of his nightmare into mimeographed or printed form for wider distribution. Occasionally a respectable publication prints a subtle and reasonably persuasive distortion of fact by competent persons who are either misinformed or ill-intentioned.

All of these scurrilities, whether expressed in a private letter or published in a book, are examples of "hate writing." All are in some degree annoying or dangerous. All should be dealt with—but each in its own way.

The effective treatment of material of this sort, like the treatment of most aspects of prejudice, rests primarily upon the proper judgment of its importance. Its importance cannot be measured by the falsity or vileness of the item. The question is: How many persons does it reach and whom is it likely to influence? Most of these calumnies are unspeakably disgusting, but only a few of them ever reach enough people to have any real social effect.

Let us first consider the privately circulated letter. Sometimes a well-intentioned friend displays such a letter to a Victimian. If the Victimian has not acquired sufficient perspective to see such letters for what they are, he quite naturally—and quite unwisely—becomes so enraged that he grossly exaggerates its importance. He pours broadside after broadside at this monstrous apparition, which is, in fact, hardly more than a grain of dust on his spectacles. He fails to realize that we should never confuse the *wrongfulness* of a canard with the amount of *damage* it does. Hate writing of a private nature, of which only single copies or a few copies are made, is never deserving of the tremendous interest it arouses among members of the insulted group.

A non-Victimian friend handed a Victimian a letter which contained a slur against Victimians. The letter had been written by an insignificant person of no standing in the community. The man to whom the letter was shown presented it at the board meeting of a Victimian organization. There it was discussed for an entire evening, while far more consequential matters were completely neglected. Finally one man summed up the proceedings quietly.

"Mr. Chairman," he said, "we have failed here to discuss the possibilities for promoting a course of study in the local schools to improve group relationships that would affect every child in town. We have completely ignored what we might do by way of social action to eliminate discrimination in housing, although the local housing authority greatly needs our co-operation in defending its policy of non-segregation. Everything else on the agenda has been sidetracked while thirty people discussed this nasty note, which at most represents the opinion of one bigoted fool with no influence. At the end of two hours we are still going in circles because we cannot all agree upon exactly what should be done, although there have been several very good suggestions, any one of which is probably good enough. I move, Mr. Chairman, now, what we should have moved immediately, that you appoint three people who will consider the matter, decide on a course and pursue it, without keeping all of us absorbed in the discussion of an item that does not amount to a hill of beans in comparison with any of the large projects we have been overlooking."

This man's remarks contained excellent advice. In every community a few people should dispose of each case of a letter containing hate writing. It should be dealt with according to who wrote it, to whom he wrote it, and the possibilities of influencing aright the few persons involved. To promote community-wide discussion of such matters is like drawing the whole town into a prolonged public argument about one uncovered garbage can and generating such tremendous excitement that no one can give any thought to the major problems of sanitation which affect the entire city. One person of sound judgment can handle the trivia of individual hate writings and of hate speaking better than large standing committees or councils. Economy of time, effort, and energy requires that such "incidents" be ruled out of order at meetings where larger matters require consideration. Delegate these incidents to a man or two who can confer with those whose assistance may be helpful. Give him or them complete power to act and dispose of each of these incidents. Otherwise the focus and range of community relations effort become so narrowed that an occasional silly screed receives a thousand times the attention it deserves while constructive projects that require vision and initiative are ignored. Incidents are a bane principally because they distract those who should be involved in large community programs.

Published hate writings—writings with hurtful statements about racial and religious groups—which receive wide circulation present a more serious situation in which the danger increases in proportion to their circulation. They should be judged as calmly as possible on this basis. You may come across objectionable articles anywhere, often where you least expect to find them. When you do, ask yourself, "Is this magazine (or paper) a vermin publication? Does it make a practice of promoting bigotry and exist solely for that purpose? Or is this an otherwise reputable periodical whose publisher is deliberately encouraging this particular kind of intolerance against a certain group? Or is this an unfortunate slip on the part of a publication which is on the whole consistently averse to the promotion of group animosities?" The action that should be taken depends on which of these categories is involved. But whatever the character of the publication and whatever steps you take, please bear in mind that what is done is done, what is published is published. You cannot undo what is past and you cannot blot out what has already been written on the mind. Never treat the matter as though you are going to use an eraser on the memories of those who have read something. No such eraser has ever been invented.

With hate sheets (well described as the "vermin press") any approach to a publisher, editor, or writer will only bring forth a worse blast than the one of which complaint is made. The standard illustrative example of the fatality of the forced retraction in this type of publication tells of a newspaper publisher who informed his readers one day, "I wrote a few days ago that the members of our city council are not fit to associate with pigs. I have received many complaints. An apology has been demanded. I wish to declare, therefore, that the members of our city council are fit to associate with pigs." The possibility of provoking an even worse attack than the original one should never be overlooked. But even though it is difficult to handle these professional hate sheets, the situation is usually much less alarming than one might at first think. This type of publication today reaches less than 1 per cent of the public. It is true that *The Menace*, the Dearborn *Independent*, and *Social Justice*, now defunct and unlamented, at one time achieved high circulations. But no publication of this type now issues even twenty thousand copies per month. At present the *entire* vermin press issues less than half a million copies a month—probably much less. Compare that with the one and a half billion (billion, not million) newspapers printed in the United States each month. Compare the entire output of the hate peddlers with the multi-millioned circulation of even one such magazine as *Reader's Digest, Life, Look, Saturday Evening Post,* et cetera, and you will realize that the vermin press is a flea among elephants.

The readers of the poison press usually subscribe to a number of such publications. It gives them the titillation that others get from soap operas and comic books. About the only thing that can be done about this putrid stuff is to educate the entire public—at any rate all but the incurable fools—to scorn hate publications. If you were to pick up one of these specimens of fantastic denunciation you would simply be revolted. There is no reason why the overwhelming majority of your fellow citizens cannot be enlightened sufficiently to share your contempt for the vermin press. Even now it is usually recognized as something beneath contempt.

Public libraries do not knowingly give hate sheets shelf room. If you should see one in a public library, it is probably there by error. Call it to the attention of the librarian, not in anger but with confidence that a mistake was made and that it will be promptly rectified. You must, however, be able to recognize the difference between a puny hate sheet and a reputable publication that happens to contain something objectionable. The librarian may rightfully point out in the latter case that one discreditable item does not disqualify a periodical in every issue of which there are many articles which the public wants and has a right to read. Unless you have a very strong case, you will have to accept that fact. But don't let that convince you that the deluge is upon us. No great harm is likely to result from a single article. To develop a flourishing dislike for Victimians in a previously friendly librarian by being unreasonable is worse than having a few people read the offending piece.

The technique for handling books containing objectionable material is not unlike that applied to newspapers and magazines. Fortunately there are relatively few outright "smear" books, counterparts of the vermin press. Usually unfair or distorted references are confined to brief passages. Almost all American book publishers conscientiously adhere to a code of ethics which stress the rights of the individual to be heard. Publishers and editors are scrupulous but not infallible. Like any self-respecting person, the publisher resents and resists coercion—particularly when the pressure is the result of minor and inadvertent lapses.

If you see the manuscript or galley proof in advance of publication you are fully justified in calling the attention of the author or publisher to an objectionable line. If there is to be another edition you may ask for a change. But the ultimate right to publish not what the other fellow wishes, but what he himself wishes, is something for which an American publisher will fight to the last ditch.

Those who are involved in preparing or in purveying the printed word for public consumption need no license from the government of the United States or from any group of its citizens to do so. One may plead with publishers, argue with them, and carry one's case even into the courts if the item is libelous, obscene, or otherwise unlawful. But a publisher's right to make his own ultimate decisions must remain inviolate in a free country. Otherwise it will soon cease to be free. If ever there were a case where the golden rule applies, it is here. Any of us can become a publisher. As a publisher, each of us would insist that when all has been said, discussed, and argued out, the final decision on what to publish must be his. People who are at heart totalitarian, who believe that their own complete, infallible rectitude makes it advisable that they control the hands and lips of others will never understand *equal* freedom under law. Nevertheless equal freedom is the basis of democratic society. Publish what you will. Accord others the same right to publish or refuse to publish as their conscience, not yours, prescribes.

A Victimian organization proudly announced in the public press recently that it had persuaded a certain publisher to abandon publication of a book. That was stupid. It penalized a co-operative publisher by telling the world that he contemplated publishing something which would promote intolerance, but thanks to the self-advertising agency he will not publish it. It also gives an impression that the organization has assumed the right of censorship. In America we do not like snoopers and censors. Insofar as any of us needs to direct the activities of others by persuading them to refrain from publishing something, we are well within our rights in urging that incorrect statements be changed or omitted. These measures are, however, necessary evils in a society that cherishes security against prying and demands freedom of speech. It is to the ultimate disadvantage of minority groups to create an impression of exulting in being censors.

There are, of course, hate-filled books which are published with the open intention of poisoning and perverting minds. What to do about such a book when it appears is a perplexing problem. Whether or not there has been argument in advance with the publisher, once it has been printed and distributed, the utmost wisdom is required to deal with it advantageously. It is thoroughly permissible to make known to book merchants that there are such-and-such reasons why this book is injurious to wholesome democratic human relations. You have a right to persuade him, if you can, to refrain from selling and promoting the book. But the final decision is his. If he cannot be convinced, nothing that could be construed as a threat should be made. If he's half a man, he will resent and resist coercion. Above all avoid public clamor against the book. The more you denounce it, the more it will prosper. That is a truism in the publishing business well substantiated by actual cases. There was, for example, *Elmer Gantry*, by Sinclair Lewis. Fifteen years ago the librarian of the Mount Vernon, New York, Public Library told me that a month after *Elmer Gantry* had been published there had been less than ten calls for it at the library. Then the most popular minister of Mount Vernon denounced the book before his Bible class of six hundred men. There were two hundred calls for the book the next week.

What should you do about prejudiced articles in reputable publications such as your daily newspaper and the magazines you read? The very first thing to remember is this: *When an objectionable item has appeared, do not deal with it through the columns of the newspaper.* Write to the editor in friendly fashion in order to educate him aright on the subject but tell him that your letter is not for publication. It is true that there are times when your cause may be served by the appearance of precisely the right type of letter. But it is difficult to know when that is, and it is even more difficult to write the proper letter. There are few people who can write as deftly as the person who sent the following letter to a well-known magazine:

> TO THE EDITOR OF ———
>
> *As a Catholic subscriber to ——— I was shocked to find an issue carrying the grossly misleading and insulting reference to Catholicism in the ——— advertisement.*
>
> *I had subscribed to ——— not only because of my admiration for its scholarship and culture but also because of my conviction that in these disturbed times it is our responsibility as citizens of a democracy to make a positive effort to develop as much insight as possible into the point of view of other groups. That responsibility, it seems to me, is incumbent upon all of us.*
>
> *I do not want to think that the ———'s slur on the Catholic Church represents the thinking of the editors and publishers of ———. On the other hand, you printed a thoroughly unfair advertisement. You could have refused it.*
>
> (SIGNATURE)

That is a courageous dignified letter. It was published with this reply:

> *We can well understand the feeling of Miss ——— in this matter. We have, on previous occasions, refused advertisements which seemed to us to be appealing to anti-Catholic prejudice. The cartoon in the lower right-hand corner of the ——— ad seems to us to place it quite clearly within that category. It appeared in our pages only because of the kind of carelessness in checking that happens once in a long while even on a carefully edited magazine. It is quite out of keep-*

*ing with the whole aim and tenor of our policy and the high
level of responsibility we try to stand for and encourage in
dealing with the group life of America. We greatly regret
the incident.*

EDITOR

This letter to the editor is a model of clear statement without
rancor, invective, or exaggeration. If the editor is fair-minded, a letter
of this kind is almost certain to have the desired effect. If he is not,
a blistering tirade will not help; it will only make him feel more
self-righteous. No editor or publisher can wipe out what appeared
in yesterday's columns. In a periodical the all-important thing is
tomorrow's issue. The trickle of spiteful writing that may have
flowed under the bridge yesterday is of no consequence compared to
the torrent that might flow tomorrow. Educate the editor of your
publication if he needs education, and your reporters and feature
writers. Keep them informed about the issues of the day that interest
you. Don't be surprised if they come under the influence of hostile
and intolerant people if nothing positive is done to counteract such
influence. But don't argue with them in their columns. That is poor
policy.

If you are convinced that some public statement ought to be
made to the readers of an offending publication, go to an organization actively engaged in combating prejudice. You may insist that
someone do something about answering the canard—but *don't* try it
yourself without help unless you are an expert in journalism.

On October 3, 1945, a columnist who interprets with a dash of gall
and spleen events which he imagines have transpired or suspects
may be about to happen behind the scenes in Washington, stated
bluntly that a certain general had been dismissed from his command
for having slapped a Victimian soldier. He even named in this connection several distinguished Victimians. The anti-Victimian sentiments of this columnist had been reflected in previous writing of his
but never so unmistakably that an issue could be made of his bias.
This time, beyond a shadow of a doubt, he breached the truth. The
slapped soldier was certainly not a Victimian and nothing could
have been more fantastically absurd than the columnist's imagined
Victimian plot against that highly admired army officer.

A popular columnist is an asset to his syndicate and to his newspaper. People like to read "the dirt," and a writer who can skillfully

blast reputations by clever innuendo without becoming guilty of libel appears to be a particularly good drawing card for some newspapers. It has become a lucrative business with its own pat technique. Smear artists *falsify* without lying by simply omitting relevant facts; they imply untruths by juxtaposition without enabling the offended to protest effectively. For example: "Now this lawyer Houston has a brother who once worked for a newspaper which employed a communist, So-and-So. So-and-So was involved in several communist organizations. Houston has been nominated for . . ." You will note that Houston is not a communist and it has not been said that he is one. But the reader is expected to get the impression that Houston has had definite communist connections. By such literary sleight of hand the skillful reputation wrecker can do an astonishing amount of damage to reputable, innocent people.

The presidents of several Victimian organizations wrote to the publisher of the large daily which published the columnist's dream story of the slapped soldier. They asked to see the publisher. Had he granted their request it is probable that an amicable understanding would have been reached. Instead, he published their protest in the Letters-to-the-Editor Column and refused to discuss the matter with them. That disposed of step one of a process which we shall call "Dissuasion." The average publisher or editor is sensitive to public opinion and consultation is usually possible. In this case it was not.

Although few Victimians read that objectionable column when it appeared, within days the matter was being discussed at meetings of their various organizations. Telephones carried the facts from home to home. Letters and phone calls from hundreds of Victimians came to the managing editor of the newspaper. This was step two in dissuasion. (The publisher kept himself inaccessible.) Here was a clear-cut lie. A retraction was certainly in order. But against the stubborn insolence of a tremendously wealthy publisher the rightful resentment of Victimians was of no avail.

The facts continued to spread. A number of organizations began to discuss them. What right had any newspaper to publish a hate-inciting falsehood against a group and then compound the injury by refusing to recant that lie? Within a week it was no longer a problem for Victimians alone. The mayor of the city spoke out. Labor organizations, veteran organizations, and thousands of individuals—the public, in fact—protested. That was step three. Individuals began to cancel their subscriptions and advertisers, although it was far more of a loss to them than to the newspaper, began to withdraw their advertising. At last, while protests were still mounting, the columnist on October 18 announced that, "On the evidence, our statements . . . were untrue. We regret having made them." All other steps having failed, maximal, legitimate pressure brought a retractio..

You may rightfully ask why I have called this process "Dissuasion." Is it not coercion? The answer is that the adverse pressure which developed in this case was not the result of boycott or of urging anyone to cancel subscriptions or refuse advertising. Everyone who took a position did so because *he himself* resented that newspaper item. Any preacher who told his congregation, "Don't buy that newspaper," *would* have been using coercion. But the speaker who said, "Here are the facts. I am not going to buy that newspaper. You do as you please," was still using dissuasion. Beyond this one should not go. No picketings. No mass meetings. No appeals to hysteria.

In cases of this kind dissuasion consists of 1) consultation with the publisher or editor, 2) protests by phone and mail, 3) informing larger and larger numbers of people why the policy of the newspaper is being questioned, 4) the withdrawal of support from the newspaper by those who are convinced that its policy is inimical to public welfare. That is a fair, democratic procedure. Avoid coercion that involves anything more drastic than is implied by dissuasion. The diminution of circulation and advertising is useful in dissuasion only as proof positive and convincing that the public is genuinely averse to the periodical's policy. If that is the only kind of proof which a publisher will believe, he should receive that kind of proof.

There is another type of hate literature that deserves attention. It is the fly-by-night filthy screed that sometimes attains the dignity of type but usually is the product of a mimeograph machine or carbon paper. Because these bits of scurrility generally conceal the name of the sender, it is difficult and sometimes impossible to trace the source. Many cities now have ordinances which prohibit the printing and distribution of anonymous literature which "exposes any individual or any racial or religious group to hatred, contempt, ridicule, or obloquy unless the name and address of the person responsible for its issuance is clearly printed on it." Such a regulation does not interfere with freedom of speech, since it does not forbid the publication of the item but merely requires its publisher to accept responsibility for it.

A state statute prohibits anonymous hate literature in all of Florida. Laws of this kind obviously do not make it impossible for crackpots to send out poison-pen notes. Nothing can prevent a man from occasionally sneaking into the mails whatever he will. But if someone makes a habit of sending out anonymous hate literature, or if a pile of it is laid out in such a place as a tavern for people to help themselves, or if a merchant is passing it out to his customers, the police can intervene, confiscate the copies, and by penalizing an offender make him reluctant to continue the practice. You might check up to see whether your own city has such an ordinance. It should. The Philadelphia, Pennsylvania, ordinance on this subject is a good model bill.

The state of Oregon issues an official *Voters' Pamphlet*, in which candidates present their views of the reasons why they should be elected to public office. Among the candidates for Congress in 1940 was Kenneth A. Brown. He was then thirty-one and a member of a well-respected family. He was also an isolationist whose political platform had an anti-Semitic tinge. Into the Oregon *Voters' Pamphlet* Brown inserted some venomous statements about the Jews. Not that it helped him any; he failed by a very large margin to secure the nomination he sought. He did, however, secure for his defamatory ideas publication in the official *Voters' Pamphlet*, which was mailed to every voter in the state of Oregon.

In 1941, the very next year, Oregon adopted provisions requiring its Secretary of State to exclude from the *Voters' Pamphlet* any statement "which in any way incites, counsels, promotes, or advocates hatred, abuse, violence, or hostility toward, or which tends to cast ridicule or shame upon any person or group of persons by reason of race, color, religion, or manner of worship."

This raises the much-discussed question, "Why do we tolerate any speech or writing against racial and religious groups?" Why not prohibit it altogether by law? Attacks upon such groups destroy our national unity. They endanger the security not only of the attacked groups but of our entire nation. Since we have libel laws to protect individuals, why not have libel laws to protect groups? If the state of Oregon ruled that kind of abuse out of its *Voters' Pamphlet*, why not forbid it in everything published in Oregon?

One state, Massachusetts, does have a group libel law. It was adopted in 1943. In the six years since it went into effect it has been invoked only once, and that case was dismissed on a technicality. Indiana in 1947 adopted a slightly different law, aimed at hate organizations rather than hate publications. It is likely that both of these laws will be declared unconstitutional if a serious attempt is ever made to enforce them.

On December 5, 1941, the New Jersey Supreme Court declared unconstitutional "the New Jersey Race Hatred Law" which had been on the books since March 6, 1935. That was a group libel law which was so broad and all inclusive that while it would have applied to a rabble-rouser's excoriation of Victimians it would also have included thousands of cases it was not intended to include. Among the things the New Jersey legislators forbade were all books, speeches, articles, circulars, pamphlets, and even "statements" which in any way promote hostility against racial or religious groups. The law was so poorly conceived that anyone who sold a book or magazine without carefully reading its contents before the sale ran a risk of violating it. A father telling his child why his religion was better than another was, even though he probably was unaware of the fact, violating that group libel law. It was properly declared null and void.

There are many obvious reasons why all group libel laws are both unenforceable and dangerous. To determine whether or not something said about a racial or religious group is true the amount of evidence that would require examination is colossal. If it is said that such a group is trying to control the public schools or to corrupt our magazines or to get us into a war or promote atheism, can it be left to a judge and jury to weigh all the evidence and bring in a verdict about that entire group? Can anyone really gather all the relevant information? It is not only the defendant in a group libel suit who is being judged; the whole group whom he defamed is likewise weighed in the balance. It is clearly better to leave the decisions concerning racial and religious groups to the court of public opinion than to a trial court. To give to hate mongers a courtroom as a sounding-board for their views is a sure way of giving their canards enormous circulation.

In considering facts about groups, the prejudices and partialities of those who examine defamations are sure to enter. Assuming that an anti-Victimian writer were haled into court on a group libel charge, what kind of jury will try him? Mr. Jones, a prospective juror, is asked by the writer's attorney, "Do you have any objections to a man's disliking the Victimians?"

Jones says, "I have."

The defendant's attorney says, "I admit that my client dislikes Victimians. We claim, however, that he did not libel them. But if Mr. Jones here objects to dislike of Victimians, he is prejudiced against my client."

Jones cannot serve on that jury.

The next prospective juror is Brown. Brown says, when questioned, "I have no objections to anyone's disliking the Victimians."

Brown therefore may serve on the jury.

Since the case revolves around the truth or falsehood of certain allegations concerning Victimians, jurors would have to be impartial in their attitude toward Victimians. But what kind of jurymen are these who have no objections to racial and religious hatred? How will they decide an issue fraught with hate mongering? This is not an academic or theoretical question. It can be deadly important. Think of a Negro who has been pointing out the mistreatment of his people and faces a hostile jury on the charge that he has libeled the white race. It is perfectly possible that group libel laws would lead to that, particularly in times of emotional crisis.

Fear and panic could bring laws intended to deal with rabble-rousers and hate writers. But in times of tension honest crusaders, crying out against corruption, would be caught in the net of those laws. They would be adjudged guilty for criticizing, however inadvertently, a racial or religious group. Liberals and spokesmen of minority groups would be most likely to be thus penalized by a hostile regime. Group libel laws can become powerful boomerangs. Members of all racial and religious groups should forego the desire to defend their status and reputation against hate mongers through the group libel formula.

Proponents of group libel laws fail to recognize the reason that slandered individuals rarely sue for libel. In the atrocious article (mentioned before), wherein Victimians were said to have taken vengeance on a general, four prominent Victimians were mentioned by name. They were accused of an act of skullduggery of which they could not possibly have been guilty. The whole story was based on a total falsification of readily verifiable fact. The defamed individuals did not take any legal steps. They did not even issue statements denying the accusation. Obviously these extremely astute men of great political experience preferred not to dignify the calumny by giving it recognition and still greater circulation. That defamation, like innumerable others, was soon forgotten by all but those who were intensely interested in it. A legal suit, even though won by these four men, would have aggravated the injury. It would have engraved the lie in public memory, where it would have remained regardless of the verdict.

Why should groups be exposed to the kind of courtroom rehearsal of insults against themselves which discerning individuals consider more hurtful than helpful? Individuals or organizations, when they sue for libel, may be awarded large sums of money to recompense them for damages received; slandered racial or religious groups would not even receive that satisfaction, since it is obviously impossible either to collect damages or to distribute them in the case of a race or a religious fellowship.

The ultimate safeguard against hate promoters has been well described in the following sentences which appeared in *Freedom of the Press*, a report of the Commission on Freedom of the Press (University of Chicago Press, 1947): "Modern life brings its own sophistications and develops a knowing sales resistance to the more usual varieties of deceit. Tough immunities can bear tough assaults, and there is a general presumption that a sound civilization develops and enjoys using an increasing tough immunity." Continuous education of the public concerning the evils of intolerance and the evil motives of those who capitalize upon intolerance is the only reliable antidote to hate writings.

If democracy is to be preserved, the right to express opinions must remain as great as possible. We already have laws against speech and action which *create clear and present danger* to the public welfare. If anyone tells his hearers to take up arms or commit violent acts against a racial or religious group, it requires no new laws to arraign him at the bar of justice. In our libel laws protecting individuals and organizations, in laws forbidding obscenity, and in various other statutes and ordinances we already have adequate protection against certain highly objectionable abuses of the freedom of speech and writing. Laws which would impose additional restraints would impair the framework of democratic human relations.

To deal properly with hate writings you should cultivate the ability to evaluate the effect of each objectionable item. Proper perspective is indispensable to avoid exaggerating or minimizing the importance and influence of malicious books, articles, and statements. In taking any corrective steps be guided by the distinction between incorrigible hate mongers and respectable publishers and writers guilty of errors which they will readily correct if properly approached. Above all, bear in mind that it is more profitable to educate the public toward dislike and rejection of scurrilous attacks upon racial and religious groups than to offset any particular bit of obloquy.

CHAPTER 4

Ruffians

The word "intolerance" is not susceptible to precise and scientifically accurate definition. Each of us has his own complex concept of its meaning and many a speaker befuddles both himself and his audience by speaking of intolerance as though *feeling* a prejudice, expressing it *verbally,* and *committing intolerant acts* were one and the same thing.

Before we discuss the handling of ruffians—and especially since we shall be considering the legal action which can be taken against overt intolerance—it is wise to understand quite clearly what different forms intolerance takes. To prevent confusion it is convenient to classify the indications of intolerance under the following four headings:

1. *Disliking Victimians.*
2. *Attacking them verbally.*
3. *Discriminating against them in employment, housing, et cetera.*
4. *Inflicting malicious injury, because of group prejudice, on the persons or property of members of the disliked group.*

1. There is little to be said here about disliking Victimians. That involves the whole problem of what to do about prejudice, and as such is the *general* subject of this book. True, unfriendly feelings *might* lead to abuse or even violence. But should those suspected

of intolerant attitudes be grilled by the police and ordered to become fair-minded or else be jailed? That would be disastrous. No freedom-loving nation ever inflicts a penalty for what resides only within the head and the heart. We can and should work for the elimination of prejudiced attitudes in every way possible. It is worth pointing out here, however, that objectionable sentiments per se are not subject to *legal* controls except in a police state.

2. Verbal expressions of intolerance may be as mild as dishwater or as deadly as nitric acid. Courts should and can deal with the most menacing. They cannot be expected to cleanse every mouth and pen so thoroughly that no unkind word will be spoken because of unwarranted aversions. A rumor has circulated in this country, presumably to the glory of communist Russia, that in Russia a man was actually sentenced to eight years in jail for using an ugly epithet addressed to a member of a nationality group. That is not so admirable as it sounds. If true—and I doubt its veracity—it would indicate a barbaric, backward conception of justice, a throwback to the age when hanging a man for stealing a loaf of bread was considered just punishment. Eight years in jail for a harsh word is not, in the sight of highly civilized people, a mark of advanced culture, but, rather, a token of ruthless, terrorizing despotism.

Our laws already forbid the use of spoken and written language to threaten violence or to incite others to commit it. Conspiracy to commit crimes, whether motivated by racial or religious animosity or by any other motive, is likewise forbidden. You may denounce a group without incurring any penalty. But if you urge, "Let's go out and beat them up," it may mean a jail sentence.

At what point does a man's baring his teeth leave no doubt that he is going to bite? Many a man has said, "I'm going to kill that guy!" but on meeting the threatened fellow has shed nothing but angry words. The Supreme Court and our lesser courts draw the line between the permissible and the unpermissible at the point of "clear and present danger," a phrase worth remembering. To some extent it is always dangerous when people express animosity, but it is not necessarily *clear and present* danger. It may be only distant danger, which may evaporate. It may be evanescent danger. It may not be at all clear to a fair-minded jury that what was said or printed creates any *real* danger. To make a practice of invoking penal measures against everyone who says something objectionable would involve a far greater danger to our liberties than do these offenses themselves.

In borderline cases, especially where demagogues and hate writers are very careful of their phrasing, in *borderline cases* (I repeat) it is extremely difficult to determine whether or not "clear and present danger" has been presented. Those words do, nevertheless, furnish the best line of demarcation between the permissible and the forbidden.

3. About those brambles growing out of intolerance, known as "discriminatory practices," so much has been said earlier in this book that nothing need be added here. Well-considered laws, properly enforced, are a step in the right direction.

4. Unexpressed opinion never runs afoul of the law. Verbal assaults may or may not. Whether a speech or publication violates city ordinances or state statutes depends upon exactly what was said, to whom it was said, where and when it was said, and upon the actual or probable effect of the spoken or written statement. But *every* act—except in self-defense or in apprehending a criminal— *every* act which injures someone's body or damages or destroys his property is forbidden by law. It does not matter whether the ruffian is animated by intolerance. When an injurious *act* of felonious nature has been committed, to obtain a conviction it is not necessary to prove anything beyond the fact that so-and-so perpetrated it.

The following propositions are surely reasonable enough. Yet they are totally negated and denied by some defenders of racial and religious groups who are as prone to be agitators as are the demagogues attacking the groups.

1. One cannot be sure of the motives for a crime until the identity of the criminal is known, except where the nature of the act leaves no possible doubt of the motive.

2. A single act or several acts of mischief owing to group hatred, perpetrated by one or very few culprits, is not conclusive evidence of widespread hostility against that group.

3. Those who commit assault or vandalism because of animosity against a group should suffer the penalties provided by law for the offense. Unless the act was a harmless prank or only trivial

damage was done, the perpetrators should not be magnanimously forgiven if motivated by prejudice. Unless they would have been pardoned had their motive been free of prejudice, they should be held rigidly accountable for similar acts inspired by prejudice.

If a brick wrapped in a page of anti-Japanese propaganda is hurled through a Nisei's window, the motivation of the thrower is patently established. Short of such unmistakable revelation of intolerance, it must not be assumed that damage done to the property or person of Victimians is because of intolerance. The mere fact that it is a Victimian house of worship or cemetery that has been vandalized does not prove that group hatred was involved.

In Brooklyn it happened that over a period of months synagogues and rabbinical schools were entered stealthily and sacred scrolls were mutilated. Other acts of vandalism were committed. Alarmist organizations and fire-eating individuals were screaming that organized storm troopers were loose in Brooklyn. According to the panicky, a wave of anti-Semitism had broken out. Alarm grew as the desecrations continued. At last the police caught the one man who had done all this mischief. He confessed to the outrages at the nine vandalized institutions. His name was Mordecai Stanger. His age, twenty-three. His religion, Jewish.

It took fifty detectives and thirty uniformed policemen working full time to apprehend this young Jewish garment cutter who, as he put it, "was guided by an evil spirit," but who certainly was not anti-Semitic or under the influence of anti-Semites. Yet the impression that this was large-scale anti-Semitic vandalism could not be dispelled until the culprit was caught. One may well marvel at the clairvoyance, at the psychic sense, of journalists who long before the perpetrator of an act is discovered are positive of his motives. When it is heralded that a wave of anti-Victimianism has occurred, it usually turns out that a couple of delinquent youngsters with nothing but mischief in their hearts did the job.

Some people seem to extract a perverted joy from the hysteria that can be evoked by quarrels between racial and religious groups. In Freeport, Long Island, a white policeman was persecuted by people who tried to make a *cause célèbre* out of this policeman's fatally shooting two Negro brothers and wounding a third. Those determined to make "a racial killing" out of this incident were not there at the time of the fray, which took place in a lonely spot in the dead of night, but they were as sure about what happened as though they had witnessed the shooting. They claimed greater prescience and greater sense of justice than the grand jury which exonerated the policeman. They were contemptuous of a special examiner appointed by the governor of New York State who reviewed the case, because he confined the hearing to genuine evidence and refused to listen to secondhand and thirdhand hearsay evidence. The agitators would have created no ruction at all if the brothers had been white, although to kill wantonly members of one's own race is as heinous as to kill members of another.

I went to Freeport. I found that some of the assertions of those demanding the head of the officer were certainly untrue. I interviewed Negroes at random, Negroes whom I met near the place where the incident occurred. All of them said, "If I'd have been in that cop's place, I'd have shot those drunks myself in self-defense." I found that the policeman had an enviable record for decency, kindliness, and fairness to those of all races and creeds. Never before in his career of several years on police duty had he drawn a gun on anyone. After several hours of firsthand inquiry, I knew that had I been in his place I would have had to shoot to avoid having my weapon taken from me and being killed. Several policemen had been slain in that county during the previous year. It was for such emergencies that this patrolman had been given a revolver and he was the kind of man who would employ it only in an extremity. Yet he was pictured in a pamphlet as a one-man Ku Klux Klan, a trigger-happy cop who enjoyed murdering Negroes.

Until the identity of the offender is known, there is certainly no justification for an emotional spree on the assumption that a vast campaign against a group has been launched. Even after the offender has been apprehended, it requires more than snap judgment based on emotional reaction to reach the truth. Unquestionably many petty offenses, as well as many heinous crimes, are the result of intolerance. In each instance, however, the establishment of fair and equal justice comes first and we must look to responsible sources and to the most fair and impartial reporters. Of course we should be alert to the injustices committed against members of minority groups; but those who cry "Wolf! Wolf!" on every conceivable occasion are very poor guides.

Whenever an act of assault or vandalism has been committed, the first and most important thing to do is *Catch the culprit*. Omit the excitement, avoid hysteria. Apprehending the offender is worth more than practically everything else that can be done. If he "gets away with it," publicizing the event is at best of little good and probably harmful. To overturn tombstones *with impunity* is a tempting idea for numbskulls. Why remind morons through the press that if they want some fun there are all those graves unattended at night where they can commit vandalism unchecked and unpunished? Waves of desecrating cemeteries and burglarizing unguarded buildings generally grow in volume as newspaper after newspaper across the nation announces that such an act has occurred but reports no arrest. These waves abate and stop when it is made known that such and such persons were arrested, found guilty, sentenced to jail. Give the police the utmost co-operation. Arrange for sets of volunteer watchers, but refrain from drawing conclusions until the guilty have been found and questioned.

In August 1945 a headline shouted that the Springfield Plan had failed. I had been under the impression that this outstanding attempt on the part of a school system to create ideal relationships between members of the various racial and religious groups was a great success. This pronouncement of failure was based entirely upon the fact that some school children in that city had broken some synagogue windows. I wrote to a well-informed friend in Springfield and received the following reply:

> *In the neighborhood of the Kodimah Synagogue there resides a group of boys who for many years have had a record of mischievousness and minor delinquency. They have evidenced this delinquency most frequently and clearly against this synagogue and its members. There is also evidence of their having damaged a Protestant church, the public school building, and, at such times as Halloween, neighborhood stores and residences. All have been a minor type of irritation.*
>
> *Every so often the group gets a little "cocky" and acts up against the synagogue and its members. In recent weeks they evidently have been disturbing the men on the way to services and finally got fresh enough to break some of the windows in the building.*
>
> *Three or four individuals have set the example for the younger members of the group and are the ones the police*

immediately picked up when the synagogue complained.
These particular boys do not have a good record and have
been known to the police for other infractions. One of them
is over eighteen years of age and was rejected by the Army
for his low I.Q.

It is the considered judgment of our community relations
committee that the boys are not especially anti-Semitic. If
they lived in another neighborhood these same actions
would be committed against any other identifiable groups
—for example, against the Italians, Poles, or Negroes.

Here in Springfield the matter was treated primarily on
a delinquency basis and was handled as such by the police
and will undoubtedly be so handled by the court. . . .
There has been no local reaction either in the Jewish com-
munity or in the general community because the record of
this particular group of boys and their frequent involve-
ment in neighborhood disturbances are well known. I was
greatly surprised to hear that the incident has been used
elsewhere. We thought little of it here.

Usually an incident involving racial and religious conflict (or
which may be so interpreted, even if incorrectly) is viewed with a
great deal more alarm at a distance than it is in the place where it
occurs. Those on the scene know that except in the case of a riot or
something equally serious a broken window or a wall smeared with
paint has not altered the friendly relationship with their neighbors.
It takes only one lout to hurl a brick or wield a wanton paintbrush
in a city of a million souls. Life thereabouts goes on normally. But
elsewhere, if such incidents have been publicized in the newspapers
and radio, the impression prevails that the only thing of importance
that month in Littleburg or Bigtown or wherever it happened—was
that Victimians were mistreated.

When fists fly and ill will rages in a community the police and
various other local agencies go quietly, but vigorously, to work on
the problem. They do not enter the scene to advertise themselves.
Their first and foremost problem is to relieve tension, to lessen the
sense of strain. Despite any amount of intervention by national
organizations, ultimately it is the people who live there—the educators and the community leaders—who must improve the environment and the climate of opinion.

Local leaders (leaders, not cheap politicians) readily understand that creating hysteria and frightening one group or another into a sense of insecurity is highly inadvisable, since panicky persons are in no mood for better understanding and conciliation. Nevertheless, alarmists start wild rumors, with each group being told that its members have been more injured and are in far greater danger than they are. A violent incident *can* be turned into a source of continued warfare by publicity. It should not be. A program to provide pleasant meetings for the hitherto unfriendly, recreational opportunities for youth, and various new facilities is needed. These are instituted by those whose sole concern is to accomplish good results for their community. It is not dramatic, or exciting, or sensational, or easy—this work of crowding out existing hatreds with a new growth of amiable, friendly sentiment. It is not accomplished in a month or in a year. Yet, if the neighborhood is not to remain in perpetual uproar and conflict, antagonisms must be reduced, suspicions allayed, and kindly faith in neighbors nurtured by patient, diligent, exacting labor.

Incidents involving intergroup hostility are invitingly exploitable. An organization without qualms and with a periodical—which we shall call *The Denouncer*—can use any squabble to mulct the innocents. This paper magnifies the street fight into a battle and the minor brawl takes on the semblance of organized mobs threatening massacre. Eager to get into the limelight and to appear heroic, *The Denouncer* exaggerates every tiff or spat into a homicidal encounter. If a youngster is slapped or cuffed, the world is told that he was mauled and maimed, and since the world was not there to observe the facts it is often willing to accept the lurid version. Insignificant scraps and scrimmages of the kind that have been occurring frequently ever since one group of urchins bullied another on the streets of ancient Rome are magnified into bloody wars and publicized as horrible instances of racial and religious vendettas. Since fear is a sure pocketbook opener for *The Denouncer,* it loves to picture those whom it claims to protect as victims of immense hatred, rapine, and mayhem.

The wife of the rabbi of a New York town could tell *The Denouncer* supporters an apt story. She was strolling one day with another Jewish woman whom she had only recently met. As they turned a corner they saw ahead of them two boys rolling on a lawn, pummeling each other. One was dark and black-haired, the other was light-skinned and flaxen. At the moment the blond was on top.

"Just look at that vicious boy," the visitor exclaimed. "Look at the anti-Semitism in his face—the little monster!"

The rabbi's wife laughed. The blond "little monster" was her own son. The child with whom he was playfully wrestling was his best friend, brunet scion of a Christian neighbor.

It is inconceivable to *The Denouncer* and its following that someone might hit a member of a minority group because of friction that has no relationship to whether he was a member of that group or not. Even if the victim of the attack and all other witnesses present insist that nothing whatsoever was done or said to indicate racial or religious awareness, *The Denouncer* holds to its theory that if a meteor falls on a Victimian, it was hurled by an anti-Victimian.

The Denouncer, snooping around for something which will attract public attention and money, finds in instances of violence the fat it lives on—the chance to build a bonfire of the kind of scraps that yellow journalism loves and the better publications either omit or "play down." For those who would rather devour three columns about the latest murder (which has no effect on their own lives) than read one column about the progress of the United Nations (which will influence their own existence mightily), *The Denouncer* has exactly the right bait.

When an incident has occurred wherein ruffians have attacked one or several Victimians, *The Denouncer* uses whatever means it can to draw all eyes in alarm to the occurrence. Its representative issues a blast against the police for failing to apprehend the ruffians immediately. A full-page advertisement in newspapers shrieks about an alleged reign of terror against Victimians. *The Denouncer* arranges mass meetings (where funds are invariably solicited for *The Denouncer*) to decry the menace of hoodlumism now being unleashed against Victimians. More full-page newspaper advertisements are run. These have more screaming headlines—and invariably an appeal for funds for *The Denouncer*, which is soon thoroughly publicized. Through all of this its chief labor is to advertise itself. Then, when more sober heads and sturdier hands have caused the apprehension and punishment of culprits and have initiated needed communal projects, *The Denouncer* sends its self-laudatory literature to its entire sucker list, claiming all credit and glory for its magnificent accomplishment in Topsyburg or wherever the incident occurred. And while responsible agencies settle down to years of arduous work in that neighborhood, *The Denouncer* is off to other ventures.

The Denouncer makes it a policy to castigate any organization (especially a Victimian organization) trying to act sensibly and deal with the actual issues. The agencies continuously working to improve human relationships and assiduously laboring in the homes and schools of that particular city, instead of in alarmist newspaper headlines, are accused of a "hush-hush" policy and of protecting anti-Victimians. *The Denouncer* will sabotage every conscientious effort to restore harmony and good will by decent, kindly folk and will accuse them of being supine and too submissive. Those who do the most difficult work but avoid self-glorification endure constant abuse from such masters of chicanery as *The Denouncer's* strategists. Berating Victimian organizations on the ground that they are cowardly or indifferent is just part of *The Denouncer's* fun.

The most useful suggestion that can be made at this point is this: If you read in reliable newspapers or are told by creditable witnesses or get authentic information from some dependable source accounts which relate mistreatment of the members of disadvantaged groups you may regard them as true. But fly-by-night reports and statements from organizations or in periodicals which make a regular practice of "alarming" on these subjects should always be scanned skeptically. When you contribute, do so to encourage and to aid positive constructive year-around effort to improve group relationships and to better the status of the mistreated. Do not pay anyone for parading as a savior or for screeching in your ear. If he pictures a minor incident as a momentous event of vast significance, a man lacks the perspective to deal with it correctly.

Two boys were stopped in a lonely spot in New York one night and asked by several men whether they were members of a certain religious group. They replied in the affirmative and were beaten unmercifully.

It may seem splitting hairs to ask, "Which was more important, the fact that the men were anti-something or that the boys were physically assaulted?" You may say, "Oh, nonsense! Why even raise such an irrelevant question? The motive and the crime are inextricably interwoven. It is senseless to talk about their relative importance." Yet there are differences of emphases and different ways of handling such matters. Choices are made according to whether the crime and the motive are seen in proper perspective. Too many people still yell, "Racial (or religious) hatred!" when they should be crying "Crime!"

This crime of the beating of the two boys was everyone's affair. This was not the members of one racial and religious group versus the attackers. It was the case of the people of New York—all of the people—against a group of ruffians. Some think there is a great lesson to be learned by everyone by emphasizing the cause of the crime. I am not so sure of that. The strategy of terror employed by the Nazis ought to convince us that the sadistic effect of well-advertised brutality is far greater upon the baser elements of society than the effect of such things upon the good-hearted and decent public. You need not tell average Americans that two Victimian children have just been assaulted to make them abhor such a crime. They do already. And what can they do about this one? Can they become policemen and apprehend the brutes? Just what are they to do other than launch a campaign of education and intergroup co-operation to banish intolerance? But is it necessary to have mayhem and assault committed and well advertised to enlist people in combating bigotry? Have our society's morals sunk so low that average men and women can be motivated to action only by brutal conduct? On the other hand, telling the world that you can beat up two children and get away with it is a dreadful suggestion to offer the weak-minded and the delinquent. *Apprehend those ruffians and punish them.* They assaulted two innocent youngsters. Never mind whose youngsters. They are, for all that really matters, everybody's children, the more so if their assailants want the world to think of them as the children of a misprized group.

A Victimian in San Francisco, finding that his store window had been defaced with large-lettered anti-Victimian epithets, insisted on keeping these libels permanently on his window as a horrible example of something. He could not be budged. A picture was made of the besmirched pane with its infamous remarks about Victimians. This got into newspapers, even in distant cities. How this could enlighten anyone is hard to understand. How it could disappoint or discourage the malfeasor, who evidently learned his techniques of sign painting from Hitler, is still more difficult to comprehend.

It is far more encouraging to a gutter-minded scamp to find that his artistic productions receive prolonged attention and expansive reproduction than to find that they are quickly and quietly eradicated. Such advertising as the San Francisco case offered is the reverse of penalty. The perpetrator can best be chastised by apprehending him and treating him as a vandal. It is better to punish him as a common, ordinary lawbreaker than to identify him to the public as one who dislikes Victimians. Many who do not like Victimians will applaud an anti-Victimian act. No one admires a run-of-the-mill vandal.

In the summer of 1947 Norman Cousins, vice-president of *The Saturday Review of Literature,* drew national attention to an anti-Semitic incident that had occurred in an Iowa city. It involved the name of a university in which Jewish students and applicants for admission have been treated as well as in any other American university. By any standard of justice that university's long, excellent record entitles it to be recognized as one free of anti-Semitism. To muddy its name because of one unfortunate incident is tantamount to saying, "Be as fair as you like, as kindly as you like, as generous as you like to the members of a racial or religious group and the reputation you have earned will vanish in an hour if something that reflects intolerance happens, however beyond your control it may be."

It was certainly by no wish of the university authorities that an undergraduate student of dubious character and another young man, not a student, assaulted a graduate Jewish student, E. S. Cooper. Whether others on the scene had an opportunity to intervene in the swift attack I do not know. Mr. Cousins rightfully refrained at first from mentioning the name of the university, but in response to pressure from correspondents he divulged it, with the result that the university received barrages of highly unmerited adverse criticism. One of the saddest features of assaults upon members of racial or religious groups by irresponsible persons is that the names of other persons or institutions and organizations, with whom the attackers are somehow identified, are unjustly smeared.

Mr. Cooper did not report the incident to the university or to the police. When Mr. Cousins discovered and publicized the incident, Cooper insisted that there be no prosecution. There is no law under which the state could prosecute if the victim will not prefer charges. The university did all that it could (in the summer vacation period) by barring the offending student from readmission in the fall term. It is Cooper's attitude that requires analysis. He took the position that his assailants were to be pitied rather than punished, that they were victims of prevailing prejudices for which society is responsible. By the same token no one ought ever to be penalized for any crime, since every delinquent is a product of his environment. Here I quote some lines from an earlier volume of mine, *Overcoming Anti-Semitism* (Harper & Brothers, 1943):

> *If a Jew is denounced as a "Damned Jew" and bashed on the head, the assailant should be arrested and prosecuted. But neither in the trial nor in the newspapers should it be made to appear that the thug is being condemned for harboring anti-Jewish sentiments.[1] Let him be revealed as a common lawbreaker, stripped of any of the aura of martyrdom. Let him go to jail rebuked for striking a human being, regardless of the victim's religious (or racial) background. Let him be unable to parade among his fellow plug-uglies as one who had the courage to resist Jewish (or any other) insolence, and don't let anyone make a fine, gracious speech in court and have the fellow released because we Jews (or any other groups) don't bear any grudges. He didn't hit a Jew. In this country, when you punch or stab or shoot, you hit a human being. It is only in countries that have reverted to barbarism that it is a crime to injure one man and good clean fun to injure another.*
>
> *If you discover anti-Jewish stickers pasted on a window, do not become so disturbed by the anti-Semitic implication that you overlook the fact that, in violation of city ordinances, property has been defaced. If you see a man hurl a stone through a store window to emphasize an anti-Semitic speech, realize that from that moment on the man's anti-Semitism had better be ignored until after he is duly tried and punished for destroying property. American courts hold that men must be punished for their acts and not for their views. Hating is legally permissible. Hitting is punishable.*

I disagree totally with Mr. Cooper, who permitted the university to suffer damage to its reputation, which could have been avoided had he reported the attack promptly, had he instituted charges against his assailants and thus cleared the university officials from

---

[1] The same is true, obviously, of anti-Negro, anti-Catholic, anti-Italian, anti-Japanese, and any other anti-Victimian attack.

a most undeserved blame. The best procedure in any isolated crime motivated by intolerance is to treat it as any other crime. The attitude toward Mr. Cooper's religious group in that Iowa city was as good as it was anywhere in America. By his very silence he brought about a situation which gave a wrong impression to the nation.

Riots or threatened riots should be handled by the police. The procedure in such cases is discussed elsewhere in this book.

Where ill feeling between groups is on the increase and mass violence is likely to occur, the "play-it-up" tactic can only increase the tension and drive the factions into open hostility or, if it has already begun, into further depredations.

To expect no instances of juvenile delinquency or adult violence because of intolerance in a country as large as the United States is to expect the impossible. Ask any custodian of a zoo, ask any librarian, ask any superintendent of schools, and he will tell you that mischievous injury to animals, to books, to public property, and the like happens right along. Nevertheless most people refrain from such activities. There will be some cases here and there of racial and religious intolerance expressing itself in acts of hostility. Each instance must be regarded for what it is—no more and no less. But remember: *The central figure in each little drama is not the chance victim, but the lawbreaking ruffian.* Do not make it appear that his action is by, for, of, or with the consent of the general community. He represents himself only and alone should receive the opprobrium and the appropriate penalties.

Report every case of lawbreaking to the police. If it seems to involve prejudice, also report it to your community relations authorities. Let them decide, in co-operation with the police, what action should be taken and what publicity, if any, should be released to the public.

CHAPTER 5

Tricksters

Prior to the 1947 annual convention of the CIO two factions within the United Automobile Workers were maneuvering to obtain control of their union, the largest organization within the CIO. The contest pivoted around the re-election of Walter Reuther as president of the U.A.W. Some of Reuther's opponents attempted to arouse group hostility against him. A Detroit leftist labor journal published an alleged copy of a letter presumably from a well-known anti-Semitic rabble-rouser to his constituents. It read:

SPECIAL CONFIDENTIAL BULLETIN ✕247 (2-2-rks)
CONFIDENTIAL MEMO TO KEY WORKERS:

> *This is to warn all key workers in the Nationalist movement to avoid enthusiastic praise of Walter Reuther. He is doing such an excellent job from our viewpoint that any public statement complimentary to him by one of our known leaders might limit his essential usefulness.*
>
> *As much as I appreciate his value I am careful never to compliment Mr. Reuther in anything I write or speak.*

Destroy this letter immediately after reading its contents.
> *Signed*——(SIGNATURE)

A photostat of the spurious letter with a statement by a "handwriting expert" that the signature was authentic was published in a corner of one page, the remainder of which assailed Reuther in vile and intemperate language.

If ever a letter contained evidence of being a forgery, this one did. It would require amazing modesty, most unbefitting this rabble-rouser, to admit even to himself that he was anathema. For him to tell his followers that organized labor so disliked him and them that his praise and theirs would injure a labor leader's standing with labor was quite inconceivable. The letter was so patently a falsehood that it fooled few, if any. Indeed, it was a boomerang. The story was handled skillfully. It was not broadcast to the world, but through limited labor channels Reuther quietly exposed it for the miserable trick it was. There is now no possibility of its injuring the innocent.

Forgeries and falsehoods of this type are often invented to damage the reputations of admirable persons, and sometimes they accomplish their sinister purposes. The spurious items range from scribbled post cards to lengthy documents. Some of these monstrosities have deceived millions of people and have caused incalculable damage. A particularly vicious myth, reprinted in a score of languages, has unquestionably played a part in bringing about the massacre of innumerable members of one religious group. A mere mention of the name of that counterfeit document would be sufficient to remind all familiar with the facts about this cruel forgery that a total lie can be as powerful as Hitler said a lie can be. I refrain from mentioning the name of this fictitious "plot" because I believe that the only way to terminate the evil effects of scurrilities is to blot them out of the printed pages of today and tomorrow and eventually out of the memory of man. The sooner they pass into total oblivion, the better. There are books in English exposing the forgery to which I have reference. Anyone who hears of it can get full information through any capable librarian. But I would not be party to advertising it. The facts in such instances should be kept in archives, not in current circulation. Those who repeat such libels thereby commit libel. To say, "Did you hear that your neighbor's wife is immoral? Now let me tell you it is not so," is either stupid or sadistic. If someone raises the question and wants information about a certain falsehood or forgery, very well, give it if you have it. But to arouse curiosity about fraudulent documents which would otherwise be unknown is like sowing weed seed in the hope it will not grow.

You cannot beat a lie to the punch. Never seek to deny it in advance of its circulation. Nor should lies and forgeries ever be repeated in print to illustrate anything *unless they have no longer any potentiality for further harm.* If your purpose is to instill a healthy skepticism, confine your examples to instances which cannot do further harm. The case of Alfred Dreyfus, who, completely innocent, spent years as a prisoner on Devil's Island for treason while the actual culprit went unpunished, admirably illustrates how religious prejudice can pervert justice, blind a nation, and aid the guilty. The fact that Dreyfus was eventually vindicated, and that we have a clear and complete record of the case, makes this a desirable story to tell. It was, indeed, made into a magnificent motion picture. No harm can now befall Captain Dreyfus or even his memory by recounting this bit of history, which so clearly demonstrates the depravity of bigotry. But to use forgeries and canards about racial and religious groups, to prove how wrongful they are, is inadvisable. No matter how transparent they may seem to you, they may still lodge and take root in gullible minds already somewhat prejudiced.

One of the hoariest tricks of mischief-makers is the circulation of post cards or handbills presumably sent by some Victimian organization to its own members. The ignoramus's forged screed carries bigoted remarks or inflammatory instructions which any decent person would resent, and they are carefully contrived to arouse wrath against the racial or religious group allegedly issuing them. Usually the name of the organization supposed to have issued the instructions is a non-existent one, such as "The Assembly of Rabbis," "Society of New York Negroes," "The Knights of the Catholic Order," and so forth. The names of individuals are rarely used, but occasionally the forgers go so far as to subscribe the names of well-known persons of the alleged sending group. A hate organization circulated a fraudulent oath attributed to a certain Christian society in just this way.

There are two methods of diminishing the circulation of these contemptible screeds. Some are barred from the mails if the post-office officials detect them soon enough. *In localities where there are laws forbidding the distribution of anonymous hate literature* the police co-operate by confiscating the supply, if located. If discovered, the authors of these *anonymous* canards are liable to penalty. Quite often, however, a whole batch has been mailed and delivered, or is circulated by hand before the perpetration of the fraud becomes known to post-office officials or to the police. Ultimately the best protection from such chicanery is a good dose of the kind of informed skepticism that leads people to suspect malicious forgery. Items supposedly directed to members of some group but obviously calculated to arouse the hostility of others should instantly and always be suspected.

Paralleling the forged written word is the fabricated rumor. In a contest for public favor no skill is required to ascribe to the opposition things they never even dreamed of doing. When the rotten rumor factory starts working it is amazing what a stream of putrid ideas it can turn out. In a struggle between decent people and scoundrels, it is obvious who has the advantage of employing deceitful rumors. The sons and daughters of Ananias willingly and happily resort to treacherous methods which honorable people spurn.

In a city where Negro veterans had moved into a housing project the Community Chest was one of the agencies giving support to non-segregation. To intimidate the board of the Community Chest by hampering its campaign for funds, a "Citizens' Committee" launched the totally untrue rumor that the director of the Chest was receiving a salary of twenty-five thousand dollars a year. (For aught I know, he deserved even more, but the position actually paid nearer to one third of that sum and the impression of extravagance was totally deceptive.) It was also rumored that a Negro organization was paying the Negro veterans who had moved into the project to remain there.

What is the antidote to this demoralizing process? In this instance, *without making reference to the rumor*, the actual salary of the executive was publicized. Some hurtful rumors can thus be counteracted squarely by disseminating facts without giving any direct indication that they are in answer to the rumor. Some of these rumors can best be short-circuited by analogous rumors for which validity must first be established. If the public must have rumors, let them have some good ones to talk about. In a locality in which the only newspaper blatantly was anti-Negro I suggested that a committee consult other publishers about starting a competitive newspaper. Frankly, I saw no reason—since there was an acute situation—to wait until the advertising was actually withdrawn or another paper launched before getting the word around that these things were being discussed. That was a truth. It was something beneficial for the public to consider and the owner of the anti-

Negro newspaper amply deserved to stay awake nights. In some situations the best antidote to worrisome rumors is to give the opposition something to worry about.

In the face of trickery and malevolence, people struggling to further democratic conditions should not feel weak and trembly. Planning a vigorous counterattack to win favorable public opinion builds better morale than trying to deny each rumor. Another factor necessary for morale is faith in that part of the public which is still neutral. To cry, "They who are not with us are already against us!" is a blunder. However limited in numbers the active right-thinking element may be, they should never minimize their own potential strength. Where no practical means are available to determine which side of an issue is favored by latent and unexpressed sentiment, think, speak, and act on the hypothesis that "they who are with us are more than they who are against us."

You can inoculate yourself against frauds intended to arouse group hostility by cultivating a kindly attitude toward out-groups. Whenever a provocative rumor, an alleged news release, a mimeographed or printed sheet, or the like stirs animosity in you against a racial or religious group, be alert to the possibility that it stems from intentional deception. If the matter is of no consequence, reject and forget it on the ground that no one should be adjudged guilty unless *proved* guilty. If you feel that it is a matter of moment not to be lightly dismissed, seek the facts. If you are in a position to ascertain the truth or falsehood of the item, do so yourself. If you are not, get the opinion of someone whose competence and integrity you trust. Someone who is in a position to verify or disprove the allegation or who has access to those who can furnish a reliable verdict should be consulted.

Cultivating proper habits of response in one's own thinking is not too difficult, but to enlighten the public at large on this score presents far graver problems. The advice "Don't believe *everything* you hear" is not helpful if interpreted to mean "Don't believe *anything* you hear." Mere skepticism is not enough. Sound judgment requires a knowledge of how to obtain evidence and how to sift and evaluate it. An educative process that substitutes reasoning for credulity requires an army of educators devoted to the cause of truth.

CHAPTER 6

The Abusive

The finest thing I ever witnessed by way of rebuffing an intolerant person took place in a crowded railroad coach where a tired elderly Negro woman arrived at a seat at about the same moment as a young, prosperously dressed white man. She sat down and he, contesting her right to the seat, began to tell her in a loud voice what would happen to a Negro who dared to do that where he came from.

The woman was obviously shaken. Her lips trembled. She had blurted out a few defensive words when an attractive white woman, seated across the aisle, rose and said contemptuously, "Some people make me ashamed to belong to the white race. To think that a man in your comfortable circumstances, presumably educated, can stand here abusing a poor, tired woman! I am changing places with her, and I dare you to take either seat while we do it."

She took the arm of the older woman and gently helped her across the aisle. Her own manner was calm, dignified, magnificent. The feeling of the other passengers was against the arrogant fellow. One sensed that men were clenching their fists. Mine were certainly ready for action. There was no need, however, to prevent his interfering with that dramatic exchange of seats. He was glad to scurry away.

How could that poor Negro woman, browbeaten into terror by an imposing stranger, hounded by unhappy race memories, have shamed her assailant so completely as the white woman could and did? And how much more effective a gesture—that protecting hand upon the frightened woman's shoulder—was than a long argument could possibly have been.

What we need is more people anxious to help the members of other racial and religious groups in moments of tension—people who can utter a few firm words with a ring of confidence and self-assurance. If we had them there would be fewer incidents such as this one, related by Hortense Powdermaker in *Probing Our Prejudices* (Harper, 1944):

> *One Sunday night before Pearl Harbor, Mr. Soo Cheng, an economist and a graduate of one of our American universities, was driving with his family on a crowded thoroughfare in a big Eastern city. The traffic came to a sudden halt because of some jam farther up the line. The bumper of Mr. Cheng's car locked with the bumper in front of his. The man in the other car looked back and saw the Chinese family. "Hey, you yellow ——, what do you think you are doing?" A policeman came up and began shouting to Mr. Cheng to move on. He immediately assumed that it was all Mr. Cheng's fault (actually it was no one's fault and no great harm had been done), and in ugly manner he demanded Mr. Cheng's license and seemed disappointed when he could find nothing the matter with it. Finally the bumpers were unlocked, the white man in front let out an oath against those "yellow devils," and the policeman angrily told them to get moving. This was the way the Cheng family began their vacation.*

Among "the abusive" I do not include those who *in the course of conversation* introduce scurrilous remarks about racial or religious groups. These "waggle tongues" are discussed in another chapter. Bigoted, abusive speech occurs when wrath against an individual is extended to include his racial or religious group. The use of contemptuous epithets generally indicates that the abusive person's spleen is swelling with intolerance. One angry word may constitute his entire caustic performance. The abusive evoke more resentment in ten seconds than the waggle tongued are likely to elicit in an hour.

The average controversy with an abusive person is swift and emotion runs high. Whatever is done about such a situation, the lasting effect upon the abuser is very slight. There are times, however, when something should be said for the sake of spectators who witness an abusive incident. Speak in a calm, confident, firm manner when you answer a bigot, especially if you want the bystanders to sympathize with you and not with the brash spouters of intolerance. No one says that you must feel unruffled and unperturbed in such an incident. Inner tension may, and probably will, mount. But unless you can take a deep breath or two, gain self-control, and speak with self-possession, you will not do the needed job well.

Prestige is what counts in the tiff with the abusive bigot. Is he going to emerge with more of it or with less of it than his opponent? The bigot begins with an advantage. He is appealing to the bigotry of those on the side lines and he is also counting on the sense of shock and dismay the Victimian will feel. He probably has not figured it out that way, but instinctively he has become aware of the soft spot in the average Victimian where a swift verbal blow causes panic. The abusive fellow assumes that he can drive the Victimian, and those onlookers sympathetic to him, into a futile rage which will make it appear that the bully has superior status and greater prestige.

A frenzied or frantic reaction on the part of a bigot's opponent gives the upper hand to the bigot, indicating that he is right in assuming that Victimians feel themselves inferior and vulnerable. True, one would resent being called a "dirty" anything, but one would not be thrown off balance if called a "dirty Presbyterian." If one is a Victimian, however, the knife is turned in the wound when one's group is injected into an epithet. The response to abuse must be given by either Victimian or non-Victimian in a tone and manner that indicate the bigot's assumptions are too wrong and unworthy to cause consternation. A Jew who had been venomously called "dirty Jew" replied with a smile, "Thanks, old man. Glad you called me a Jew, because I can't think of anything I'd rather be. I'll forgive you the 'dirty.'" It was said with cheery conviction that left no verbal ax with which the other man could attack.

It is not absolutely necessary that any reply be made to an intolerant aspersion. There are occasions when a shrug of the shoulders is better than risking a prolonged altercation. But if vulgar blusterers were permitted to go about spewing bigoted remarks without any opposition, their success would encourage others. If intolerant abuse customarily met a wall of rebuke and resulted each time in the abuser's being trimmed by an apt retort, there would be less of it.

On the other hand, the abusers must not find it easy to destroy a Victimian's happiness and rouse him to impotent fury by taunts. Whether you are answering on your own behalf or intruding to protect another, remember that you should appear calm, firm, and confident in the presence of an abuser. Never be too hasty or over-wrought. You can generally get the best of the encounter by walking away when you have said something appropriate. If someone is to be left yammering and yapping after the other's back has been turned, let it be the bigot. You may not leave him speechless. He may rant on. But you can leave him exasperated and discomfited so that his prestige goes down while yours goes up. Onlookers will have less respect for him and more for his victim.

In some instances—and it is almost a matter of luck—intolerant abuse can be penalized far more severely by legal than by verbal castigation. Normally it is impractical and inexpedient to arrest a person for utterances. (If there is violence, an arrest of the *ruffian* should be made. "Abuse" here is limited to speech.) Abuse can, however, breach the peace or be disorderly conduct. That depends on the loudness of voice, the place, et cetera. What might not be disorderly conduct in a tavern may be disorderly conduct in a hospital. You may have no chance of issuing a useful complaint against an unidentified stranger, but you can report a bus driver's conduct to the company that employs him. People have been discharged from their jobs for abusive intolerance repeatedly inflicted on patrons, especially when their work was none too satisfactory anyhow. Others have been arrested and fined for unwarranted verbal abuse. It is generally better, however, not to employ such means unless the case is a very grievous one. You may convert a thoughtless disliker of Victimians into a confirmed hater.

Usually a display of abuse involves people who are strangers unlikely to meet again after the flurry. Sometimes, however, the parties are well known to each other. The most aggravating cases of friction are between persons who work in the same place or live in the same apartment house or neighborhood. Where prolonged antagonism results from abusive outbursts an intermediary may be needed to reconcile the disputants.

One day an Irish freight elevator operator in a factory building lowered the gate too soon and caught the foot of a truck driver, who thereupon let out a curse and used a derisive generic epithet. Insults involving one's racial origin cut deeper than a personal insult. But the elevator operator, realizing that the driver was frightened and upset, mumbled an apology while the latter limped off. Since he made deliveries several times a week in the building, the driver had occasion to see the elevator operator quite frequently and now and then made disparaging, intolerant remarks to others who used the elevator.

Wishing to end the hostility, the elevator operator for some time made unavailing attempts to placate the driver. After a month had passed, he spoke to a friendly truck driver. "Jerry, I don't like this feuding. No good in quarreling with fellows you work with all the time, but I can't get down on my hands and knees to Bill. He'll only kick me around all the worse. And fighting with him won't help either, though I could lick him with one hand. What do you suggest I do?"

"I'll talk to Bill," Jerry offered. "I'll sound him out and see how prejudiced he is against Irish Catholics. I won't mention you at all. When I find out how he really feels we'll talk it over some more."

Two days later Jerry reported to Ed, the elevator operator. "I talked to Bill and he's not so bad. Oh, he's got some queer ideas, but he's not hopeless. You know, I said I wasn't going to mention your name, but he brought it up and says you never apologized to him, that you even laughed when the accident happened."

"Laughed?" Ed exclaimed. "I did nothing of the kind. I told him ten times I was sorry."

"Well, he's been down on you, so I guess he didn't want to hear. I told him this wasn't doing him or you or anybody any good. Every religion says to be kind and decent to other people even if they've hurt you. Must be something in it. I felt like a preacher talking to him like that. But, anyhow, what I got out of him was a promise that if I could arrange it with you, we'd meet here Saturday noon and go out and have a bite together. O.K.?"

It was O.K. The three lunched together and friendly relations were fully restored.

Abusive explosions involving intolerance may end in intermittent warfare, an armed truce, or the re-establishment of good feeling. Which it will be depends upon the temperaments of the persons involved, their diplomatic skills, and their readiness to forgive and forget. A heart-to-heart talk often works wonders, but there is no single prescription for what to do in such instances any more than there is a single prescription that will cure every illness.

In some instances an abuser is of such prominence and influence that further action after the original incident has occurred is advisable. This is especially true in reference to public officials. The action to be taken devolves in some cases not upon the offended party but on a community organization. When supplementary action is to be taken, some very astute thinking should be done. A one- or two-man committee—the most competent available—should handle the matter. A few persons with considerable political experience and sagacity can furnish better advice than a thousand inexperienced, over-excitable, untrained minds.

A group of Victimians were discussing what to do about the recently elected president of the most important women's organization in their city of eighty thousand. She had lost her temper at two Victimian women in a sewing class conducted by the Red Cross and had shouted some disparaging remarks about Victimians. The woman in question (whom we shall call Miss Vixen) was a society woman with more ambition than discretion. No one who knew her well considered her broad-minded, but this was her first outburst of unquestionable intolerance.

In discussing the episode the following proposals were made:

"We should demand that the board of the women's club apologize for this. I move we send a committee requesting that they repudiate Miss Vixen's action and censure her."

"I am going to resign from the club and I'm going to urge other women to resign unless Miss Vixen resigns as president."

"Let's send a letter to the editor of each of our newspapers condemning Miss Vixen's action and also ask for editorials on the subject."

"We should request the chairman of the local Red Cross chapter to obtain an apology from Miss Vixen. He should appear in person at the next meeting of the sewing class and ask Miss Vixen to apologize or else expel her from the class."

Emotions mounted as the angered Victimians brooded about the insult to their group. Mr. W. had been sitting silent but attentive and made no move to speak until someone asked, "What would you suggest?"

"I suggest," he replied slowly, "that nothing whatever be done except to ask our Red Cross chairman to read at the next meeting of the sewing class a statement to the effect that the American Red Cross is supported by all racial and religious groups and that, as an

American institution, it desires good will and mutual understanding among the members of all groups."

This mild proposal evoked an outburst of disdain and contempt, but Mr. W. remained calm and unperturbed.

"You mean," he was asked, "that Miss Vixen's name is not to be mentioned, that she is to go unpunished? Don't you realize that you would merely be encouraging her and others to make similar attacks?"

"I mean exactly what I said—that no mention of Miss Vixen's name be made and that we do none of the things proposed here, except that a statement condemning intolerance be read before the women who witnessed Miss Vixen's outburst. This simple statement on the need for national unity should be published in the newspapers. Nothing more. That is ample."

During the next fifteen minutes Mr. W.'s proposal was ridiculed and denounced. Had a vote been taken during that quarter of an hour his suggestion would have been rejected by all but two or three and drastic steps would have been approved. Mr. W. listened silently to the heated debate. Finally he said, "Suppose we were to do the other things that have been proposed here. Let's consider *all* the consequences of each suggestion, not merely whether taking a slap at Miss Vixen would relieve our emotions, but *all* the consequences of each proposed move.

"What would happen if we were to demand that the board of the women's club, of which Miss Vixen happens to be president, apologize for her conduct or even ask her for an apology? The board would refuse to intervene. Certainly they are not going to issue any statement, least of all an apology. Miss Vixen was not acting as president, or as a member, of the women's club when she blurted out those words. She attends that class as a private individual, as do all the other women enrolled. The women's club has no connection with the fact that Miss Vixen laid her packages on several chairs and that when late-comers entered and moved her packages to clear the chairs Miss Vixen became angry. She spoke as a hot-headed individual, and her remarks in no way relate to her connection with the women's club. How, then, can that organization or its board take responsibility? Are they to become involved in whatever their president does in her private life? I am a member of fifteen boards. Do you think that I would accept responsibility for the un-official conduct of all those presidents? If you ask the board of the women's club to take action or pass judgment in this matter they will rightfully refuse to do so. They will not become involved. Miss Vixen will say it is none of their business and she will win out. So it will not be Miss Vixen who will be slapped. The slapped ones will be the persons who lodge a complaint with the women's club board, where such a complaint does not belong.

"Someone suggested that all women of our group resign from the club. Some have been members for more than ten years. They have been well received and well treated all this time. They have earned the good will of the other members. Is it fair to all those friendly women of other groups that the members of our group resign from their club? This is not Miss Vixen's club. Four hundred and fifty other women share it. Will resignations create more good will or will they arouse bitterness and resentment? What kind of people are we if one insult from one woman is more important to us than ten years of friendship on the part of all these other women? Miss Vixen will not be president forever, unless you are determined to hand the club over to her. Why shouldn't our women remain there and help to maintain it as the kind of organization it should be? In trying to smack Miss Vixen's cheek, why forget your own face?

"It has been suggested that this incident be aired in the press. As matters stand, at the very most less than 2 per cent of the people in town have heard that our group has been insulted by this woman. What can we gain by informing everyone that we have been subjected to such insult and abuse? Will it enhance our prestige, even if the editor or a letter writer says he objects to intolerance? Decent people already dislike such racial or religious insults. But what about the others? Are they suddenly going to be converted by a letter or an editorial or two?

"At present there is no hate organization in this city and no recognized leader among the haters. Put this story in the papers, where it will reach all kinds of people, and Miss Vixen will hear from prejudiced persons who will congratulate her and offer her their loyalty. She craves leadership, and this may suggest a following and even tempt her, once she has been put on the spot publicly, to go all out on a hate-mongering crusade. Haven't we enough trouble without that? I happen to know that Miss Vixen has called on the editor of our morning paper twice during the past week. She told him she was pushed around and thinks it's outrageous that such discourtesies as she suffered have been permitted without a protest from the Red Cross. You are welcoming publicity. What about her craving for it? We are convinced that there was no reason for her indignation. She had no right to insist on using chairs for her packages and keep the other women from sitting down on the only available chairs. But that's not the way she tells the story. While we go around telling the facts to our friends she moves in other circles and tells this story the way she wants it told. There were only thirty women present, and their eyes were on the instructor before Miss Vixen began to shout. She is ready to fight and build a following of bigots or to drop the whole thing. Which do you want her to do? What have you to gain by precipitating such a controversy?

"Even if the chairman of the Red Cross demands an apology, Miss Vixen will certainly refuse it. What, then? No one can force her to apologize. So there will be an odious scene most unfair to the very kind, decent, friendly gentleman, Mr. R., who happens to head the local chapter. Then what? Suppose she is barred from the sewing class. What a public furore that will arouse! Now she and her friends—she must have some to be elected president of an organization of more than four hundred and fifty women—will misconstrue that. Can't you hear them declaring, 'See! The Victimians control the Red Cross and everything in town!' "

Mr. W.'s analysis was too penetrating and convincing to be contradicted. It was agreed to discard the suggestions he had demolished.

"Let us," he continued, "examine my proposal and *all* of its effects. If the chairman at the next session of the sewing class reads a statement urging friendly group relations and it is published in the papers, the 98 per cent of the readers, who know nothing about this incident, will regard the statement as an ordinary message in favor of harmony and good will. But everyone who attends the sewing class or who has heard of the episode will know that this was a rebuke to Miss Vixen for her intolerant outburst. The timing of the statement and the fact that it is read at the sewing class will make its purpose perfectly clear. And what will Miss Vixen do? What can she do? Can she object to this statement, which does not mention her, and declare that bigotry is desirable? Of course not. She will have to accept the implied reprimand as best she can. Surely it is better to administer a dignified rebuke to an ill-tempered woman and to convey a positive, constructive message to the community than to create an impression that our standing in public esteem is so weak that every unsavory word disturbs us profoundly. Can we really afford to treat such an incident as if it were a terrible blow?"

Everyone present, with one stubborn exception, recognized the logic and validity of this proposal when they had thought the matter through and weighed it properly. The one objector was a fiery individual who insisted that they ought "to make an example" of Miss Vixen. There will always be some so devoid of good sense that they cannot make correct appraisals or wise decisions on anything that involves them emotionally. In this case the resultant procedure, as suggested by Mr. W., proved thoroughly beneficial. The chairman and members of the sewing circle, as well as the other members of the women's club, were extremely grateful that the matter was sensibly handled instead of being "blown up" into a fracas that would unjustifiably besmirch the club. Miss Vixen suffered great loss of prestige without any opportunity to appear as a heroine or martyr. She did not long retain the presidency of the club.

A set of specific rules on "how to counteract intolerant abuse" is no more practical than a guide on "what to do when you are insulted." The circumstances vary infinitely. Resignation from a club may be the only proper and self-respecting thing to do in one case and the most foolish and self-defeating thing to do in another. And so it is with many other moves—good in some instances and bad in others. Sound personal judgment is the final determinant. As a university president said to an incoming freshman class, "We shall teach you a great deal here which will be valuable throughout your lives. But regardless of what you learn from us, you will not get along well in this world without common sense. That only God can furnish you."

The best single piece of advice in respect to abusive incidents which you have time to think about is *Think of all the counter-measures you can.* Weigh and compare all of the likely consequences of each possibility. Never accept any proposal because it relieves emotions. It is far more important to relieve the situation.

CHAPTER 7

Waggle Tongues

A person who protests *every* intolerant word may be a hot-head, a prig, or a crackpot. In some circumstances it is not a mark of cowardice, but of culture, to let an objectionable remark pass without remonstrance. When Ecclesiastes spoke of "a time to keep silence and a time to speak," he may well have been thinking of the wisdom of choosing the proper time and manner to answer the waggle tongue's tommyrot. But the advice offered by the sophisticated preacher of the Bible would have been more illuminating had he explained *when* to be *silent* and when to speak.

Mrs. Tenney, a brilliant young woman active in community relations work, had remained silent at a dinner party when a woman whom she and her husband were meeting for the first time spoke of members of another race as mentally inferior to white people. It was an incidental remark. The conversation quickly drifted to something else.

Driving home, Mr. Tenney said to his wife, "I was watching you when Mrs. Hammond put in that nasty crack about colored people. Why didn't you speak up?"

"And spoil the chance of ever changing her mind?" asked Mrs. Tenney. "Had I spoken up, Mrs. Hammond would have defended her opinion. If I had won the argument, it would have been to my satisfaction but not to hers. She would have disliked me for embarrassing her among her new acquaintances. She looks like a sincere, capable person. I think we can change her views on several things.

When she made that quip about racial inferiority, I put it down in my little mental notebook. And what do you think I did while we were getting our wraps?"

Mr. Tenney smiled. "Knowing you as I do, I'd say you made a date with Mrs. Hammond."

"Right! When we know each other better, I'll introduce Mrs. Hammond to Dr. Sanford and to Mrs. Taylor, who are as intelligent as any white person she ever met. One of these days Mrs. Hammond will be working for our Interracial Commission. That's not a promise, John, but I'll try hard."

In less than two months Mrs. Hammond had abandoned the notion of racial inferiority without having been forced to recant, apologize, or even to recall the invidious remark. Her mentor, Mrs. Tenney, is one of the few—there are altogether too few—who is concerned enough about racial and religious prejudice and astute enough to undertake the *re-education* of mildly prejudiced individuals. One worker who takes the necessary pains to bring one other person into an intergroup organization is worth a hundred disputants who do nothing more for the cause than administer rebukes or who indulge in heated arguments if, when, and as anything displeasing is said in their presence. Get someone to contribute a dollar or a deed on behalf of those whom he has disparaged and you will have accomplished infinitely more than anything that could be achieved in a spat with him.

When we speak of a waggle tongue here we do not mean a hardened bigot. The person we are talking about is somewhat prejudiced, to be sure. He may be—and probably is—a bit malicious. But often he has no more real animosity than Mrs. Smith, who gossips freely about a neighbor to whose assistance she would rush with food or clothing if that neighbor were in need. The waggle tongue may add and embellish, but in the main he merely repeats (or thinks he repeats) what he has heard from others. We have already dealt with some phases of the problem he presents in "Beware of Quicksands." Our present question is what to say to him in person.

The suggestion made in some recent novels and films that racial and religious prejudices can be banished by challenging *every* prejudiced remark emanates from wishful thinking and not from scientific comprehension. This idea of "hit them *every* time" reveals the same old juvenile misconceptions about the nature of prejudice that makes some people who do nothing but snarl at the prejudiced think they are doing a whale of a good job. They haven't. One might as well say that what is needed in order to inculcate courtesy is to have more people denounce discourtesy more vehemently whenever it occurs. If you are emphatic enough about expressing your resentment, you may well succeed in keeping people from making certain types of remarks in *your* presence. But that isn't enough. That alone will not prevent their continuing to think as they have in the past, nor will it stop them voicing intolerance when you are not around. People who have acquired any social polish avoid slurring a group when a member of that group is present. Yet the same people will feel free to make derogatory remarks when no member of that group is on hand. If a minister assumes that none of the people whom he knows tells smutty stories simply because no one tells risqué jokes in his presence, he is the more deceived.

Mrs. Tenney has developed a method for handling the waggle tongue. She does not wait for him to inject a bigoted remark or a derisive joke before introducing the subject of racial friendship. She would rather not approach the subject with that handicap. Her preference was expressed thus:

"I like to tell people about the splendid things Negroes are doing for all of us, of their contribution to art, to music, to industry. I first get the ball rolling in the right direction and then build up the case for equal opportunity and for co-operation between whites and Negroes. Why should I run smack into someone's prejudices and wave my little flags in front of his blind spot when I can get to the better side of that person and have his own decency and fair-mindedness working on my side? I have had many a person agreeing with me and helping me convince others who would have battled me forever if the first time we discussed group relationships was right on the heels of an unfortunate remark that person had made."

Don't be persuaded that you must invariably call the intolerant to task for an objectionable remark then and there. Raising objections to a prejudiced assertion that involves no implications for action is not the enormously important matter it is generally believed to be. If someone says, "Let's not buy from that Victimian," or "Let's break his windows," or anything involving action, speaking up at once obviously becomes mandatory. But it is not denunciations hard on the heels of prejudiced statements which have created whatever good will, mutual understanding, and fair play now exist between members of various racial and religious groups. The countertirades, acrimonious exchanges, and swift rebukes—the scoldings and rantings of those who cannot brook an unkind word—are decidedly minor contributions to the bettering of human relations. Their effect is often bad. *There is a time to be silent as well as to speak.* No one can deal properly with waggle tongues until he understands that simple fact.

Whenever intolerance is indicated in a company of people by something that has been said, you have to choose quickly between three alternatives:

1. *Let it pass without a rejoinder.*
2. *Make brief comment and then dismiss the topic, or*
3. *Discuss the mistaken opinions at length.*

The time, the place, the occasion, the personality of the offender, and the seriousness of the allegation should be considered in deciding what to do. Disparaging things are sometimes said when it is inexpedient to enter an objection. If, for example, something defamatory is said at a meeting where those present are dealing with important matters and would resent loss of time in an extraneous argument, it is unwise to precipitate a debate with a bigot. Speak to him after the meeting. Do not feel that honor or virtue requires that you nullify every intolerant word you hear by an immediate counterblast, or that the ill effects of prejudiced remarks *can* be expunged by calling further attention to them. All too often the opposite occurs and a statement that would have left no impression becomes deeply ingrained in the memory of all present by an ineffectual rebuttal. The permanent effect of each intolerant word or phrase or paragraph upon the basic attitude of those who hear it is trifling. Even an impassioned denunciation against a group will not turn fair-minded people into bigots or go very far toward increasing the prejudices of those already prejudiced. Its chief importance is that it reveals the attitude of the speaker. Often it is best to rebuke him privately. Do not overlook that possibility.

An Ohio manufacturer who was representing his trade group at a conference in Washington, D.C., in connection with the war effort, permitted an unsavory jest by the chairman to go unchallenged even though its implications were highly insulting to the Ohio man and his co-religionists. The joke drew laughter from most of the twenty men from various parts of the country who had come together to form a unit for co-operation with the government.

When the session adjourned for a few hours, the offended man approached the chairman.

"I think you ought to know," he said, "that I didn't like that joke you told, although perhaps it's because I'm a member of the group whose reputation it injures."

"Don't be too sensitive," said the other. "Jokes don't mean anything. You shouldn't take a thing like that seriously."

The two men lunched together. The Ohio man again referred to the hurtful jest. "It made me uncomfortable," he said, "and I hope you won't spring anything like that again. Not while I'm around, anyhow."

"Of course I won't," said the other. "Now that you've made me think about it, I'm not a bit proud of having told it. But I certainly do appreciate your taking it up with me this way instead of doing it in front of those fellows whose respect I have to have if we are to do this job."

In combating prejudice, to win an argument is a penny's gain; to win an ally is to acquire a fortune.

Sometimes a few apt words can accomplish a great deal more than an argument. Irony, sarcasm, or humor are far more likely to accomplish your purpose than a lengthy, serious response.

At a board meeting of a Florida bank one of the members observed that people of a certain religious group are less likely to meet their obligations fully than others.

"I move," said another member of the board solemnly, "that hereafter no member of that group be granted a loan by this bank."

The others looked in astonishment at the proposer of the motion. He was the most highly respected man in town, and a member of the disparaged group.

Then they all broke into laughter, except one man whose face turned a fiery red.

"I'm terribly sorry, Mr. A.," he said. "That was a stupid thing I said. I apologize to everyone here."

No burst of indignation or lengthy dissertation could have revealed to the members of that board the folly of prejudging applicants of loans on the basis of race or religion so convincingly as the suggestion by a man of impeccable character that all members of his own group be barred from loans.

However, the quick-witted retort that exposes the folly of intolerance, like the soft answer that turneth away wrath, does not always suffice. It is sometimes advisable to do a lengthier job of enlightenment on the chronically malicious waggle tongue. If it *is* necessary to challenge an intolerant statement, the attack should be against the basic assumptions underlying the bigoted remark.

It is deceptively easy to pander to bigotry without realizing it. Compare these two ways of handling a situation. One is the usual response of a person confronted by prejudice. The other is a technique of handling the waggle tongue that should become far more frequent.

Jones (to Smith): Have you noticed that the Victimians are taking over all the restaurants in our town? Soon they'll have a monopoly. I don't like it.

Smith: Monopoly? There are five or six Victimian restaurants, but how about the one at the hotel and the one at Fourth and Herald streets? I can name you seven or eight others not owned by Victimians.

Jones: Yes, but there are more Victimian restaurants now than there were twenty years ago. The way they're gaining, we won't have any restaurants not owned by Victimians.

Smith (good, patient, honest, decent, tolerant, and well-meaning Mr. Smith): Now be reasonable, Jones. The Victimians have only a third of the restaurants and, come to think of it, I remember four more the Victimians don't own——

At this point Brown enters and the conversation develops in a new direction.

Smith (to Brown): Billy here has been complaining that the Victimians are taking over too many restaurants in our town.

Brown (with a grim glance toward Jones): And what did you tell him?

Smith: I showed him how many restaurants are not owned by Victimians.

Brown: Why did you do that?

Smith: He's entitled to know. After all, the facts are against him. Why not put him straight?

Brown (turning to Jones): Well, the truth is that the Victimians in this town *don't own a single restaurant.* In all of America the Victimians own *no* restaurants. The Victimians, taken collectively, mean all of them, and there isn't one restaurant, kitchen, barn, or chicken coop in America owned by "the Victimians." Some Victimians have acquired restaurants; a few may own a string of them. The truth is you don't like their achieving any sort of success.

Jones: Haven't I got a right to repeat what's being said and to find out whether it's true?

Brown: You have as much right to repeat this on the grounds of searching for the facts as I have to say that you and your wife drink and then ask everyone I meet whether it's true. You do take an occasional drink.

Jones (angrily): You wouldn't do that. No one is saying that my wife and I drink.

Brown: Not yet they aren't, but by the time the story's gone around they'll have you pictured as too drunk to stay in business. How did this other thing get started about the Victimians? Someone started it. And then, since most people know nothing about the nature of intolerance, even good-hearted people pick it up and pass it along innocently. I can get everyone in town talking about whether or not you and your wife are heavy drinkers, especially if I get a hall to address audiences and put out a magazine, like hate mongers do.

Jones: O.K. I'll admit that the fact that a rumor gets around doesn't prove it's true. But I don't want Victimians to run all the restaurants.

Brown: What's to keep you or anyone else from opening one? Every Victimian is subject to the same laws that you and I are. But what you evidently want is free enterprise for yourself and your kind and something very different for those you don't consider your kind.

What *is* it you want, Billy? You cannot by law forbid Victimians to acquire property by transactions that are legal for other people. How do you propose to divest Victimians of what they properly own? What do you intend to do when you have gotten everybody to hate Victimians by this miserable trick of adding up two and three and making eleven out of it? Before you go further with this kind of talk, I want to know right now where we are all going to end up because of it. Let's not have confiscation and looting creep up here in America. If plundering and pillaging are to become acceptable notions in the United States, let's know it. Let's face the issue before the public's sense of morality and justice has been wrecked. Before you go on creating ill will by this prejudiced balderdash, offer your solution *now*. If the only thing you can possibly accomplish by this sort of talk is to create hatred, dissension, and chaos, stop right now!

Brown is right. He is concerned *now* about the *results* inherent in bigotry. Intolerant talk is never innocuous in its consequences, however innocent the credulous are who spread it. If Jones had not believed that there is something wrong in the success of anyone except those of his own kind, he would not have become worried because men of other racial, national, or religious backgrounds own restaurants. He does not recognize his prejudice or stop to visualize the kind of country he would have to live in if its basic idea resembled that of the Fascists: "Only our kind have a right to life, liberty, and the pursuit of happiness."

A certain amount of loose talk about racial and religious groups will continue despite all efforts to put a complete stop to it. Anyone attempting to mop it all up would be wasting a great deal of time that could be spent to much better advantage. Each of us should acquire a balanced, judicious perspective so that he can readily recognize how serious and how injurious any particular statement or rumor or snide joke is. The best contribution we can make to ending intolerant talk is to be careful in our own conversation about the reputation of groups other than our own as we would be where esteem for our own group is involved.

If each of us talks about racial and religious groups with good will and respect, we shall build a pattern of thought that will seep gradually but increasingly into the minds of waggle tongues.

CHAPTER 8

The Frustrated

All of us at times have been victims of someone's fury when the wrathful person was the one most responsible for his plight. A schoolmate of mine who had the day before been engaged as a clerk in the college library told me that he had been on the job about an hour when the librarian summoned him to a remote part of the stacks where some books were disarranged.

"Is this the way you do your work?" demanded the irate librarian.

The student was nonplused. "I came to work here only an hour ago," he stammered, "and I've been kept busy the whole time in the reading room."

"All right," said the testy librarian. "I'll forgive you this time, but don't let it happen again."

You can surely recall instances when you felt a bit guilty about something that had occurred and were eager to blame the occurrence on someone else. I recall once stumbling in the dark over a suitcase and wondering angrily "Who left this here?" The realization that I had placed it there myself was keenly disappointing.

A businesswoman seeking escape from her unhappy home life became a habitual drinker. Eventually days went by when she was too intoxicated to perform her duties as a merchandise buyer. Having lost her job, she sank into despondency.

Skillful treatment has cured her of alcoholism. Since her return to work she has been no less successful than she was in her pre-alcoholic career. Conditions at home remain unchanged, but she has found a new outlet for her frustrations. She now shuns the bottle, but when she wants to forget her quarreling parents and maladjusted children she rails against Victimians, against whom she previously had displayed no animosity. During the tirades she relieves her injured ego much as she formerly did by intoxication. Both forms of escape have served to let her forget for brief spells the muddle and bickering of her family. Not that she would admit the connection. Clinical observers, however, have no doubt of it.

Psychologists say that this woman's group hatred results from *projection.* When a great number of people heap their rage upon an innocent group it is because they have individually and collectively projected their misdirected wrath to a scapegoat. Many primitive peoples, seeking atonement for their sins, would take a kid from the fold, heap imprecations upon it, and, thinking their sins were now upon its head, dash the terrified animal over a cliff. No doubt this provided some emotional release for the superstitious mob that plucked the fleece of the animal and howled curses. Nobody today advocates badgering and tormenting a goat and hurling it to destruction as a means of securing salvation. Yet only yesterday millions of people were murdered and millions are today being wronged senselessly by a transference of blame just as primitive and brutal.

How much all of us are in peril of being penalized for frustrations that are not of our making and how inclined we all are to inflict our own frustrations upon the innocent is indicated by this statement of Dr. Lawrence S. Kubie, chairman of the Public Education Committee of the New York Psychoanalytic Institute. "Transference," he says, "is a universal phenomenon. It plays some role in every human relationship. . . . It is one of several forces which distort human relationships by giving rise to inappropriate feelings, making people hate those against whom they have no grievance, love those for whom they have no valid basis for affection, and fear those who are no threat to them." (*The American Scholar,* winter 1947–48.)

In moments of frustration it is well for all of us to remember a dream described by Olive Schreiner wherein she visited hell. There she saw people running around with spades digging pits.

"Why are they doing this?" she asked.

"Because they think they will rise when their neighbors fall into the pits."

"How will they rise?" she asked.

And the answer of her guide was, "They will not rise."

All of us suffer frustrations and in scores of obscure ways all of us react to frustration. We are fortunate when these reactions assume the form of minor foibles or are channeled into productive activities. But when the frustrations are such that they inhibit acceptable social behavior and burst out in dangerous and destructive actions, both the individual and society suffer. We have learned a great deal about the care and treatment of individuals who, under the stress of conflicts, become a physical danger to themselves or others. We know much less about handling those who, under similar stresses, attack the principles of society by converting their frustrations into intolerance, prejudice, and eventually violence.

There are some Olympian political and economic thinkers who say that the only way to diminish intolerance is to remove every source of frustration and misery. That, no doubt, would be an ideal solution. No one will deny the desirability of eliminating unemployment, poverty, and all other kinds of hardship. The elimination of these evils is an excellent goal—admirable even if it had no effect at all upon intolerance. But even the most utopian of these dreamers has yet to tell us how all frustrations can be prevented. Can every man be assured marriage with the woman he prefers? Can every soprano sing the prima donna's role? Can every runner be acclaimed winner in the race? Can all forms of competition be destroyed so that none will lose or grieve in defeat? No social reformer can assure us that his system or any other will remove the roots of all frustration. And if he could, we could not wait for the dawn of his millennium to end the prejudice of today.

There *are* methods of diminishing racial and religious intolerance other than the total elimination of all social causes of frustration. Just as a boys' club can lessen the extent of juvenile delinquency in an underprivileged district, certain specific measures can abate prejudices. True, poverty is the primal cause of juvenile delinquency. The boys' club does not put a stop to poverty. But how shall we ever have the kind of people who will create a society free of poverty if we go on breeding criminals by neglecting youngsters who, through boys' clubs, can become capable, intelligent, socially minded men? What blather it is—no matter in what pretty salons it sounds high-brow—to talk glibly about eliminating prejudice by herculean measures while refusing to help make a somewhat better environment out of the present one. Who is going to change the present swamp into a fertile field if we do not do some reclamation work right now? The sincere worker soon recognizes that we have no choice but to use every means at our command to lessen the extent of intolerance even though we are incapable of removing forthwith all the economic and other sources of frustration.

A New Jersey man of considerable influence in his city was unhappy about the disadvantages suffered by the Negro part of the community. He discussed it with his friends, some of whom explained that the Negroes' situation was owing to deep-seated economic conditions and that the only way to really help them was to revolutionize the social system. They made no practical suggestions; they merely talked glibly and did nothing. A thousand years of that kind of theorizing in conversation or in books is as unavailing as it is sometimes insincere.

But this man was determined to do something. He called together leaders of the Negro community and talked with them. He invited several of the white members of the Community Chest board and heads of organizations, which could do something constructive, to talk matters over with the Negroes.

"What are your needs?" was the simple question that opened floodgates.

"No place for our sick to convalesce. When they leave the hospitals after severe illness they return to unsanitary rooms where they get worse rather than better. No place for our old folks. No place for our children to play. Not a place in town where a Negro can swim. No decent facilities for social services—and poverty that makes it impossible for us to provide them ourselves."

The list of frustrations was long. If only from a financial standpoint, steps toward the elimination of all of them could not possibly be undertaken immediately.

"Give us a list of priorities," said the white men. "Tell us what you need first. We'll fight for it at City Hall, in the Community Chest, at the banks, in the Chamber of Commerce. We can't get all the things you need and deserve right now, but we can stop the continued neglect of the Negroes in this city; we can get constant improvements for you."

That spirit has already taken hold in some cities. But remember this: Never work *for* Negroes or *for* any other racial or religious group. Work *with* them. Lady Bountiful is a nuisance in intergroup relations. You cannot aid people unless you get close enough to them to understand them and unless you plan matters so that they, too, can help, and help not only themselves but the entire community. Any move in the field of intergroup relations which perpetuates chasms of inequality creates new frustrations. People are not frustrated by the lack of bread alone. The lack of decent respect—or the lack of opportunity to *win* respect—is in itself a source of frustration. We can certainly eliminate some of the frustrations caused by intolerance by the simple expedient of working along with the disadvantaged to remove the handicaps. That is one side of the picture—and the most important one.

But how shall we treat the frustrated who are here today and who *will* be here until we are able to eliminate the roots of their frustrations? I wish I could offer a prescription for curing those who because of their frustrations turn against racial or religious groups. I wish that it were possible to aid the intolerant to overcome their own prejudices by some simple therapy. But this is an instance where diagnosis is comparatively easy while methods of cure are yet to be explored. When you encounter a soured, cantankerous creature spitting gall against a racial or religious group you may be quite sure that failure to resolve personal problems has much to do with his or her group antagonisms. Research has already proved that rigid minds—those at odds with all who do not conform to their own tastes—rank high on the list of haters. But social science has not as yet collected sufficient data to prescribe reliable techniques. In treating the frustrated who explode in the wrong places we are still in the trial-and-error stage.

Mrs. M., a widow, had endured several disastrous misfortunes. At forty-five she was teaching school. Childless, she lacked a goal in life. She taught only because it provided a salary, enough to maintain a rather bleak existence. The school in which she taught was in a Victimian neighborhood. Annually she asked to be transferred to a more desirable school; annually her requests were refused. She developed an antipathy toward her undernourished and sometimes ill-behaved children. The prejudice did not reveal itself sufficiently in the classroom to arouse censure, but it added slowly to her bitterness.

A program of intercultural education was launched in Mrs. M.'s school. She attended several lectures by a very attractive and well-informed lecturer, a woman whose own broad-minded attitudes were contagious. Mrs. M. was not too embittered to realize that she would be far happier if she accepted the proffered program. She began to apply it to her classroom. Having done an about-face, she found the needed release for her emotions and drew profound satisfaction in working to improve the lot of her Victimian pupils in and out of the classroom.

In instances such as this there may be the key to valuable possibilities. One *can* compensate for frustration by promoting friendships to far greater advantage than by cultivating hatred. The tolerant know that full well. The greatest service we can do for the intolerant is to convince *them* that it is so.

Whenever we encounter intolerance in individuals it is well to discover the extent to which frustration and transference are at the root of it. If group hatred has become a compensating mechanism, we can accomplish much less in a short space of time than when the animosity is not linked to the person's self-esteem. If, for example, an employee thoughtlessly indulges in scurrilities against a racial or religious group, a few heart-to-heart talks may change his attitude and correct his conduct. If, however, his vituperation emanates from a craving to show his own superiority (as a relief from a sense of inferiority) by convincing himself that he is better than all members of some group, the employer may be able to compel him to refrain from abusive talk on the employer's premises. But he will not be able to alter the employee's basic attitude. There are many instances in which the frustrated can be restrained from expressing their frustrations in blunt words and deeds. To change their mental processes is a very difficult task requiring painstaking therapy.

Intolerant outbursts are usually mistaken and mischievous outlets for inner tensions. Unable to find personal fault in a successful competitor one can resort to an insulting group epithet. Habitual intolerance ranks with alcoholism, sexual promiscuity, crime, and other types of anti-social conduct which make those who resort to such misconduct all the more maladjusted. But the false sense of satisfaction which the perverted ego derives from spewing hatred does furnish an illusory, temporary relief. Deep-rooted intolerance cannot be shed as simply as one removes clothing. Where it plays an important role in the individual's psychic structure, intolerance cannot be exorcised without substituting other compensations. Here we have a problem as perplexing and perhaps more difficult in itself than the gravest economic problems. To say that we can secure tranquil human relations and universal friendship by merely improving environment is to overlook the imperative need for moral insights, religious values, and personal adjustments.

What can you do about the individual frustrated bigot when you encounter him? In the first place, you can understand that he is the victim of his own frustrations. That in itself will spare you needless annoyance by transmuting your resentment to pity. If he is a stranger or a casual acquaintance, the chances are that you can do little beyond that to *help* him. The person who because of his frustrations has become a violent bigot needs the services of a skilled pastor or psychiatrist. It may, however, be necessary to *stop* him *at the moment.* You have no alternative then but to treat him as you would another bigot—as an abusive person, a waggle tongue, or some other type, depending upon the circumstances.

On the other hand, if you have frequent or prolonged contact with a person whose intolerance rises from frustration, you may be able to correct his attitudes. It is not an easy or a quick process. It depends greatly upon your capacity to judge the causes of his difficulties, your insight into his character, your ability to handle a delicate problem tactfully. You will certainly *not* adjust his point of view by sitting down for a heart-to-heart talk beginning, "Look, Joe. The trouble with you is you're frustrated and the reason . . ." You *may* be successful if you are able to approach the problem indirectly, to point up the fact that insecurity leads to aggression of many types, and that often the aggression is directed against wholly innocent people. You cannot, of course, profitably personalize the matter, but instead must depend upon the bigot's ability to draw the proper conclusions himself. The technique *sometimes* works. It cannot be harmful and, if it succeeds only occasionally, it is still worth trying.

CHAPTER 9

Self-Haters and Self-Doubters

I was in England in November 1946, not long after the bombing of the King David Hotel in Jerusalem had taken British lives. Members of the Stern Gang in the Holy Land had put to death several British soldiers. These attacks angered the British, but the average Briton, true to his sense of fair play, did not blame his Jewish neighbors for the guerrilla warfare of the Sternists. Yet in senseless reprisal for events in Palestine a few Englishmen did damage several synagogues in England.

I shall never forget a remark made by a British Jew who should certainly have had better sense than his statement indicated. Speaking of arson perpetrated against a local synagogue he said, "Well, we asked for it."

What dreadful misunderstanding of responsibility there is in that assumption! Practically all of the three hundred thousand Jews living in the British Isles abhorred the killing of British soldiers in Palestine. The occurrences were entirely contrary to the wish of this very man and of the other Jews of his city, yet he assumed that the British Jews were responsible for the outrages, that they "had asked for it." This foolish belief by Victimians themselves that they are responsible for acts of other members of their groups, acts which are loathsome to themselves, is an invitation to the unreasonable members of other groups to blame all Victimians and hold all accountable for misdeeds in which they have in no way participated. How can they expect others to recognize the limits of liability if they themselves are so illogical? If people cannot themselves recognize when they are not at fault, how shall others do so?

In the light of what I have already said about the right of a man to be proud when his brother does something praiseworthy and yet not be penalized for a brother's wrongdoing to which he has in no way contributed, it is to be expected that people can give a dinner in honor of a coreligionist and yet not be shamed and humiliated—and certainly not be maltreated—if some of their coreligionists act badly. It is unfortunate that many Victimians do not understand that intolerance is invariably unjustified, since it always hurts innocent folk. To be intolerant toward the members of one's own racial or religious group is as bad as any other form of intolerance.

Joe R. had developed an oversensitivity about his own group's reputation. Whenever he came across a newspaper report or heard comment that indicated turpitude on the part of a member of that group he became wretched. His conversation was punctuated with unhappy references to instances of wrongs committed by a co-Victimian. One of his associates in business, Baxter, a non-Victimian, accepted Joe's view of the matter and agreed that "your people ought to do something about this misconduct."

Joe and Baxter were talking to Bert, a co-Victimian, one day and he became irked by their attitude. "Don't worry," he said, "about that Victimian you read about in this morning's paper—I mean the one who was guilty of rent gouging. Don't worry about him. I shot him."

"You shot him?" Joe exclaimed in horror.

"Well, no. I only beat him up."

"Now you're kidding," said Baxter. "Why should you beat him up? You don't even know the fellow."

"You're right. I didn't beat him up. I just went to his safe, took out some money and gave it to the tenants he fleeced."

"You couldn't do that," chorused the others.

"Why not?"

"It's against the law."

"Well, I had to do something. You fellows are always saying that people ought to do 'something' about any of us who misbehave. What *could* I do? What do you *expect* me to do? Of course I didn't do anything. But what is the 'something' you think we Victimians ought to do?"

It is thoughtlessness that leads people to remark that members of a racial or religious group ought to do "something" about wayward members of their group. They never say what that "something" is. They do not realize how unreasonable they are being. They are unwittingly intolerant, for they are saying in effect that even the most decent, moral, law-abiding, and admirable members of the group deserve blame for things they have not done and which they are powerless to prevent. They thus assume a right to be prejudiced against the innocent on the ground that they demand of them not only innocence but omnipotence. As members of that very group they are as responsible as any other members of it, if such responsibility exists. If "something" ought to be done, why don't *they* do it instead of saying that others should?

The truth is that a social or religious group should, and as a rule does, maintain religious and educational organizations for inculcating ethical standards. They provide guidance for their youth and take whatever steps they can to instill virtues. Some go beyond these normal requirements by promoting better trade practices among businessmen, codes of conduct for hotel guests and the like. But there is no conceivable way in which to prevent renegades from violating the group's standards.

Racial and religious groups cannot take the law into their own hands without violating laws in the process. Social pressures have no effect on recalcitrants. Beyond educational measures and the social processes already employed, racial and religious groups have no more power or influence upon the conduct of their members than have those who are not members of the group. Often, in fact, the disapproval of others has greater influence upon members of a group than has the disfavor of coreligionists or members of the same ethnic or racial group. A great deal of injurious self-hatred would be eliminated by realization of the fact that no one should assume responsibility or be asked to assume responsibility in matters beyond his control.

On several occasions when a crime has been committed I have been asked by troubled persons whether the guilty one was a Victimian. My reply has been, "I don't know and I don't care to know. It is irrelevant and immaterial to which group he happens to belong. If he is not of your group, he belongs to another. Why should that group be disparaged by introducing an intolerant generalization?"

It is bad when members of any racial or religious group are in-

fluenced by canards against members of other groups. They, however, do at least derive a sense of spurious superiority. Those who
believe defamatory allegations injurious to the reputation of their
own groups haven't even that illusory satisfaction. When they
generalize adversely concerning their own group they develop an
inferiority complex, which they may seek to compensate by believing
that they personally are superior to the other members of their
group. They end up in self-hatred, for they cannot completely
divorce themselves from the feeling of guilt that they attach to the
group as a whole.

In a thrilling article, "Why I Remain a Negro" (which appeared
originally in the October 11, 1947, issue of the *Saturday Review of
Literature* and was republished in condensed form in the January
1948 issue of *Reader's Digest*) Walter White, referring to many of
the 12,000 white-skinned Negroes who annually "pass" into the
white fold, said, "Some of the most vehement public haters of
Negroes are themselves secretly Negroes." Many a self-hater, who
has gone the whole way and disengaged his identity from that of
the group into which he was born, practices a fanatical intolerance
to convince himself and others that he is not a member of the
abused group.

If a man cannot speak up kindly and appreciatively of his own
group, something is rotten in him. When you find yourself engaged
in conversation with a person who berates his own group, suggest
as seriously as you can that he ask some social scientists to study
his case thoroughly in order to determine how such a splendid person
as he came from such terrible stock.

A Victimian, who has inherited a large fortune from ancestors
who were eighteenth-century pioneers, was complaining to a friend
about the fact that some less fortunate Victimians of recent immigrant vintage cluster occasionally on sidewalks of a certain
thoroughfare in his city. "It creates a lot of prejudice," said the
wealthy Mr. I. somberly.

"Not necessarily," said the other; "not unless people scrutinize
them with an eye to their group affiliation the way you do. By the
way, I saw in yesterday's newspaper that you were the largest
real estate taxpayer in town. It was blazoned across the page in a
large headline. You saw it, didn't you?"

"Yes. What of it? It shows that I am contributing most heavily
to the town's upkeep."

"In the minds of prejudiced people who don't like any of our group to be richer than they are, it creates envy, jealousy, and ill will. Why don't you give away a large part of your wealth and cut down on the prejudice?"

"That's preposterous," retorted Mr. I. "I can't help it if people develop prejudices that are wholly unjustifiable."

"I agree there," said the other. "I don't care how they feel about you, but think of all the poor devils who don't have wealth but are getting the envy and malice that certainly they themselves don't create. I tell you what we'll do—you forgive them the prejudice they create and they can forgive you the prejudice you create. Both kinds of prejudice are wholly unjustified."

Many a self-hater wishes he were not a Victimian. He accepts the thesis that a run-of-the-mill Victimian is a low-grade misfit, but attempts to prove that he and his special variety of Victimian are different and fit for decent society. He generalizes as glibly about segments of his own racial or religious group as the intolerant do about the whole group. He is willing to prejudge the ethical, aesthetic, and intellectual qualities of large numbers of Victimians on the basis of their nationality, cultural, linguistic, or other characteristics, which have no genuine relationship to personal integrity, but insists that such specious thinking should not be employed adversely against himself. The self-hater needs reorientation and a change of heart in reference to intolerance as much as does any other bigot.

The self-hater should not be confused with the self-doubter, who bears no prejudice against his own group and may even have a false sense of superiority about it, but fears prevailing prejudices to such an extent that he accepts defeat and frustration where he need not. He dares not venture even where no danger lurks. A rebuff or two discourage him too greatly. Oversensitivity brings him needless unhappiness. Many a Victimian, who succeeds in the normal course of existence, still loses opportunities for friendship and pleasant relationship even where these are available. To crowd in where one is not wanted or to make bold advances where they are unwelcome is highly inadvisable anywhere for any person. On the other hand, making sure that intolerance actually does bar the way before retreating is good practice. One of the worst results of intolerance is that its extent is exaggerated in the minds of many and therefore its ghost often operates in instances where it does not actually exist.

A minority whose members repeat to one another every bit of insult some warped person has uttered, increases the number of suspicious, fear-filled self-doubters in its rank, especially when children and young people are fed upon these morsels of gall and wormwood. Such a group will find it increasingly difficult to face others with the confidence that is indispensable to gaining their respect. Rehashing favored tales of petty intolerance against one's group merely adds needless woe and fear. Many a story of encountering prejudice is treasured as a family heirloom, whereas its rightful place is the wastebasket. If a story promotes nothing but self-doubt, forget it quickly.

Mr. C. and his family have summered for many years on an island near New York City. The cottage next to theirs has been occupied by two middle-aged ladies, the Smith sisters, whom the C. family admired but who appeared aloof.

"I wonder," said Mrs. C. several times, "why the Smiths treat us so coldly. They never smile or say 'hello' when we pass."

"I guess they just don't like people of our religious group," Mr. C. would reply. "Evidently they fear that if they are cordial we would expect to associate with them and they'd rather keep us at a distance."

One night after midnight Mrs. C.'s mother fell down a flight of stairs and was badly injured. Frantic inquiry revealed that no doctor could be found on the island that night. Mr. C. rushed out of the house to arrange for a boat to fetch a doctor. When he returned an hour later, he found that his mother-in-law had been put to bed and that one Smith sister was upstairs nursing her while the other Miss Smith was taking the best of care of Mrs. C., who had suffered shock and exhaustion in her own efforts to serve her mother.

"We saw the lights go on all over your house," explained the elder sister, "and from the sounds we heard we feared there had been some trouble and thought that you might need some help."

Mr. C. was deeply moved, for he had imagined his wife and mother-in-law alone in a deplorable situation. From then on a friendly relationship developed between the Smiths and the C. family.

One day Mr. C. said to the Smiths, "Now that we have gotten to know each other so well, I have a confession to make. We thought you ladies were terribly stiff and even hostile. The fact that you never spoke to us during the first few years we lived here made us think you might even be prejudiced."

"You didn't speak to us either," they replied.

Self-doubt of one's own group, as well as self-hatred, results from being too keenly conscious of its being a Victimian group, without compensating confidence. In both cases the prejudices of an unfriendly prestige group have made a deep personal impact—much deeper than need be—and have not been resisted by sufficient inner fortitude. There is a highly important distinction between the self-doubter and the self-hater. The self-doubter feels profoundly pessimistic. He feels that his life is hopelessly constricted by a wall of immovable prejudices, but he condemns those prejudices as unwarranted and unjust. Burdened by galling frustrations owing to the minority position of his group and its lowly status, he believes that his group is intrinsically not one whit inferior in virtue to its neighbors. The self-hater, on the other hand, has become so imbued with the prejudices of the prestige group that his attitude toward his own group corresponds to that of its other defamers.

Therapy for a self-hater begins with realization that he is actually prejudiced against his own group, even though he may have thought he was critical of only a segment of it. Prejudice knows no such boundaries. He must learn to avoid spurious generalizations about even segments of his own group and extend to them the same fair-minded respect that is due to all racial and religious groups. If he has criticisms to offer and suggestions for improvement, he should employ the religious, educational, and social channels of that group to influence aright those whom he dislikes, rather than "wash dirty linen in public." He should be reminded that the world has no respect for those who court admiration for themselves by stigmatizing their own kin.

The self-doubter is like a frightened child, shocked by events or by magnified reports of events that have created a trauma. In many instances bitterness furnishes morbid compensations in his distorted thinking. In extreme cases a martyr complex makes the self-doubter hysterically sensitive to every new indication of prejudice against his group and closes his mind to heartening developments. Reassurance and renewal of faith in the members of other groups are the needed antidotes for self-doubt. The self-doubter can best be helped to a wholesome, normal frame of mind by being shown the brighter side of inter-group relationships and especially more pleasant aspects of the relationship of other groups to his own.

Never encourage self-hate or self-doubt in members of any group. These shadows which prejudice casts among the direct victims of prejudice should be dispelled by gentle persuasion, encouraging personal contacts with members of other groups, and by a frank facing of the wrongfulness of despising or disdaining one's own group. Members of prestige groups can be highly helpful in correcting the warped thinking of self-haters and self-doubters. It is, however, a task that anyone can undertake with some profit provided he can remain kindly and patient in spite of irritating reactions.

CHAPTER 10

Firebrands

Twelve years ago, as the national chaplain of the Jewish War Veterans of the United States, I had an opportunity to reply to an article in the *Jewish War Veteran* which bore the title "I'm Going Down Fighting." The writer had taken a very pessimistic view of the effect of Nazi propaganda and presumed that what was happening in Germany would happen in the United States unless he and other Jews prepared to battle it out in the streets. It was a fiery article sneering at those foolish enough to believe the problem of anti-Semitism in America might be met calmly. The author was ready to punch anyone who uttered an anti-Semitic remark and to meet every sign of hostility in a bellicose manner. He did not represent the views of the Jewish War Veterans but spoke only for the few who had worked themselves into hysteria. Had his views prevailed, there undoubtedly would have been widespread street fighting in the United States. Incalculable damage would have been done to relationships between Jews and Christians.

In my reply I said that I did not intend to "go down fighting," that indeed I had no intention of "going down" at all. Anyone can tempt disaster and even death by courting them in a suicidal mood. Inviting battle where defeat in a clash would be inevitable is good histrionics but poor policy. I advocated a course of self-controlled conduct and the establishment of such friendly relationships between Jews and their neighbors that there would be neither any need nor any occasion for physical combat. Developments of the past decade have proved that the advocate of "militancy" was wrong and that security for Jewish-Americans lay not in street fights or riots but in constructive efforts to increase friendship and good will between Jews and their neighbors, such as have successfully been made between Jewish and Christian groups throughout the United States.

For a time, however, Nazi propaganda in America was intense. The German-American Bund was formidable. Provocation of Jews by anti-Semites was galling. Anti-Semitic agitation in some localities was terrific. Harrowing events in Germany naturally led to grave fears. Fear generally leads to mistaken strategies, not only by exaggerating the menace but by dulling the edge of reason and by diminishing capacities for clear thinking. Frenzied appeals to Jews to "fight fire with fire" and "go down fighting" might well have led to bloody encounters.

In 1940 I learned that some New Jersey men were planning to organize an effort to invade and break up a meeting which was being planned by an anti-Semitic rabble-rouser in a New Jersey town. I spoke to one of them and found that he was laboring under a totally wrong concept of what had occurred in Germany.

"We're not going to take it lying down," he said heatedly, "as they did over there. The Jews of Germany did nothing and you know the result. Some of us who fought for our country in the world war are not going to stand by while our reputations are destroyed by rabble-rousers and our lives wrecked. We're going to fight now."

This totally mistaken legend about the apathy and idleness of German Jewry in the face of the Nazi threat has no basis in fact whatever. The Central Verein Deutscher Staatsbürger Jüdischen Glaubens was created in 1893 and the Verein zur Abwehr des Antisemitismus three years earlier, to combat anti-Jewish propaganda. Both of these functioned continuously until abolished in 1934 by the triumphant Nazis. During their existence they held innumerable meetings and distributed many tons of literature. Their techniques and propaganda themes were wrong. They lacked skill and psychological insights. While their enemies were diabolically clever, German Jewry's defenders devoted most of their energies to campaigns to disprove each of the Nazi lies about the Jews, a strategy which for many reasons is doomed to failure. More than two hundred lawsuits against anti-Semitic speakers and writers were won in the courts but newspaper accounts of the trials spread the anti-Semitic infection. The anti-Semites had slush funds out of which they paid their fines; they did not mind a few months in jail, and often gloried in the opportunity to pose as martyrs. Penalties were considered the hazards of a devious profession, since each case brought them into prominence and gave them opportunities to peddle their wares among people who would otherwise have completely ignored them. Nazis were able to assume the roles of patriots protecting Germany from the Jews, as a self-sacrificing service to non-Jews. To say, however, that German Jewry was stupidly indifferent to anti-Semitic propaganda and made no effort to ward off catastrophe is nonsense.

As explained in *Der Führer*, by Konrad Heiden (pages 585–86), the Nazis knew the value of propaganda by word and propaganda by deed. They welcomed violent encounters between Jews and Christians. The Jews were deliberately made to appear as foes of Christians. Moreover, the Nazis recognized in disturbances a means of wrecking law and order, thus injuring the republic. In this they were abetted by the Communists, who gave them battle in the streets and together they were able to undermine Germany's short-lived democratic government. While it was not the policy of the responsible Jewish agencies of Germany to indulge in heckling at Nazi meetings, irresponsible persons did so and precipitated a number of brawls. *The American Jewish Year Book of 1932–33* (in the chapter on Germany) reported: "The past year, therefore, saw a great number of minor clashes between Jews and Nazis, which were sometimes followed by arrests and trials; few of the latter led to an outcome which acted as a deterrent against reoccurrences of disorders." (Page 56.) My New Jersey friend and others were advocating the very measures which in Germany had proved disastrous. Having made a careful study of what had really transpired in Germany, I was anxious that the same errors should not occur here.

I asked him how many people were likely to attend the rabble-rousers' meeting, which was to be held in a hall. He guessed there would be three hundred. My guess was that there would be less than a hundred, and, knowing the quality of the speakers, I suspected that the audience would be more bored than impressed.

"Do you know," I asked him, "how hard it is to get out a crowd and how little opinions can be changed at one meeting? If you provide drama and excitement you will do for those anti-Semitic organizers what they could never accomplish without you. Moreover, you will be breaking the law. If anyone is arrested it will be those who invade the meeting. You will turn the police and the public against you."

The meeting was held. There was no attempt to interfere with it. The attendance was about fifty; it was a listless affair and the only meeting of its kind attempted in that town. There have been rare instances of interference with anti-Semitic meetings in the United States but fortunately very few. Had there been many, the American scene would have seethed with increasingly fierce clashes, exactly what the anti-Semites desired. They dared not make it a one-sided affair with themselves always the aggressors. The police and the public would not have tolerated that. But if Jews had foolishly formed strong-armed squads of their own and launched assaults, the outcome would have been dreadful.

Only those who want chaos dare overlook the law of emotional dynamics, which is described by J. H. Dennison in *Emotional Currents in American History* (Charles Scribner's Sons, 1932):

> *It is a well-known law of emotional dynamics that when two antagonistic currents of feeling are once started, each act of violence on one side raises the voltage of the other, so that by continual retaliation an emotional charge of such power is rolled up that neither reason nor justice can control it. Each side becomes blind to the merits and just claims of the other, and in place of a group of fellowmen sees only a horde of treacherous brutes and devouring monsters.*

In the world of today, seething with insecurity, wars, and fears of war, no racial or religious group in America should, regardless of the provocation, precipitate violence. To commit bodily injury, except in actual self-defense against another's weapons or fists, or to invade another's property (even property rented for a meeting) is an invitation to greater self-injury than anyone's tongue or pen can inflict. The answer to every suggestion of taking the law into one's own hands should be "No," a firm, undeviating, categorical "No." The response to an outrage should not be to go out and commit an outrage of one's own. It should be the arousing of public sentiment by all decent people of a community to demand genuine law enforcement. Whoever advocates violence as a means of protecting or aiding a racial or religious group should be written off as an irresponsible hothead. The peculiar predilection of a hothead is to leap from a frying pan into the fire. If he does it with his own personal affairs, that is *his* misfortune. But if he happens to belong to a disadvantaged group, he may start a mere pebble of intolerance rolling downhill and so produce an avalanche. He is always trying to do good, and his sense of righteousness makes it difficult to deter him, even when he has been warned of the dangers of his plan.

The cry of the hothead is always, "So you believe in doing nothing!" He thinks that nothing is being done unless it appears in the newspapers. Excitement and agitation are delicacies craved by his appetite. In an attempt to control or appease the hotheads it is possible to become involved with them in ventures that would fizzle out and create far less damage if level-headed people refused to co-operate in any way with them. The answer should be plainly, "If you are going to do this, you will have to do it without our participation. We intend to make it known that we are opposed to your proposal."

Among the hothead moves that should be spurned are "marches" on legislatures. ("Pilgrimage" is a trick substitute for "march.") The appearance at city halls, state legislatures, and congress of groups of orderly citizens to demonstrate their desire that a specific piece of legislation be enacted is perfectly proper. But it is the manner of organizing a large delegation to call upon legislators and the conduct of those in the expedition that determine whether they are peaceably inclined or whether the intent of the organizers is to create disorder and ructions, interfering with the proper processes of the legislative body. The rightfulness of a law is in some respects proportionate to the extent that the citizenry desires it, but it is not proportionate to how much clamor, noise, and disorder can be created by a claque. In the last analysis lawmakers have solemn responsibilities and should never forego their own judgment to appease a disorderly mob.

The very use of the word "march" in connection with a delegation going to visit a legislative body is suspicious. Usually those who advertise a "march" are planning to appear as heroes in the public eye and to whip up fanaticism that can be diverted to their own ends to help them acquire an undeserved leadership. One of the more contemptible tricks used by such organizers is the misuse of the names of reputable, well-established organizations. Unable to secure the official co-operation of the organization, they announce that among the marchers there will be members of this, that, and the other organization. A few misguided members of each of these organizations have actually consented to participate—but only as unrepresentative individuals. In this connection they have no more right to use the names of organizations to which they happen to belong than the promoters of the "march" have a right to exploit the names of those organizations. A prompt, sharp denial by an organization whose name has thus been misused is in order, together with a statement—if such be the case—that it *does* favor the legislation which the "march" is presumably supposed to aid.

What should you do about hotheaded proposals?

1. Avoid becoming personally involved in activities advocated by the irresponsible ("marches," street fighting, breaking up meetings, et cetera).

2. In discussions with individuals or groups try to persuade them that non-violent methods of dealing with interracial tensions are always superior to inflammatory means.

3. Work for enactment of laws and for law enforcement that will protect the rights of all minority groups.

4. Keep cool and remain careful under the cross fire of group tensions.

PART FOUR

Allies and How You Can Help Them

CHAPTER 1

Best of All Allies—The Democratic Tradition

The word "democracy" has come to mean all sorts of things to all sorts of people. Increasingly it has become a convenient tag for propagandists of all nations. But in spite of attempts to debase the word, "democracy" remains a priceless symbol to Americans. However vague its meaning may sometimes seem and however many counterfeit doctrines may be stamped "democratic" to gain approval, in America democracy still remains the coin of the realm. We have no substitute term to represent our social and political philosophies. It means to us the American way of life at its best. As Stuart Chase has said, "Democracy is not primarily voting. Democracy is not even the Bill of Rights. Democracy, as I should like to define it, is a condition where people believe that other people are as good as they are, and, given the opportunity, would be as smart as they are."

The heart of American democracy is common consent, rather than force and duress, the right of the people to govern themselves for the benefit of all the people. This is an ideal; it is not an achieved reality. American democracy *has* imperfections and failures. To insist that it is already perfect, to deny the necessity for any change, is to give aid to those who hope for the failure of the democratic way.

There are those whose conception of the rights and privileges of our system is such that they hope to reserve them for a select few. Many Americans would include no more than their own racial group or their own coreligionists or their own "kind of people" under the umbrella of rights that belong to *all* the people. They are willing enough to let every man shoulder a gun in time of war; in fact, they insist on that. They are quite democratic enough to make demands on *everyone*, but the rewards and the privileges they would reserve for *themselves*. That does not satisfy democratic standards. It is those who would circumscribe the rights of others who make it possible for carping critics to ask, "What is this limited form of democracy which denies to large segments of the American population the enjoyment of life, liberty, and the pursuit of happiness that democracy presumably provides for all alike?" So long as inequalities are deliberately preserved, the enemies of the democratic system will ask that question—and to those deprived of opportunity the question will be a bitter one.

One rainy day ten years ago an elderly gentleman I know taught his niece an excellent lesson in democracy. They were sitting in a car parked near a junk yard. Looking at the battered automobiles, the pieces of wrecked machinery, and other trash, the old man murmured, "Beautiful, isn't it?"

"It's ugly! It's awful!" cried the girl. "How can you say such a ridiculous thing?"

Her uncle smiled and repeated calmly, "This is really beautiful."

The girl was of German birth. When Nazi persecution began she was brought to her uncle's home in a suburb of New York. Homesick for her native land, she disparaged her new environment. The parks of Berlin, she said, were more attractive. She missed the handsome mansions she had seen in Germany. She recalled longingly the magnificent old castles above the Rhine. She found America ugly in contrast with the Germany she lovingly remembered. On this dismal day her uncle had suggested a ride. Reluctantly she accompanied him. When he chose a route that skirted junk yards and factories she became the more petulant, and at last protested that he might at least have taken her where the landscape was less ugly.

"But I wanted you to see," her uncle explained, "what I consider beautiful. To me European castles and mansions are saddening. They make me think of the millions of serfs and of the poor, destitute peoples who have supported their proud rulers in luxury. I see nothing beautiful where human rights are denied and where opportunity to better one's condition is unobtainable. Millions of those whose ancestors had lived for generations in ignorance and poverty were glad of the opportunity to come to this country. Their own prospects in Europe were hopeless. They came here because they expected something better.

"It was hard for immigrants who had no money—usually nothing but their bare hands and a willingness to work, in fact—to get started on satisfactory careers. Some of us went around with burlap sacks collecting paper, rags, and other worn-out things that were being thrown away. Some of us earned and saved enough money to buy a horse and wagon to collect larger discarded articles. It is a long time since I collected rags and wastepaper and broken furniture. At nights I went to school. I had always wanted to be a cabinetmaker and I learned how to be one. Finally I had my own little shop. I was able to rear a family in a modest but comfortable home. My children went to college. They were good children. They live nice, useful lives and I still earn enough, too, as you know.

"That is what these junk yards mean to me. To me it is still beautiful that out of worn-out automobiles and from old scrap iron men are salvaging what would otherwise be worthless. To me it is beautiful that these workmen here are making a living. Look at them. They are people of little education; their parents did not start them off with money, or even any special opportunity. But they are able to educate their children better. These men are citizens of a country where every man's vote counts as much as anyone else's. You are looking at free men with liberties beyond price. In this wonderful country we have homes, hills, valleys, scenery, farms, or whatever you may want to look at as lovely as you will find anywhere. But to me even the slag heaps, the mining towns, the worn-out factories, and the tenements are beautiful because here live the people with the greatest blessings on earth. It's opportunity that counts and we have that here. If you care only for appearances and for the looks of things, you will never understand the greatness of America. When you discover that beauty is much more than what the eye can see, you'll love America as I do."

Only the unthinking disparage the accomplishments of the United States because complete democracy has not yet been achieved. The full realization of its potentialities requires a state of human relationships that has not yet been attained anywhere. The *Report of the President's Committee on Civil Rights* puts it well: "At varying times in American history the gulf between ideals and practice has been wide. We have had human slavery. We have had religious persecution. We have had mob rule. But no fair-minded student of

American history, or of world history, will deny to the United States a position of leadership in enlarging the range of human liberties and rights, in recognizing and stating the ideals of freedom and equality, and in steadily and loyally working to make those ideals a reality. Whatever our failures in practice have been or may be, there has never been a time when the American people have doubted the validity of those ideals. We still regard them as vital to our democratic system."

We have no reason to be smug. While searching for evidence that democracy is a reality in the United States and that we are truly concerned about the rights and opportunities of *all* the people, it is well to remember that pronouncements and laws are no substitute for facts. The fine declarations may be hollow and the laws may be dead letters. The final proof of democracy resides in experience. Nothing matters so much as the daily experiences of people. Incidents such as this one in the life of Rabbi Henry Cohen of Galveston, Texas (described in the *Reader's Digest* of February 1939), are far more important than glowing orations about democracy:

> One day, more than twenty-five years ago, word came to Henry Cohen that a Russian, named Demchuk, in a Galveston prison had sent for him. The prisoner had been a revolutionist in Russia and had escaped as a stowaway. Now he had learned that his family was starving; and he was to be deported on the next ship. Back in Russia he would face a firing squad. The immigration officer in Galveston could do nothing. Washington could do nothing. Yet something had to be done quickly.
>
> Bicycling back from the jail, Henry Cohen suddenly stopped in at the store of a friend, borrowed $100, pedaled swiftly to the station, barely catching a train for Washington. His bike he checked in the baggage car. In Washington, Cohen pedaled down Pennsylvania Avenue to the Department of Labor. "I'm sorry, Dr. Cohen," said the Secretary. "The man has to be deported. We can't make exceptions." Rabbi Cohen turned away heartsick.
>
> Then he made for the White House and, within an hour, was telling his story to President Taft. The President, too, said, "No exceptions," and added, trying to soothe Rabbi Cohen, "You Jews are wonderful. I don't know of any

people who will do as much for their own creed as you do."

"My own creed!" said Cohen, "What do you mean, Mr. President? This man is not a Jew! He's a Greek Catholic!"

President Taft jumped. "A Greek Catholic! You came all the way from Texas to intercede for a Greek Catholic?"

"Certainly," said Rabbi Cohen. "He's a human being, isn't he?"

Taft rang for a secretary. "Take a telegram to the immigration office in Galveston: 'Release Demchuk in the custody of Rabbi Henry Cohen.'"

Back in Galveston, Cohen got Demchuk a job at his trade in a boiler factory. Eventually Demchuk got his family out of Russia.

If democracy is to live and serve as a goad to progress in the United States, let's make sure that we don't merely work for it in the abstract. Genuine concern for our neighbors of all faiths and all races, in the person of real live people whom we can help, is the best indication of our love of democracy.

Citizens of a dictatorship need know very little; they are told what to do. Their lives are rigorously regulated. Where every citizen has a measure of free will within the law, a great deal of understanding and even wisdom are needed by each individual. The citizen must realize that democracy is not the quickest method of obtaining results, although in the long run it is the surest way to serve the best interests of all and of conserving gains. In a democracy we do not burn down the house to get rid of the rats.

Speaking at a National Labor Service conference Dr. Eduard C. Lindeman said: "Perfectionists are, indeed, often the greatest enemies of democratic achievement. They ask for all or none and oftener than not take none. The believer in democratic process who is also a believer in social action invariably asks two questions, namely: (a) What is desirable? (b) What is possible at any given time, possible, that is, without running the risk of going so far as to cause a negative reaction?"

No democratic right is more highly prized than the right to convert others to our own beliefs. But battering rams, brickbats, and insults are not democracy's tools of suasion. All too frequently harsh, indignant self-righteousness—however right it may be—hardens the lines of conflict, sets group against group, and plays into the hands of the most prejudiced. John Dewey, the leading exponent of democracy in education, once said, "Intolerance, abuse, calling of names because of differences of opinion about religion or politics, or business, as well as because of differences of race, color, wealth, or degree of culture are treason to the democratic way of life. For everything which bars freedom and fullness of communication sets up barriers which divide human beings into sets and cliques, into antagonistic sects and factions, and the democratic way of life is undermined." In the growing struggle to extend civil rights, the short-sighted desire to crush and humiliate the opposition is as inappropriate as it is self-defeating. The religious attitude of seeking redemption and salvation for all, including our opponents as well as ourselves, is the true spirit of democracy.

While demanding full equality of opportunity for *all* we dare not forget that those who oppose our efforts are likewise citizens, fully entitled to participate in government and at liberty to espouse their conceptions of democracy, however wrong we may consider them. In this connection a statement of one who was the very embodiment of democracy, Abraham Lincoln, holds timely meaning for us today. "As I have not felt," said Lincoln, "so I have not expressed any harsh sentiments toward our Southern brethren. I have constantly declared, as I really believed, the only difference between them and us is the difference of circumstances. I have meant to assail the motives of no party, or individual; and if I have in any instance departed from my purposes, I regret it."

Proper appeals to the American tradition of democracy are important in combating prejudice and in eliminating discriminatory practices. How successfully the democratic ideal will be invoked depends upon how many of us want the American way of life to be increasingly democratic. Too many are content with lip service, too many willing to salve their own undemocratic practices with insincere tributes to an ideal.

The practice of democracy is more than the passive enjoyment of its rights. It is the active support and defense of the rights of all, the willingness to contribute time and effort to sustain those rights. If you want your contribution to the welfare of all to be effective:

1. Know American history. Study the decisions made by the ballot and by our courts in which progress toward greater democracy have been promoted or impeded.

2. Practice democracy in your personal relationships.

3. Give your backing to the adoption and enforcement of properly framed laws which assure equal rights and equal opportunities for all.

4. Defend the basic freedoms, especially freedom of speech, even when the exercise of these freedoms by opponents is irksome.

5. Never forget that without the maintenance of law and order democracy is impossible. No rights are of any use where life itself is destroyed or jeopardized.

6. Place loyalty to the principles of democracy above loyalty to any racial or religious group. Work for the principles which assure those rights to all individuals and to every group.

CHAPTER 2

The Role of the Non-Victimians

On March 12, 1949, the delegates to the American Bowling Congress refused overwhelmingly to alter a constitutional provision of the ABC which limits membership to white males. They had heard an impassioned plea by the Reverend Charles Carow of the Brooklyn Catholic Youth Organization who, for the fourth consecutive year, offered an amendment opening ABC membership to "all peoples." In addition, a number of interested organizations had urged the association to permit the enrollment of colored members. But of the more than five hundred delegates only three voted in favor of Father Carow's amendment.

According to newspaper accounts, "Father Carow predicted that the fight against racial discrimination in bowling would continue but said that he would not take part in it any longer." He said, "Some of the groups which have pressed this matter may become hot-tempered now and resort to tools that are not for me to employ."

What happens in the American Bowling Congress may be of small importance to most of the people in the United States. The incident itself, like hundreds of others, may have gone almost unnoticed outside of the small groups directly concerned, but its significance far transcends its effect upon the lives of a few sportsmen. Here, clearly outlined and expressed in its simplest terms, one sees in miniature the development of a socially destructive conflict. Many of the most dreadful chapters of history can be explained in terms of conflicts as simple as that in this incident. The pattern can be expressed in a few sentences: Unjust treatment of racial and religious groups creates a mounting tension. Unless adequate adjustments are made under the leadership of sensible people, bitter factions are built and directed by fanatics. Violence and distortion are the inevitable results. In the holocaust which follows everyone suffers; no one is safe.

Today the evidence of mounting social pressures is all about us. We can see it as clearly in our own back alleys as in the capitals of the world. Everywhere the downtrodden, the disenfranchised, the unhappy are moving toward a place in the sun, are demanding the opportunity to live more freely, more abundantly. In this period of discontent and uncertainty, when the old, inadequate forms are being swept away even before the new have been built, it is foolhardy to think that inertia alone will carry us through to a satisfactory future. Our fate—as individuals and nations—in the coming years depends in large part upon our leadership, upon our attitude toward change, upon the spirit with which the favored and the dispossessed meet and deal with each other.

The problems of our times are directly reflected on our very communities. We are everywhere faced with critical problems—problems of cultural unity which are fundamental to the survival of our democratic system. *All* of us face these same problems. Those who believe that they need not share the problems because they do not personally suffer the discrimination directed against minority groups are preparing the way for disaster. By rejecting their responsibilities they are thrusting the situation into the hands of reckless adventurers anxious to assume roles either as defenders or foes of the Victimians. The adjustments and improvements so essential to progress will fail to materialize unless people of all groups and conditions—Victimians and non-Victimians alike—make group relationships their mutual concern. The non-Victimian who smugly thinks that he can afford to ignore the inequality and injustice which Victimians endure is like the man who says that disease and ill health are no concern of his.

In her column of April 22, 1949, Eleanor Roosevelt commented on an excursion of a few senators into the alleys near the Capitol. In these slums Negroes have been crowded into houses which have been condemned as unfit for habitation and should be torn down. Here the only running water available to the tenants is in most instances a faucet in the yard. Poor food, poor housing, and lack of sanitation make the children living in these squalid quarters easy prey to disease. But a whole people cannot be confined to a quarantined section and sealed off there. Nor can the diseases which are bred there. The effects of consigning members of a racial group to such wretched living conditions are direct and inescapable. To shrug them off by asking, "Am I my brother's keeper?" is not only callous; it is perilous.

During recent years there have been heartening examples of intense interest taken by non-Victimians in the hardships endured by Victimians. Among those who have made the betterment of group relations their life work Marjorie Penny is a notable example. Miss Penny gave up an art career to establish Fellowship House in a desperately poor neighborhood of mixed population where in 1938 race riots were likely to occur. How greatly she succeeded in her efforts is indicated by the fact that, together with Maurice B. Fagan, Miss Penny received the 1948 Bok Award for contributing the greatest good to Philadelphia. Her influence has been felt not only in Philadelphia but in other cities where Fellowship groups have been established and where the pattern of Philadelphia's Fellowship projects is being followed.

The completely altruistic devotion of this woman to her cause has been duplicated by other non-Victimians who became seriously concerned about the bitter hardships resulting from discriminatory practices endured by members of a racial or ethnic group in their community. An aroused doctor, lawyer, merchant, mechanic, housewife, or journalist—it may be someone in practically any walk of life —proceeds to do all that is within his or her power to remedy matters, or at least to perform some humane services for Victimians. Sometimes the help of others is obtained on a haphazard basis. In other instances the sympathetic non-Victimian has formed an organization. Many of the national and local agencies working in the field of group relations could have scored few of their successes were it not for the intensive and devoted assistance of scores of non-Victimians.

Whether we will it or not, we must share the future together. What we do to prepare for that future we must do together. In some senses and in some situations we are all Victimians. Those who are least affected by discrimination and prejudice in no sense escape the problem. To the extent that any of us is less discriminated against than another, his responsibility is greater

How? How can you, the "non-Victimian," best work to end the injustices which threaten *you* and *your* security? The answer is almost apparent. What others can do, you can do—and most of this book is devoted to a discussion of specific activities. But you can do more. You can recognize the special advantages you have in the struggle. You can learn to use your position as a weapon. You can be effective in places where the Victimian finds it most difficult to plead his cause.

It goes without saying that in order to combat intolerance and racial and religious discrimination you need not become a "social reformer." Intolerance, fanaticism, and self-righteousness of any kind are a source of irritation to everyone—including the friends of a cause. Persistence and perseverance are necessary—and fearlessness, too, when the issue is vital. But to crusade simply for the sake of crusading, to speak bluntly merely for the sake of being blunt, or to take an embattled position only in order to be dramatic, is to do a disservice to the cause. Zeal must always be tempered by good judgment and a sense of values.

Better than any lecture against intolerance are good examples. The owner of a large Syracuse factory promoted a Negro worker to a position in that factory that had never before been held by a Negro. That in itself is not particularly significant, but the way in which the factory owner handled a potentially difficult situation is admirable. "I gave the man an office near my own. I saw to it that he was brought into important conferences. I gave him a respectful hearing. You see, he was a man of outstanding ability—a fact which too many people failed to see because of his color. I took particular pains to let everyone on the staff know that I regarded his opinion highly and that I felt he deserved every courtesy I could extend to him. Perhaps it is not a pleasant thought, but it is nevertheless true that the fact that the head of the firm respected this man made it easier for others to accept him as a member of our staff. Because we made a special effort to demonstrate the soundness of that relationship and because the man himself was a capable and intelligent person, it is now much easier to place well-qualified Negroes in responsible, well-paying jobs."

One of the most memorable examples of the effective use of his position by a non-Victimian occurred many years ago in the Senate of the United States.

On March 4, 1875, Blanche K. Bruce, a Negro, was to take his seat in the Senate. Those familiar with the details of Reconstruction history will understand how it happened that Bruce had been elected as a senator from Mississippi. In keeping with the customs of the Senate, James L. Alcorn, the senior senator from Mississippi, should have accompanied the new senator from his seat to the front of the chamber for the induction ceremony. When Bruce's name was called, however, Alcorn was very busy reading a newspaper. Bruce started up the aisle alone. Then one of the most prominent members of the Senate, Roscoe Conkling of New York, stepped forward and said, "I see you are without escort, Mr. Bruce. Permit me. My name is Conkling." Not only did Senator Conkling escort Bruce forward for the ceremony, but he also looked after his interests for several days until the new senator had become familiar with the rules and routines. Bruce served on four Senate committees, befriended by a distinguished senator who cared enough about the responsibility of courtesy and decency to spurn the inequality imposed by the color line.

As a non-Victimian you will learn how to take advantage of situations such as this to improve cultural relations. You will also learn to differentiate between situations which can be turned to advantage and those which cannot. You will not become embroiled in every tiff and spat in which there is a suspicion of prejudice. You will understand that you need not and should not defend any member of any racial or religious group against justifiable criticism arising out of his own objectionable behavior. It is the extension of blame to the other members of his group to which you should object. You must be ready to make that distinction yourself, and for others. Regardless of how many individuals in the group have the bad characteristics of which you speak, there is no justification for using the group's name in that connection. By using the name of any group wantonly—by even implying that it is the group rather than the individual who is at fault—you are denying a basic element of our democratic tradition.

You will learn to be circumspect in your activities—but not so circumspect that you are ineffectual. Merely mumbling, or even proclaiming, good-will sentiments and anti-intolerance slogans is not enough. There is among Victimians considerable resentment against those who pose as foes of intolerance but discreetly limit their contribution to lip service. An industrialist who is on public record as opposed to prejudice, but still refers all applicants for jobs to a personnel manager who refuses to hire a Victimian, should not be acclaimed as one who promotes good will between groups. For Victimians whose lives are handicapped by innumerable incidents of discrimination it is small consolation to know that certain important people have expressed lofty sentiments about improving group relations. The question that inevitably arises in the mind of the Victimian is, "But what have you *done* about it?"

It sometimes happens that a person becomes so convinced of the importance and justice of his own cause that he neglects to apply the principles of fair play to *all*. I have known people who, while known to be champions of the rights of some minority groups, assail another particular group. For example, I was recently consulted about an article in which a certain religious group was harshly criticized because of the stand taken by many of its leaders on a certain public question. I advised the writer, a stanch defender of other minority groups, to deal directly and solely with the issue and to present his argument without referring to the name of the group concerned. By doing so he was able to state his case all the more cogently. He simply discussed the question itself without saying things which would create group prejudice.

We have already discussed stereotypes and their role in developing and stimulating prejudice. Stereotyping is one of the most common forms of group criticism and you will have many opportunities to discuss it with your friends. Here again a nice sense of proportion is invaluable. You must not become unduly excited about incidents which do not merit such serious attention. For your own benefit and for the benefit of the cause you can function most effectively when you approach a problem calmly and with a pleasant and affable manner. There are those who become dreadfully excited, for example, when they hear a dialect joke. To my mind, this is a mistake. True, some dialect jokes do perpetuate stereotyping, but some actually create a warm feeling toward the group to which the main character belongs. It is your job to know the difference. It is also your job to point out the difference to the offending person in such a way that he will be convinced and not antagonized.

You will not always be in the position of combating something. If you are to be successful you must look for, and find, the positive side of the question. Just what *you* can do will depend largely upon your own circumstances, abilities, and opportunities. Often you will be able to create the opportunity yourself. Helen Hall Jennings describes in *Sociometry of Group Relations* (American Council on Education) an incident which illustrates the use of opportunities. Sally, one of the pupils in her school, was a rejected child. She was not "in" things very much. Mrs. Jennings observed "that she stood around on the edges to watch, as if hoping to be asked to join, that she brought books from home to share with the others, that she offered to help on occasions only to be turned down." She was in effect undergoing the typical rebuffs experienced by many Victimian children.

When the time came to choose new chairmen for the classroom committees, Miss L., the teacher, mentioned to Catherine, one of the class leaders, that Sally would make a good chairman for the housekeeping committee. "Catherine agreed and actually nominated Sally at the appropriate time. Sally was elected and showed her pleasure with a 'big smile' in Catherine's direction. That afternoon something was planned that called for more books than there were to go round; the children were asked to sit with whomever they wished to look on with. Miss L. was interested to see Sally go immediately to sit with her new friend, while Catherine received her graciously, smiling and making room for her right away. After that Sally was able to take her part in the group activities happily and was increasingly accepted by others."

It usually requires little more than thoughtfulness and kindness to achieve your purpose in bettering relations between groups. Wherever you are, you will find ample opportunities. In May 1948 seventy-five young men from eleven colleges formed a new national fraternity, Beta Sigma Tau. The name stands for "Equality, Understanding, and Unity," and it is to be the realization of these ideals that this "intercultural fraternity" is dedicated. The enthusiasm of the non-Victimians who were instrumental in setting up the new organization was as great as that of the Victimians. Describing the organization in an article in *Collier's*, January 8, 1949, Howard Whitman reported that, "While most of Beta Sigma Tau's membership is white Protestant, as is the population of the United States, it includes Catholics, Jews, Mohammedans, Negroes, Chinese, and Nisei." It is inescapably true that the success of such an organization as this depends more upon the co-operation obtained from non-

Victimians than from persons who cannot for *group* reasons hope to enter the well-established Greek fraternities.

While there is much that you can do as an individual, the greatest contribution that you can make toward eliminating prejudice and its ill effects is in the larger fields of better employment opportunities, educational facilities, housing, recreation, and other requirements of good living. These should always be your primary objectives. In handling problems of this sort, where hardened social patterns are to be broken and action to be effective must be taken on the part of many, it will be necessary to combine your efforts with those of others in order to play your part. The best way to link your efforts with those of others seeking to curb prejudice is to join a community relations organization and to persuade others, individuals and organizations, to support its activities. (See Part Five.) These organizations usually find it much more difficult to secure active members and assistance from non-Victimians than from the Victimians for the very apparent reason that the latter are more poignantly aware of the prevalence of prejudice and the injuries it inflicts. Without an adequate proportion of non-Victimians, however, any inter-group organization is seriously handicapped in its work. It needs to bring together persons of all racial and religious groups in the community. Your participation is certain to be of value. Through the inter-group organization you will be kept informed about the current problems of group relationships, about opportunities to secure desirable legislation, about movements to foster educational programs and to lessen group tension, and about many other practical programs designed to stop discrimination. By attending the meetings of such an organization, by reading its bulletins and serving on its committees, you will not only keep yourself informed but you will render a service to your community as well. If there is no such local organization available, or if it is inadequate, your job is to interest your friends in the creation of such an agency or in the improvement of the existing one.

Your own welfare requires a solution of the grave problems that now exist in American life because of racial and religious prejudices. Never be deceived by the fact that there are groups which feel the burden of intolerance more than your own does. Our nation needs national unity and the wholehearted support of its entire citizenry. It needs the respect and good will of peoples throughout the earth. We cannot maintain national unity and universal esteem unless the

democracy we preach is practiced. In addition to the moral considerations involved, in addition to the simple requirements of justice,
there are reasons—reasons of enlightened self-interest—which should
lead every non-Victimian to participate in personal and organizational efforts to banish racial and religious intolerance.

CHAPTER 3

The Role of Victimians

If your racial, religious, or ethnic group has suffered a great deal of abuse, you are likely to be deeply perturbed whenever ill will is expressed against the group. Members of groups whose status is secure are much less likely to be emotionally upset by similar criticism.

To live in morbid fear of insults is to encourage needless anxieties. A popular minister once received several phone calls from persons who thought he had said something in his radio sermon about "the hypocrite Jew." He protested that he had never even contemplated anything of the sort. Carefully he scanned the typed pages from which he had read his address until a quotation from Matthew 6, 42, gave the clue. He had quoted, "Do not sound a trumpet as the hypocrites do." The complaints were owing entirely to deceptive oversensitivity which had turned a *d* sound into a *j*.

An amusing example of imperturbability, on the other hand, is furnished by the story of a British sailor on a warship, transporting a captured German officer. The German, who spoke English fluently, was given permission to stroll the deck. As he turned to the sailor who had been assigned to serve as his guard, he said, "Your British Parliament is ridiculous."

The British tar disregarded the remark.

A moment later the German said, "And your Navy is the worst in the world."

The Briton smiled complacently.

"And as for your British sailors——!" The German stopped short and expressed his contempt by spitting over the rail.

At that the sailor drew himself up and stepped between the German officer and the rail.

"See here!" he said firmly. "I don't mind your insulting our Parliament or our Navy or our men. But don't spit in our ocean."

A Victimian woman revealed similar self-possession in handling an incident which occurred while she and another Victimian woman were shopping in a grocery store. A third woman was riled about something and was telling the grocer what she thought of Victimians. The first Victimian woman left her friend, quietly walked over to the woman who was spouting intolerance, and whispered something into her ear. The tirade against Victimians stopped abruptly. Obviously embarrassed, the anti-Victimian paid for her merchandise and hurried out.

"What did you tell her that stopped her like that?" the other woman asked her friend.

"I told her that there was a spot of dirt on the seat of her dress and that she was drawing very unfavorable attention."

Indifference to pinpricks is a saving grace. How deeply one is insulted often depends upon how readily one allows the insult to penetrate. Thin-skinned people gasp in dismay where the placid barely blink. The man who can laugh off an insult or who can cap it with a humorous exaggeration has a great advantage over someone whose marrow freezes at an unkind word. A quick-witted leap into the absurd often turns the tables.

"Your people are too ambitious," said one man.

"That's just what I tell them," said the other, "but usually I tell them at ball games when they're rooting for the losing team."

To be able to take intolerant remarks in stride one must learn not to overestimate their importance. What would you have done to retain peace of mind in this instance had you been Clarence Wilson, a Brooklyn district attorney? Mr. Wilson had entered a restaurant and had taken a seat next to a man who was halfway through his meal. The latter, resenting the presence of a Negro at his table, got up and left in such a huff he neglected to pay his check. How would you have acted had you been in Wilson's place?

Mr. Wilson picked up the neglected check, paid the cashier, and continued his meal. A few minutes later it occurred to the white diner that he had overlooked the matter of payment. He returned to the restaurant, where he was told what Mr. Wilson had done. Looking at Wilson, he saw no arrogance or rancor, but rather a friendly face, expressive of good will and warm understanding. Ashamed of his own conduct, he came over, shook hands, said he was from the South, and because he had become accustomed to strict segregation, he had acted impulsively. He offered assurances that he would never repeat the offence. However, Wilson's paying his bill would have infuriated a Southerner had it been done in a smart-aleck spirit. *What* is said or done often matters less than *how* it is said or done.

What would you have done in the following case?

A frantic mother ran from her home into the street screaming that her baby was choking to death. She had reached her doctor's office by phone and was told that he was performing a surgical operation and could not come immediately.

Utterly bewildered, she appealed to the first person she saw, a passing fireman.

There wasn't a cab in sight on the unfrequented street. Phoning around for doctors might get no result for an hour.

"I'll get a car," said the fireman, "and we'll take the baby to the hospital. Bring it down and be ready to leave."

The fireman ran to the fire station two blocks away. The fire chief's car was there but not the chief. Risking censure, the fireman "borrowed" the car and took the woman and child to a hospital a mile away. They arrived in time. The child's life was saved by removing the obstruction in its windpipe. The woman was most grateful.

But on the anxious ride to the hospital, while her child was gasping in agony, she gave vent to latent prejudice. In that moment of desperate need she could not forgive the doctor's inability to rush to her aid. Referring to him, she said, "You can't expect a Jew to help you when you're in trouble."

The fireman did exactly the right thing.

"I'm a Jew myself," he said in the kindliest manner, and that was *all* he said.

The woman was instantly apologetic. I dare say that while a woman's baby is strangling a lecture on the evils of intolerance would be inappropriate. Strangely, that fact is not evident to everybody.

Incidents of this kind, if properly handled, provide opportunities for demonstrating character rather than for argument. They should not be deflected into harangues about intolerance, democracy, or anything else. In such a situation a Victimian has a splendid chance to demonstrate stability, character, or poise on the part of at least one member of the disparaged group. By restraining anger and by remembering that a soft answer turneth away wrath, Victimians have frequently won admiration for themselves and for their groups. What better can one do than to show oneself in such a moment to be a person of culture and refinement?

We cannot control other people's actions but we can train ourselves to react so as to deserve respect.

The readiness of some Victimians to become furious whenever their group is defamed is understandable but nonetheless regrettable. A fiery reaction is especially unfortunate if it is because of an embittered feeling that every non-Victimian is prejudiced. When a Victimian ascribes to *all* non-Victimians the intolerance and hostility he finds in *some* non-Victimians, he is guilty of the same misleading processes of stereotyping of which he is a victim. Non-Victimians are urged to retain faith in the ultimate goodness and decency of Victimians *as a group,* liking some Victimians and disliking others as individuals. By the very same token, Victimians must retain faith in the essential fairness and kindness of non-Victimians *as a group,* retaining their willingness to distinguish between prejudiced and unprejudiced individuals. If millions of persons who had nothing whatever to do with an outrageous act of bigotry are made to share the blame simply because they belong to the same racial or religious group as the bigot, the spiral of hatred and ill will has no conceivable ending. To live in a morbid atmosphere of anticipated "martyrdom," to expect to be treated unfairly by the members of other groups, to cultivate excessive resentment in oneself and in others, is to promote one's own brand of inverted intolerance. A wise rule is never to ascribe disappointments or failures to racial or religious prejudice in any instance unless that assumption is clearly supported by the facts of that particular incident.

Every human being encounters some injustices. Nobody always receives all that he merits. Those whose groups enjoy preferred status have less reason to suspect that disappointments are due to racial and religious prejudice. Victimians, on the other hand, must be careful not to ascribe every misadventure to intolerance. A well-known and apocryphal story has provided a name for this kind of hypersensitivity. A Victimian, having put a penny into the slot of a chewing-gum vending machine and having failed to receive anything for his coin, stood back aghast. "Ah ha!" he cried, "so you hate me too?" That is "slot-machine resentment." Only a neurotic misfit could be driven to such an utterly absurd conclusion by a persecution complex, but some Victimians do draw false and scarcely more reasonable interpretations of events from "slot-machine resentment." Brooding over discourtesies, mistreatments or disappointments, they wrongfully interpret the smallest slight as evidence of intolerance. If a non-Victimian looks askance at them, says anything rude or refuses a request, they are quick to cry, "Prejudice!" Sometimes they are right; more often they are entirely wrong.

Tod Byrnes joined the staff of a large industrial concern as one of its junior executives. The very first morning he asked one of the other junior executives whether he might lunch with him. Two others joined them.

The waiter heartily recommended the beef stew and the others ordered it. The day was Friday. Byrnes ordered fish. As he did so, he thought the others glanced at him oddly. As the meal progressed he noticed that no attempt was made to draw him into the conversation. He proffered a few words but felt repelled. There was an unmistakable attitude of unfriendliness, tempered only by a rather strained air of tolerance. Byrnes drew his own conclusions.

All the next week the aloofness continued. Byrnes plugged away at his job, went out to lunch alone, and felt wretched. Everyone treated him with politeness and civility but without warmth. He was meticulously courteous, scrupulously considerate, and as helpful to others as he could be, but for several weeks the invisible barriers remained. His persistent efforts to treat others kindly brought some result. In time the atmosphere improved. About a month after he had joined the staff, however, there was a sudden change. His colleagues became quite cordial. There was no longer a sense of distance. It seemed that almost overnight unsmiling acquaintances became genial friends.

Some time later Byrnes said to one of the other junior executives, "You fellows certainly had me worried. I decided that you didn't like Catholics and that there was nothing I could do about it."

"We didn't know you're Catholic."

"You didn't?" asked Byrnes in surprise. "Then why did you give me the cold shoulder?"

"We'd been hoping Bob Williams would get the vacant job you took. He'd earned it. Someone got the bright idea favoritism was at work and that everything would be made soft and easy for you. We resented that. Later we saw that you worked as hard as anyone could and that you knew your stuff. Then Williams was sent to that swell new job in the Chicago office the chiefs had been planning for him right along. So, of course, the picture changed completely. You'll forgive us, won't you?"

"You bet I will," said Byrnes. "But I wish I hadn't jumped to false conclusions."

For every time the average Victimian actually suffers from intolerance he has a dozen opportunities to help others overcome prejudice. By taking advantage of those opportunities he can, if he will, benefit both himself and his group. Which is better, to become bogged down in self-pity or to pay heed to the plight of others? Is it more sensible to spend great quantities of time, effort, and emotional energy directly in attempts to counteract a slur against one's group or to expend at least part of this effort to build good will by being helpful to others? I would urge, "Don't be a whiner. Be a benefactor."

In a New England city in 1942 a woman came to the pastor of her church asking for help for her people abroad. She explained that she was of Russian descent and that her brothers and sisters still lived in Russia.

"Now," she said, "the Nazis have invaded the land where my family lives. They have no doubt fled from their homes and are in need. Russian Relief drives are being organized throughout the country. I would like to help. But there is no campaign started here. I am a stranger. I have no influential friends. What can I do?"

The minister thought awhile and finally said, "I suggest that you go to the Jewish Center and see Mrs. Stern there. She has had a great deal of experience in organizing relief work. Mrs. Stern is well acquainted with Jews and Christians who are always ready to help in a good cause."

The woman called on Mrs. Stern.

"Let me see, now," said Mrs. Stern. "I do not know why our city has been tardy in getting a campaign under way for Russian Relief. Evidently each one was waiting for someone else to undertake it.

But there should be no great difficulty. We shall need a chairman. There are four or five people who would serve very well. I'll phone them. We shall need the co-operation of women's organizations. We can call a meeting of the presidents of a number of them. We shall need a headquarters where we can set up an office and where contributions of clothing and other supplies can be brought. I know of a vacant store in a good location whose owner would probably let us use it without charge for some time. The co-operation of the newspapers we can get through several members of the newspaper staffs. The mayor, no doubt, will issue an appeal." She went on to plan a campaign.

Within a month a Russian Relief headquarters had been established and contributions were coming in. The woman who had been so unhappy that there had been no Russian Relief campaign in her city was working there daily. One day she came again to see her minister.

"I have a confession to make," she said. "I am a White Russian. All my life I have hated Jews. My people did not know Jews but they despised them and taught me to think badly of them. When you told me to go to the Jewish Center to ask for help, it was the most difficult thing I ever undertook. I don't know how I did it, because I had such a hatred of Jews. But my people, my own flesh and blood, were hungry and cold and they needed help. So I thought it was my duty and I went. And now I feel that I must tell somebody. And so I am telling you." Her words became slow and measured. "As long as I live, after what I have just seen, I shall never again be able to hate Jews."

Much of the good will and friendliness that exist in many neighborhoods between members of different racial and religious groups is owing to myriads of good deeds performed by members of various groups for members of other groups and for the community at large. No one is moved to such profound gratitude by the deeds of some eminent person as he is by someone's lightening his own burden. A simple neighborly deed has a far deeper effect upon a person's attitude than a reminder that the great So-and-So was a Victimian.

Let us assume that a church has burned to the ground on the same day the newspaper carries a report of some unfavorable remarks about Jews made by a speaker at a local club. Which would be a more desirable item in the next day's newspaper? A statement refuting what the speaker had said or an announcement that the local synagogue had offered the use of its building and facilities to the Christian congregation for the period of its emergency? "Why not have both?" someone asks. For my part I would say that one impression is better. I would not confuse it by an apologetic defensive reply to that speaker. Public-relations experts always advise concentration on *favorable* publicity. That requires doing things that deserve favorable publicity. But is publicity the criterion for conduct? Is it asking too much to expect people to do things that are admirable whether they are publicized or not? There is certainly nothing wrong with publicity that cements good will in a community. But the good deed done without the hope or need of rewards is better. In building good will toward people of different racial and religious groups, deeds are mightier than words.

Doing friendly, helpful things for people of other racial and religious groups is an excellent antidote against the deforming pride of race or creed, against blind fanaticism, against clannish narrowness of spirit that threatens to mislead every group into an embattled isolationism. When the Roman Catholic Church of St. Helena, New York City, raised funds for a Jewish and a Protestant family bereaved by the death of two firemen in a burning warehouse, when Jewish soldiers in Texas volunteered to take over the work of Christians on Christmas Day, when thirty-five Negro children of Jamaica, New York, undertook to clothe and care for a Jewish refugee child in France, when any institution shelters and befriends members of another racial or religious group, and whenever the bonds of affection are extended to include others than "one's own kind of people," good will is not merely preached. It becomes a vital, active force benefiting the givers as well as the recipients. If, in the anxiety to defend one's own group from calumny or abuse, one overlooks opportunities to extend sympathy or congratulations, to console and to assist, to brighten the lives of members of other groups, one neglects the greatest gains that can be made.

Suppose you wanted your own group to win the Nobel Prize, as the Society of Friends of the United States and Britain did in 1947. It is inconceivable that the Nobel Prize would ever be awarded for self-service. The Society of Friends received the award for "its great humanitarian work." The Quakers were so distrusted and hated two centuries ago that they suffered persecution, imprisonment, and death. But ultimately their devotion to human ideals has won them the gratitude of mankind. As conscientious objectors, they have accepted scorn and abuse in time of war. Refusing to bear arms, their young men served as guinea pigs for medical science and braved death as ambulance men in battle and disaster. Theirs is an impressive record of bringing relief to the victims of war, plague, and famine. I cannot imagine a genuine Quaker obsessed by self-pity or overwrought because of insult. He would be too busy figuring out what he might do for others, even for those who reviled him.

I cannot conceive of a committee that would be more helpful to the Victimians of any city than "a committee on cordiality to non-Victimians." There are many occasions when even a note of congratulation or of sympathy is an investment in lasting friendship. The best time to think about the principal of a school or a teacher, or an editor, or a hospital superintendent, or anyone else whose opinion toward one's group matters, is not when there is a complaint to be made but when something can be done to establish mutual respect and confidence. Get enough of these and there will be far fewer occasions for complaint. If Victimians are all too busy to be present when a hospital or school has open house, no one will complain openly. Nothing may be said publicly about it, but a precious opportunity has been lost. Contributions of money cannot substitute as good-will builders for personal participation in the welfare of the community.

In an Illinois city of about a hundred thousand I lunched with twenty of the leading Jews of the community. I asked them whether it might not be advisable to set up an organization for community-relations activities in order to counteract intolerance and to maintain the best relationships with their non-Jewish neighbors.

"Oh no," they assured me unanimously. They had a committee of three men to take care of "all that."

"We take care of everything," said the three proudly.

I urged upon them the idea that two or three or ten people cannot take care of the matter of group relationships on behalf of thousands. "You need to activate the whole group toward improving their own relationships. A tiny committee whose activities are limited to what it does itself is like a political party with a few candidates but no members or voters."

"Oh no!" they replied, "everything is fine here. Really, we take care of everything."

The conversation around the table drifted along.

"There's one religious group here," said one man at length, "from whom we've been sort of distant for about five years. Not that there has been any actual friction, or anything of that sort, but they have been standoffish, and they were very friendly up until just about five years ago. I think it's that new man who's been doing it, the head of their biggest church."

"Yes," said another. "You know, when he was being inducted here they held a big public ceremony. It was thoroughly publicized in the newspapers. Prominent members of all Christian denominations were there. But, as it happened, there wasn't even one Jew present. I don't doubt it was resented."

"It seems to me," I remarked, "that you three don't take care of everything. You have not been educating your people to participate when participation is desirable."

Recently I was told by a troubled Victimian that the editor of the local newspaper was evidently ill-disposed toward his group. My reply was a question that startled him: "Have you ever done anything for him?"

He looked blank for a moment and then said, "Oh yes. We've sent him pamphlets. We've talked to him. But it hasn't had any effect."

"You mean you have tried to do something *about* him, or even *to* him? But what have you done *for* him?"

"You mean we ought to give him a *gift?*"

"Certainly not. But when he has written a good editorial or published a praiseworthy feature story on any subject, does he receive from members of your group the honey he deserves, or can he expect only vinegar?"

"That's a good idea," the man conceded. "Maybe we ought to give him moral support when he does take a liberal stand, even if it's not about our group and surely when it directly concerns us."

I recall one instance when the members of a Victimian men's organization invited an unfriendly journalist to speak to their club. They arranged a dinner meeting, made certain that a few guests would be at the head table whom the journalist would be happy to see there. He was given the choice of his own subject. A half hour's entertainment was arranged. Members were told not to ask spontaneous questions. Four or five good questions were prepared on the topic in advance. The whole evening was on a pleasant plane. Everyone, including the journalist, enjoyed it greatly. It was almost inevitable that his attitude toward Victimians was improved by the experience. Relationships established in this sort of way have lasting benefits.

No minority group can establish itself properly in a community if it creates the impression that it is a belligerent, unfriendly lot of self-seekers. To be sure it must carry on a battle from time to time when its rights are violated or to eliminate discriminatory practices. But without friends, without allies, without admirers, no minority can win out. There is no better practice for a minority group than to be concerned about the welfare of others and about winning their regard. Beware of leadership that does not care a hoot about the good or bad opinion of others. For every gain achieved by such leaders there will be a dozen losses. The most dangerous type of leadership is that which exults in ruin and recklessly invites a fight sure to end in self-destruction. In January 1948, when Moslems and Hindus were rioting in India, a young Moslem officer shouted to a gathering of his coreligionists, "Let us go down in chaos! But at least let us take India down with us!" People who talk that way are emotionally unbalanced. Not only should they not be given leadership, but they should be scorned and rebuffed.

The ideal kind of leadership is well exemplified by Booker T. Washington, one of the hundred Americans included in the Hall of Fame. He ardently believed that with a racial or religious group, as with an individual, God and man help those who help themselves. He believed that freeing Negroes from their economic slavery was a job to which Negroes could contribute more than others. He believed that by their own efforts Negroes could win the respect and co-operation of others. What he was least willing to have Negroes overlook or neglect were those things that they could accomplish for themselves and for their neighbors.

A characteristic event in Booker T. Washington's life occurred one day when he happened to walk by the Varner mansion. Mrs. Varner did not know him by sight and asked him to chop some wood. He removed his coat, took the ax, cut the wood and carried it into the kitchen. A servant recognized him and told Mrs. Varner that the man who had done the chore was the president of Tuskegee Institute.

The next morning Mrs. Varner called to apologize.

"It's all right, madam," Washington replied. "I like to work, and I'm delighted to do favors for friends."

Mrs. Varner became a valuable friend of Tuskegee Institute. She obtained from her wealthy acquaintances thousands of dollars for the school.

By tact, patience, and perseverance, Booker T. Washington throughout his life accomplished far more than he could possibly have achieved by a bellicose air or a bristling manner. Doors that would have remained firmly closed against a battering ram opened at his gentle knock. Not that he turned away when attempts were made to discourage him. Not that he refrained from speaking the truth firmly and unequivocally. But he was too busy working for genuine gains to rend the air with ineffectual bellowing. Booker T. Washington is an enduring example of responsible leadership which rests its faith on toiling hands and refrains from idle blustering. In two generations his disciples have tripled the production of Southern Negro farms. People need food as much as they need civil rights. Booker T. Washington was a masterful leader of his people because dreams did not make him oblivious to immediate needs, while practical considerations did not make him forget the dreams.

"What can we do for ourselves? How can we make our own lives noble and admirable? How can we fully deserve the esteem we want?" are questions which should never be neglected by those who feel disparaged, disesteemed, or mistreated. Demanding rights is easy enough, but unless demands are backed by moral force and endorsed by strong friends, they go unheeded, especially when it is a relatively small group that is seeking to improve its status.

As a Victimian it is only *occasionally* necessary for you to fight, and fight hard, for your rights or for the rights of others. But it is *always* necessary for you to exercise self-control in your relations with others. As a member of the community it is your duty to do your share to see that it is a healthy, democratic community—a duty that is fulfilled, not by a narrow defense of your own position, but by a genuine concern for the welfare of all. That concern for the *total* community should always be apparent.

If an outburst of intolerance has been directed against your group, evaluate its importance in terms of your group's status. Usually the incident is of trivial consequence. Act as one too self-assured to suffer panic or fright.

Don't let your mind dwell upon personal incidents of intolerance against your group and don't narrate them needlessly to other members of your group. Such rehashing breeds inferiority complexes in yourself and in your group.

Don't cry, "Prejudice!" unless you have adequate reason to attribute a discriminatory act to prejudice. Bear in mind that false charges of prejudice have sometimes been launched by rivals and competitors to injure innocent people maliciously. Don't wail. Investigate.

Don't miss opportunities to do praiseworthy things which win for your group the respect and good will of members of other groups. Slanders can be offset by building at all times additional assets of public esteem.

CHAPTER 4

Workers in Their Own Fields
and How We Can Help Them

TEACHERS

Would it be possible in the school in your neighborhood to include in the traffic squad a Chinese captain, a Negro vice-captain, and a Filipino lieutenant? That happened in a San Francisco school recently. In that school some of the children speak Spanish at home. Others speak Italian, Armenian, Greek, Finnish, French, Russian, or some other language. That particular school has a cosmopolitan population, far more so than most schools. There are other public schools in which there is no mingling of races, cultures, religions, and languages. Many of us received our education in a homogeneous atmosphere, among pupils all—or nearly all—of whom had the same ethnic background as ourselves. Others of us rubbed shoulders (or deliberately avoided rubbing them) with children whose cultural heritage differed greatly from our own. But whatever the make-up of the school itself, merely being together in a classroom does not create companionship or mutual acceptance. It may create friction.

From the time when American public schools came into existence until 1930 or 1935 everyone accepted the "melting-pot" theory. American educators believed that racial and religious tensions in the United States would gradually disappear simply because group differences would melt away through everyone's becoming "Americanized." The existence of various racial and religious groups on the American scene was therefore ignored. Pupils crammed all kinds of facts into their heads, but the obvious fact that there are many points of cultural difference between the various kinds of Americans was never officially recognized by teachers. Time would blot out these differences; why call the children's attention to them?

The melting-pot theory failed, however. It failed because the ingredients in the pot stubbornly retained very distinctive features that refused to evaporate. Why the theory that all Americans of the future would in time be almost identical was so thoroughly accepted is now hard to understand. Not only have there been islands of imported cultures which have refused to dissolve, but all kinds of Americans differing widely from each other have been born and bred right here. The persistence of such distinct types as the Navajo Indian, the Tennessee miner, the Vermont villager, the Negro share cropper, the Texan rancher, the Pennsylvania Mennonite, and scores of other American varieties clearly disprove the melting-pot theory. Ours is a multi-cultured nation and in the foreseeable future it cannot be otherwise. Unless they stay at home and close the shutters, Americans are going to meet a lot of Americans unlike themselves. Will they accept those unlike themselves as fellow Americans or will they reject them? National unity and domestic tranquility will not survive if the children and youth of today refuse to accept distinctive groups as full-fledged members of the American community.

Intercultural education has been conceived and is being developed to foster in children a friendly, appreciative attitude toward their fellow Americans of other creeds, colors, and ethnic origins. Its primary aim is to make American life wholesome by making social variations understandable and acceptable. Otherwise group differences will be sources of constant irritation and frustration which will inevitably endanger the rights and prerogatives of all.

The school which accommodates a medley of ethnic cultures is most likely to feel the impact of the present demand for intercultural education. A school in which there is a diversity of cultural patterns may become the scene of a dangerous riot if ill will develops along the lines of group cleavage. The situation is sometimes so explosive that even a poorly handled attempt to promote harmony may create tension resulting in serious disturbances. In *They See for Themselves* Spencer Brown relates an occurrence in a district where the Christian Front had created considerable anti-Jewish feeling. In a deliberate effort to overcome harmful propaganda, a teacher opened a discussion with this question, "Supposing I were to say to you, 'Last night

I heard a Jewish speaker give a lecture on Communism.' Would that mean that all Communists are Jews?"

The teacher had made the mistake, so often made by well-intentioned but unthinking people, of expecting the class to give the correct, logical answer, the one he was seeking. Mr. Brown tells what happened.

"Three students immediately shouted, 'Yes!' The rest of the class period was a fruitless wrangle in which the teacher tried to persuade the three of their error; nobody learned anything from the discussion except the teacher, who wisely decided that the whole approach had been wrong and resolved not to try it again." Mr. Brown explains that in an atmosphere saturated with prejudice, the very word *Jew* was sufficient to set off the conditioned reflex of belligerence, closing the doors to persuasion and conversion. "Only after arduous process of study in less-inflammatory" areas could the discussion of Jews in this classroom have been helpful. "Had the three been sent among their neighbors to investigate and report on social problems, with no particular emphasis (or even mention) of the Jewish people, some good might have resulted."

Intercultural education can be a boomerang if it leads to seeing others primarily as members of groups, emphasizing only their peculiarities and increasing social distances. An intolerant teacher is certain to do more harm than good. Presented by a teacher who is free of prejudices and who will set a good example, intercultural education puts group differences into proper perspective and helps pupils to recognize their fellow pupils primarily as fellow human beings and secondarily as members of racial and religious groups. This all-important distinction in emphasis requires knowledge, skill, and ingenuity on the teacher's part. To develop these essentials in *teachers* is a major function of intercultural education.

Efforts to determine what the schools can do to discourage bigotry and to develop teaching skills were pioneered by the Bureau for Intercultural Education, whose directors have been Rachel DuBois, Stuart Cole, and H. H. Giles. If any one event can be said to have been the first noteworthy experiment in intercultural education, it was probably a project conducted in 1925 in the Senior High School of Woodbury, N. Y. It was an organized attempt on the part of a number of teachers in one school to remove prejudice by gathering facts about the participation in American life of various groups in the population and by presenting these facts to their pupils.

Considerable impetus to the adoption and furtherance of inter-cultural education came from the successful program of education for citizenship of the school system of Springfield, Massachusetts, which included a community program. John Granrud, then super-intendent of schools of Springfield, assisted by Clyde R. Miller, pre-pared the Springfield Plan and with the aid of school supervisors, principals, and teachers, put it into operation after a committee representing all levels of the public schools of Springfield had spent six months of 1939 studying the proposals.

The Springfield Plan is much more than an attempt to combat intolerance. Its philosophy is expressed in the phrase "living, learn-ing, working, and thinking TOGETHER," as Clarence L. Chato and Alice Halligan pointed out in *The Story of the Springfield Plan*. In the schools this philosophy is practiced "by experience in demo-cratic living and by studying the principles of democracy and the relations of human beings with one another."

Several books, pamphlets, and articles and a motion picture by Warner Brothers publicized the story of the Springfield Plan on a tremendous scale. This aroused widespread desire to emulate the plan elsewhere. Unfortunately it also led to a serious error on the part of many who arrived at the conclusion that a pattern for educa-tion had been created which could be quickly copied point by point by all schools. Dr. Granrud and others who administered the Spring-field experiment made no such error. They knew that even in Spring-field intercultural education had made only a beginning; that even there considerable enrichment and improvement of the program were needed, and that while the philosophy and aims of the Spring-field Plan could be applied elsewhere, every school system would require a plan adapted to its own needs, fitted to the conditions, problems, and resources of each community desiring a program of intercultural (or citizenship) education. Identical programs can-not be successfully undertaken, for example, in a homogeneous com-munity and in a heterogeneous community. A community that has no teachers trained in intercultural education, embarking for the first time on such a program, cannot duplicate the program of an-other community where activities guided by experts skilled in inter-cultural education have already been under way for several years.

Every school superintendent and his assistants should study the local situation together with the projects, techniques, and materials that have already been produced in the field of intercultural education. There must be a fitting of curricula to local realities and possibilities. School authorities resent misguided clamor for intercultural education as much as a village fire department would resent a sudden public demand that a type of fire-fighting equipment be installed simply because it has been used successfully in some metropolis. *Intercultural education is a program for educators,* who in the last analysis are the only ones who can put it into practice.

What, then, can you do to promote intercultural education? First of all, it is necessary to understand what intercultural (or intergroup) education is. These names do not imply a prescribed course of study, such as history or geometry, which can be added to the curriculum as something to be studied two or three hours per week. They represent a learning process in which the pupils while engaged in their regular studies or engrossed in special projects discover the worth of human beings unlike themselves—the joy of mutual understanding, the satisfaction of co-operation with people of all groups. Becoming informed about the peoples who make America, studying the contributions of groups to their own community, making pictorial maps of peoples represented in their own ancestries, writing and enacting a documentary play, listening to leading citizens of various racial and religious groups, learning the games and songs, and tasting the foods of various peoples, reading the biographies of persons representing American cultural and racial groups, exchanging letters, making scrapbooks, viewing ceremonial objects, and visiting institutions of various racial and religious groups—these are *some* of the projects that make for better understanding. More important than any of them is the spirit of the school, the code of fair play covering sports, games, office holding, and classroom conduct in which the pupils strive to treat all other pupils as members in equal standing, judging them solely upon their merits and without group bias or prejudice. The subtle weaving of intercultural education into studies such as history, geography, literature, and art requires the utmost skill. The best program is not one that emphasizes an idea here or there, but one which creates such a spirit of friendliness and understanding for persons of diverse racial and religious backgrounds that one senses on coming into the school building that here democracy is alive.

As agencies caring for the children of a neighborhood, the schools can contribute greatly to community improvement. The benefits of intercultural education are reaped by the community long before the school children grow up. Each child brings into its home the elements of better understanding instilled and enjoyed in the classroom. Informally and without organized effort the democracy-centered school influences parents. To be most effective, however, this natural influence of the school upon the community should be supplemented by direct adult participation.

Hand in hand with intercultural education should go community improvements. In *Democratic Human Relations,* Hilda Taba and William Van Til remind us that "in a district marked by racial, religious, ethnic, and socio-economic problems, an approach which stresses the cultural contributions of Italians or Negroes or Jews, but which does nothing to improve the community, is as efficacious as a mustard plaster applied to a cancer. Educators have recognized this fact and, with others, are trying to achieve community improvement—a slow and frequently disheartening task."

An encouraging example of the effect of intercultural education upon a neglected community is furnished by the Joseph E. Hill School in Philadelphia, which is situated in an underprivileged area where housing is extremely poor. When asked during an assembly program what changes they would like to make in their homes the children responded eagerly. They wanted running water, window-panes, plaster on the walls, and unbroken doorsteps. With the aid of older pupils, parents, and other residents, pipes were laid and repairs were made. From this yearning of the little children there came a federation of interracial groups, community councils, church groups, and other agencies. Within a reasonably short time one hundred and twenty-nine pupils had co-operated with their elders in repairing homes. The president of the Hill School Parent-Teacher Organization met frequently with a group at a community center. The group included two homemaking consultants, appointed by the extension department of the Philadelphia Public School System. Effective sewing, knitting, crocheting, painting, and repairing projects were some of the products of these group meetings.

The first thing anyone should do for intercultural education is to learn something about it—especially how complicated a process it is. The novice should understand the subject thoroughly before making any move. The second thing is to realize that intercultural education is an instrumentality which can operate in a community only if those who operate the school system want to use it. The third thing to do is to co-operate with the school authorities in providing the right kind of intergroup relationships in the community at large, so that the results of intercultural education in the schools will be enhanced by the homes and by all community agencies.

Before advocating intercultural education it is essential that you become familiar with the present program in your local schools. If you happen to live in Detroit, Cincinnati, Pittsburgh, Philadelphia, St. Louis, Springfield (Massachusetts), Gary (Indiana), Kalamazoo (Michigan), Denver, Minneapolis, Cleveland, South Bend (Indiana), Newark (New Jersey), San Diego (California), White Plains (New York), or in one of a dozen other cities, you will find that the job of introducing or initiating programs of intercultural education has already been done. The schools in these cities are fully embarked on intercultural education programs.

If the school authorities of your community have not awakened to the possibilities for intercultural education or if they have been indifferent to them or even if they are adverse to undertaking such a program, assist in overcoming their opposition. They should be urged to do their part in implementing the July 6, 1944, resolution of the N.E.A.: "The National Education Association believes that teachers and educational institutions of this country have a heavy responsibility for educating the youth to understand the achievements and problems of all groups, and an obligation to develop a determination to remove the causes of group conflicts." Enough copies of the N.E.A.'s and other organizations' publications on the subject of intercultural education should be purchased to make a collection available to local teachers and school administrators. Get your club to build a collection and promote its circulation. Your local librarian will help you. Consult her.

A well-informed group, representing various elements of the community and using a co-operative, friendly approach, may expect a favorable response from school authorities. Nothing could be better than to have within the promoting group teachers who have attended intercultural workshops which are held every summer in various parts of the country. If you and your friends are in earnest, arrange scholarships for local teachers—or, even better, for school administrators—to attend one of the several workshops conducted every summer by organizations specializing in intercultural (or intergroup) education. You will need the help of persons within the school system who are likely to be well disposed to intercultural education and who have favorable contacts with the highest school authorities. It is helpful to have speakers on intercultural education to address parent-teachers' meetings. Most important is a circle of teachers and laymen who discuss the subject and who continuously inform others about the advantages of intergroup education. For literature on the subject, write to the Bureau of Intercultural Education, 157 West Thirteenth Street, New York City, or to the Commission on Educational Organizations of the National Conference of Christians and Jews, 381 Fourth Avenue, New York City.

CLERGYMEN

A minister in a remote town in eastern Pennsylvania once asked me how often I had officiated at shotgun weddings. I replied that although I had performed several hundred wedding ceremonies, I knew of no instance among these where the bride was already pregnant.

His reply was, "I've got to get out of here for the sake of my daughters. Alice will soon be twelve, and the custom hereabouts is for couples to indulge in complete love-making until the girl becomes pregnant. It's a survival of bundling. Usually it is not until a birth is expected that a marriage ceremony occurs."

"Have you preached against this?" I inquired.

"How can I?" asked my friend, who incidentally is a courageous man with great social vision. "How can I? Some of the finest men and women in my congregation were married to each other that way. This is no secret sin hereabouts. Many of the young people are aware that their own mothers conceived them before marriage. Shall I estrange these youngsters and their parents by declaring that the children were born in sin? Here, as long as marriage occurs before the child's birth, no eyebrows are raised. You don't change a thing like that by direct attack. And you don't launch such an attack if you expect to go on ministering to these people."

To what extent a spiritual leader may defer to the beliefs and mores of his community is a moot question, endlessly debated. In *Christianity and Progress,* one of America's most distinguished preachers, Dr. Harry Emerson Fosdick, complained that "everywhere the Christian minister turns he finds his dearest ideals and

hopes entangled in economic life." The ever-present attempt to confine the man in the pulpit to a discussion of inconsequential matters
drew this rebuke from Dr. Fosdick: "Do you ask us then under these
conditions to keep our hands off? In God's name, you ask too much!"

A few years prior to the Civil War, Rabbi David Einhorn of Baltimore, Maryland, publicly advocated the abolition of slavery. His
views evoked threats of violence against him and against his synagogue. Dismissed from his pulpit by a frightened congregation,
Rabbi Einhorn fled to Philadelphia, where he continued to denounce
slavery. But in Philadelphia his congregants had no reason to fear
reprisals. Sermons that were anathema in Baltimore drew overwhelming approval less than a hundred miles away. The same elo-
quent clergyman said the same things to audiences which, except
for their attitudes toward slavery, were quite similar. In the one
instance he elicited wrath and in the other support. In one locality
he promoted better understanding of a grave social problem, while
in a spot where his message was far more applicable the chief responses were resentment and fear. Capable and intrepid clergymen
of all faiths holding pulpits south of the Mason and Dixon line in the
pre-Civil War years often had to choose between a measure of
silence on the chief problem of the day and moving North.

Even were all clergymen in the United States identically minded
in abhorring the mistreatment of Victimians, they would not decry
discrimination in the same way and to the same extent. A clergyman
whose white congregation accepts colored people into church membership and welcomes them in all activities of the parish house need
not fear the analogy of the beam and the mote which plagues every
liberal pastor of a strictly white congregation. And what of the Negro
minister who sincerely believes that it is better to maintain separate
Negro denominational churches? The attitudes of ministers differ
widely. It is unfortunately true that one occasionally encounters
bigots in clerical sheepskins who even contribute to racial and
religious antagonisms. When discussing what "the clergy" does and
can do regarding racial and religious discrimination we should
remember that while the overwhelming majority of Protestant, Catholic, and Jewish religious leaders of the United States are stanchly
averse to intolerant speech and deeds, individual clergymen can be
found at every point of the good-will and bad-will spectrum.

This is not an apology for the shortcomings of weak or prejudiced
clergymen. Any preacher who wishes to oppose hate organizations

will find ample support among his colleagues. In practically any instance he can cite pronouncements of his own religious group. A clergyman who will not take a public stand against hate mongering is either sympathetic to the hate mongers or much more cowardly than a man of God should be.

In 1923 Lloyd C. Douglas, author of *The Robe* and other best sellers, wrote an article on the Ku Klux Klan for *The Christian Century*. Said Mr. Douglas, "The question for us to decide is not: What will it do to me personally, if I do my bit toward discrediting this thing? The question is: Am I for, or against, a program of organized hate? If I am against it, and keep silence for policy's sake, may God have mercy on my soul!"

On September 30, 1948, Francis Cardinal Spellman and Rev. John La Farge, editor of the Catholic weekly *America,* averted hostility between Jews and Catholics which might well have developed as a result of a newspaper item which originated in Madrid, Spain. An American motion picture had been barred there. The reasons cited by the newspaper correspondent (as presumably furnished by the ecclesiastical member of the film censorship board) were revoltingly anti-Semitic. Without waiting even a day, these notable American Catholics vigorously repudiated the ideas allegedly expressed in the censorship board's order.

Said Cardinal Spellman: "I do not know what was actually said in Spain, who said it, or why it was said, but I do know that it is untrue to say that the Christian attitude to 'stimulate love among individuals, societies, nations, and peoples' does not extend to people of the Jewish race and faith. Catholic doctrine follows the Commandment of God: 'Thou shalt love the Lord thy God with thy whole heart and thy whole soul . . . and thy neighbor as thyself.' This is the 'Christian attitude.' This, I repeat, is Catholic doctrine in Rome, Jerusalem, Madrid, and in Kabul. It was Catholic doctrine 2000 years ago. It is Catholic doctrine today, and will be Catholic doctrine forever."

The very next day the president of the Spanish Board of Film Censors declared that the picture had been banned because its subject matter—anti-Semitism—is no problem in Spain. This explanation may be too sanguine, but regardless of the Spanish Government's faults and regardless of severe criticism that may rightfully be leveled against it, the undeniable truth is that during the period when millions of Jewish lives were being snuffed out by the Nazis, many thousands of Jews were welcomed and sheltered in Spain. It is reassuring to note that American Jews were not provoked by this single news release out of Spain concerning motion-picture censorship into forgetting what Spain had done for Jewish refugees. They did not burst out with denunciations; they waited in dignified silence to see what Catholic authorities in the United States would say about the incident.

"Case closed" can never be written over any disturbance by any amount of bitter protest on the part of Victimians. The balance *can* be restored, as it was in this instance, by prompt action of people outside the injured group. The clergy of all faiths can do— as they have done in many instances—tremendous good by defending groups other than their own assaulted by the intolerant. The Federal Council of Churches of Christ in America has an admirable record in combating anti-Semitism and other forms of intolerance.

The minister, the priest, and the rabbi have exceptional opportunities to promote friendship and to build bridges of understanding between the members of various religions. Countless Protestant ministers, Catholic priests, and rabbis are recognized as stanch defenders of minority groups in their communities. As an accredited spokesman of his group, every clergyman has boundless opportunities to make his own group appear selfish and bigoted or generous and sympathetic. Whatever the clergyman does reflects favorably or unfavorably not only upon himself and the members of his own congregation, but also upon the whole religious fellowship.

In 1912 a young priest was conducting services each Sunday in a small chapel in California. Trap shooting was then becoming a popular sport and a skeet range was set up not far from the chapel. After the service one morning the priest walked out to the range.

He might well have broken in on the sportsmen with an angry tirade. "How dare you disturb the Sabbath with this outrageous shooting? Have you no consideration for those who are trying to worship near by?"

The sportsmen would probably have been shamefaced and apologetic. Yet resentment against the priest and against Catholics as well probably would have been the aftermath. Here is what actually occurred, as told by John Ladd in *The Catholic World:*

The men stared at him.

" 'Gentlemen,' said he gravely, though a twinkle persisted, 'I find my sermons are punctuated in the most awkward places by the sound of shots coming from your skeet range. My congregation's attention is distracted from the sacred rites on which it should be fixed. If you would therefore do me the favor to tell me at what hour you quit your sport, I shall be glad to celebrate Mass at a time that will not interfere with your pleasure.'

"The men looked at the priest with sudden contrition. A distinguished-looking shooter, whom the others had addressed as 'judge,' stepped forward. 'Please accept our apologies, Father,' he said with deep feeling. 'We didn't know there was a Catholic church in the neighborhood.'

"'Well, it's hardly a church,' murmured the priest with a smile. 'It's just a small chapel that our good people around here built themselves out of rough lumber. I'm only here on Sundays. Would one o'clock in the afternoon be all right?'

"'You put us to shame,' continued the judge warmly. 'I happen not to be of your faith—I am Jewish—but no matter what the creed, God's message comes before such idle sport as ours. I assure you, sir, that hereafter our skeet shooting will wait until *your* services are over.'

"That was the beginning of a long friendship. Father Lacombe soon discovered that the group of men who had broken rudely, if unwittingly, in upon his holy offices consisted of some of the most prominent citizens of San Francisco, forty miles to the north." Among them were Catholics, Protestants, and Jews, respectful of the others' faiths.

Father Lacombe's parishioners were very poor but the men of all faiths whose friendship he had won contributed generously to erect a church. "By next spring, just as the fruit pickers were coming back to Portola Valley for the season, a stately chapel . . . reared itself before their astonished eyes. A deep-toned bell called them to solemn Mass, and at the altar . . . stood Father Lacombe in rustling vestments." Among the worshipers were Father Lacombe's influential friends who called themselves "The Family."

"The years passed. World War I came. Father Lacombe went as chaplain to bring aid and comfort to the boys in service. More years followed and 'Steve' Lacombe answered the 'Final Call.' Another priest came to Our Lady of the Wayside.

"But every year The Family, old members and new, make a pilgrimage to attend a morning Mass. At such times they take over the lay duties of the day." A stranger would be astonished if he knew that the silver-haired gentleman who passes the plate to him for his offering is a Jewish jurist, and that it is a Protestant doctor who stands at the portal to welcome him. "During the services, he might see the priest pause a moment, then bow his head and ask the congregation to remember in their prayers one whose name is unmistakably Jewish."

A nation in which an episode such as this is not unusual will remain a strong united nation despite wars of dogma and clashes of group interest.

Never in American history has the clergy undertaken a more vast or more important job of social engineering than is required for the elimination of racial and religious tolerance. In a statement endorsing the report of the President's Committee on Civil Rights, the Commission on Justice and Peace of the Central Conference of American Rabbis urged a program of social action, but noted that "federal pressures will never be able to sterilize the seed bed of [these] prejudices. Since the cause is largely the moral weakness and ignorance of individuals, the remedies must be largely in the hands of our homes, our schools, and our churches."

As Rev. Dr. James V. Thompson has aptly said: "From the standpoint of discrimination, religion has its greatest opportunity as well as its deepest responsibility since our basic beliefs about God and man are the source of some of the most strangling kinds of persecution as well as of the deepest and most enriching fellowships."

The World Council of Churches, meeting in Amsterdam in 1948, recognized that the Protestant churches "must call society away from racial prejudice and from the practices of discrimination and segregation as denials of justice and human dignity." There has been no compromise or mincing of words in official statements of leading Protestant, Catholic, and Jewish bodies, representative of enormous numbers of communicants. It is in the smaller subdivisions, in regional conferences, in the local ministerial associations, in the preachments of individual ministers, and in the grass-root situations, where actual form and substance must be given to broad statements, that considerable lag exists. It is where neighbors meet in the flesh that the moral leadership of the clergy must be more clearly and unequivocally asserted.

The religious approach to the eradication of racial and religious prejudices is especially desirable because it is rooted in historic tradition. It envisages the present struggle as more universal than a clash between one set of neighbors and another. People are urged to side with the right for the noblest of reasons as Kathleen Macarthur says in *The Bible and Human Rights* (Published by the National Board of the Young Women's Christian Association):

> *Feelings of pride and fear, of prejudice and dislike, vanish under the fire of God's convincing spirit. Gradually we become able to see our fellow men in the light of God's superior standards of human worth and merit. The equality due to men seen in this perspective of the Christian appraisal of human worth is of a higher quality than any equality that must be gained by force or even by law. It is the recognition of an already existing equality, based on brotherhood, and there is no question of any man's right to enjoy it. It is complete acceptance of the truth that God has made of one blood all people of all nations. Though never fully attained, this ideal of equality at the heart of our democracy, inspired by the combined resources and teachings of Judaism and Christianity, is man's best hope for a good life and a good society.*

Here are some of the things clergymen can do to combat intolerance and discriminatory practices:

1. Dispel prejudice through sermons, discussion groups, and in conversation with their own congregants.

2. Invite representatives of other groups to address their own congregants.

3. Participate with clergymen of other faiths in conferences for the advancement of the public welfare.

4. Give preference to those books, pamphlets, leaflets, and other educational materials from their own denominational sources which further respect for people of all creeds and races.

5. Promote an interracial basis for church and synagogue membership and end segregation in religious schools.

6. Take active part in promoting fair practice legislation, designed to secure equality of employment and educational opportunity.

In the last analysis it is, of course, true that what a clergyman can accomplish on behalf of any worthy cause depends upon what backing he receives from his congregation. The power of the clergy to accomplish worthy objectives depends upon the leadership they exert, and leadership without a following is meaningless. If a congregation and its affiliated organizations are sufficiently interested in a program of assuring fair treatment for *all* Americans, the spiritual leader of that congregation will accomplish a great deal in the community at large, whereas otherwise he is quite powerless. To my mind, nothing is more inappropriate than criticisms on the part of the unchurched and unsynagogued who, lending no assistance to the liberal leaders of those institutions, decry failure to take more liberal positions. A nation gets the kind of clergy it deserves. While the pulpit preaches to the pew, the men in the pew and the man who should be in the pew can uphold or tie the arms of the minister.

WRITERS, CARTOONISTS, AND OTHERS

Blatant phrases, clearly and unmistakably discriminatory, can be banned by law. The laws can be enforced so that this kind of public display and encouragement of bigotry is impossible. The more subtle type of announcement, however, is much more difficult to eliminate. Even so, many newspapers and magazines are today doing an excellent job in prohibiting even veiled attempts to publicize discrimination in their advertising columns.

Those who are anxious to flaunt their bigotry seem willing to resort to all sorts of dodges. What could be more simple, for example, than the trick of certain restaurants in an area where it was forbidden to advertise the sale of beer? Signs appeared in their windows reading, "Peer sold here," or "Good Vere." Euphemisms of this sort are usually obvious to even the dullest person. No skill in deciphering cryptograms is required to understand the codes of willful discriminators. And yet even those most concerned with the problems of prejudice are sometimes satisfied with such transparent maneuvers. A western hotel association won praise from unsophisticated Victimians when it urged its members to "assume a brotherly attitude in all things racial and live up to the ideals embodied in the Bill of Rights"—and in the same bulletin, cautioning against the use of "discriminatory terms" because they are forbidden by Minnesota law, advised, "Just state 'refined clientele.'" In other words, don't run afoul of the law. Here is a key phrase to serve your purpose: "Refined clientele." In the trade of social discrimination there are

many tricks. Of these, "Gentleman's Agreements" are the most no-
torious.

A survey of anti-Semitism in the United States in 1948 by the
Anti-Defamation League reported that "throughout the country,
with the possible exception of the Northwest, gentlemen's agreement
patterns, and in many instances restrictive covenants, continue to
run their anti-Semitic course." (*How Secure These Rights?*)

This has occurred subsequently to intense popular interest in
Gentleman's Agreement, a best selling novel and a prize-winning
motion picture, which in the opinion of some enthusiasts were to
bring a cessation of that sort of thing. In the main the desirable
residential areas of our country have always been available to
Jewish homeowners and tenants, with only spots here and there
closed against them. The plight of the Jews in this respect is as
nothing compared to that of the Negroes. The impression conveyed
by this prize-winning picture—which somehow failed to appeal for
admission of Negroes into exclusive neighborhoods—was that Jews
are excluded just about everywhere that "the best people" live.

The scenarist in *Gentleman's Agreement* permitted one character
in the picture to express the opinion that it was unwise to publicize
anti-Jewish prejudice. However, he was promptly told, in effect, that
his was an exploded, mistaken notion and that the right way to
destroy covert prejudices is to bring them into the open on as large
a scale as possible. That view is not the whole truth. Few psycho-
analysts would claim today that it is only necessary to show a person
his inner hidden guilt and denounce it to reform him. Unless the
discovery is accompanied by skilled therapeutic measures, such a
revelation is likely to cause worse neuroses than existed previously.
Reminding children that they have been naughty makes them anti-
social more often than it improves their conduct.

We would certainly not attempt to eliminate such social sins as
adultery, heavy drinking, black-marketeering, and fostering specific
prejudices, by notifying people that if they indulge in them they will
be in the excellent company of the most admired people in the
community. Anyone who has had any experience in appraising
group attitudes knows that John Doe fears that he is cheating himself
whenever he feels that everyone else is cutting a corner while he
alone walks the straight-and-narrow path. That applies doubly when
the persons practicing discrimination in a motion picture are not
objectionable characters but the most glamorous and most envied

segment of society. The average movie-goer looks to certain types as his models for social conduct. Show him the Victimian fully accepted in such a circle and you build greater esteem for the Victimian.

In the book and motion picture we have been discussing, a Jewish family was permitted to take up residence in a restricted zone as a favor to a charming non-Jewish lady. This success does not obliterate the audience's impression that in his new surroundings Dave Goldman will be treated as coldly as a gate crasher at a wedding party. Nothing was presented in the motion picture to remove the logical impression that the most the Goldmans could expect from their new neighbors would be condescension and toleration. Nothing at all was said or implied about any benefit that might accrue to non-Victimians as a result of eliminating "gentlemen's agreements." Why not have a scene wherein David Goldman and his wife appear welcome in the previously airtight neighborhood, a scene in which these Jewish neighbors contribute to the pleasure of the people next door? The possibilities of a fiction plot are so many and so elastic that the correct message *can* be gotten into some spot by a deft author. At any rate, an author should never think he will demolish a certain type of prejudice if he concentrates on the job of advertising it.

No one would arouse the public to take steps to prevent juvenile delinquency if he merely showed that delinquency was bad for the poor delinquents and that out of compassion we should improve their lot. Every worthy book, article, and play on the subject emphasizes the baneful effects of delinquency upon society at large. Any book or article, fiction or non-fiction, intended to reduce the extent of prejudice should demonstrate as clearly as possible that prejudice is a thorn in the side of the *prejudiced* even when pride, greed, and stupidity blind the arrogant to that fact. For the most part it is far better to produce a drama, a novel, or a motion picture that shows happy people free of prejudice getting real enjoyment out of their association with those of other races and religions than to take a negative approach to the subject.

I am not asking that prejudice and discrimination be glossed over or "hushed up." But if the desired results are to be achieved by a story or novel, implications and suggestions must be fully analyzed to avoid "boomerang."

No doubt a measure of hearty appreciation is owing to novelists, playwrights, scenarists, actors, journalists, and others who have taken an unequivocal stand against intolerance, even when they do not correctly evaluate the themes they employ and their treatment of them. It would be unkind and unfair to fail to recognize the sincere attempts that have been made by American writers to combat prejudice. Their attitude on the subject of racial and religious intolerance is, with few exceptions, ahead of the nation as a whole. Craftsmen and artists of press, radio, stage, and screen during the past decade have been among the foremost advocates of genuinely democratic relationships without regard to creed or color. Both for their work and for their personal practices in this connection, many of these public-opinion molders deserve "Oscars." The problem today is not how to persuade writers to work for the betterment of group relationships but, rather, how to enable them to use their talents and opportunities more skillfully. While intentions have been excellent, the truth is that much that has been produced by the American press, stage, and screen actually has reinforced existing stereotypes and reflected popular misconceptions. Certainly the mass media have fallen considerably short of their excellent possibilities. We have little to be proud of when the Writers' War Board and its Committee to Combat Race Hatred are forced to come to the conclusion that the writers of the United States, because of their habitual employment of "stock characters," are unconsciously fostering group prejudice.

Members of a Youthbuilders' club became quite indignant about a certain comic-strip character, a shiftless Negro named "Steamboat." Day after day the public was presumably amused by the antics of this dark-skinned, dishonest half-wit, but the boys found his actions less than funny.

"What can we do about this?" the youngsters asked their leader.

"Why not object to the manager of the feature syndicate that distributes this comic?" he suggested.

In the office of the feature syndicate one of the boys explained how the club members felt about that comic.

"You are overlooking something," the publisher told them. "You seem to forget that our comics also have objectionable white characters. Don't we have white gunmen?"

"Yes," countered one of the high school students. "But when do you show Negro heroes? The young lovers in your strips are always white. Whenever they are just nice, ordinary people doing the proper things that create respect, your characters are white. And certain kinds of white—not American Italians, American Jews, or American Chinese, or American Mennonites, or American Indians, or American Swedes, or many other kinds of Americans. As far as Negroes are concerned, they are never portrayed except to disadvantage. When will you bring in Negro scientists, as you show Negro porters and servants?"

After further conferences the publisher announced that "Steamboat" would not appear again in the comic strip. None of the characters in this comic strip were denouncing Negroes or saying harsh things about them. The word "Negro" never appeared.

It is by suggestion, not by direct statement, that prejudices are most often implanted.

Everyone who wants to improve the social mores must understand the limitations of his own craft. A study was made, for example, of a number of comics and cartoons. The results were disturbing. They indicated that considerably more ingenuity and knowledge of the average person's responses are needed by the cartoonist who uses his art to attack prejudice. In some cartoons the majority of the people questioned missed the point entirely. In some instances the reaction was the very opposite of the one the artist had intended. It was found that where pictures are used in broadsides, comics, cartoons, and the like, the picture itself—not the reading matter— must convey the message, for it is the picture that makes the lasting impression. To sketch the usual unfavorable stereotype of a group is damaging, no matter what the accompanying text may say. According to tests made, a banner which reads "Down with Victimians" will *not* be offset by other features of a cartoon. One cannot benefit a man—let us call him "Jim Grogan"—by drawing a portrait of a leering, ugly, moronic individual above a caption: "This is not Jim Grogan. Do not think of Jim Grogan this way. Jim Grogan is an intelligent fellow and very handsome." The tests demonstrated one thing clearly: unless he has a firm understanding of the quirks of mass psychology, the artist or writer should approach the subject of intolerance with the utmost caution.

Every type of mass communication can be used to lessen intolerance and to promote better group relationships *if it is skillfully employed,* with sufficient understanding of psychological reactions. Again using cartooning as an example, what could be more effective in exposing the absurdity of nativism than the picture by Bill

Mauldin which appeared in many newspapers in October 1945? It portrays a family of American Indians who have stopped their automobile to read a roadside poster bearing this announcement:

COMING NEXT WEEK TO THE COUNTY SEAT
AMERICA FIRST RALLY
Our Beloved Country Is Being Overrun by Undesirables
Let's Keep America in the Hands of
PURE-BLOODED AMERICANS

Under this drawing of the American Indians there is one word, "UGH!"—which says more than has been said by many a windy treatise.

In educating the public against intolerance there is great need for graphic and pictorial material with a minimum of text and a maximum of imagery. The same concepts, which should by all means be conveyed in language form to those who can absorb it profitably, should be enlivened for mass consumption in comics, cartoons, posters, motion pictures, et cetera.

The writer who desires to do his part in diminishing racial and religious prejudice need not devote an entire story or book or article to that purpose. He can probably do a much more effective job by seeing to it that a wholesome, positive attitude is reflected in all of his work. The introduction of an admirable character who is unmistakably a member of a misprized group is often possible in a fiction piece which has no relation to the problems of prejudice. Properly handled, such a character can be more effective than a dozen articles. But he must not be an "Uncle Tom" of the good old servant stereotype or some other "acceptable-in-his-lowly-place" protagonist of the group. His stature must not be heroically far above normal and certainly not inferior. Both in fiction and in non-fiction a few sentences on the values of democratic human relationships "salted in" are likely to influence readers, auditors, or spectators as cogently as a long dissertation on the subject.

Because of the tremendous audiences they reach, editors, journalists, authors, and screen writers can render great service in the reduction of prejudice. But before you bestow orchids or express disapproval of a story, article, movie, or the like, ask yourself the following questions:

Who suffers loss because of prejudice according to this article (book, movie, et cetera)? Is it only the racial or religious group against whom discrimination is practiced or is it also those who discriminate against them?

Does this bit of literature (or broadcast, movie, et cetera) intensify the habit of thinking about members of a whole group as though they should all be judged alike on the basis of their membership in that group? Or does it make one conscious that in matters of personal standards and characteristics each should be judged according to his own merits?

Does this cartoon (or story, movie, et cetera) point out something that needs to be done and furnish an emotional, dynamic, or profound conviction that will lead the average reader (listener or theater-goer, et cetera) to do what he can to remedy matters?

What will the lasting impression be? When the details have faded out and one remembers only the main points, will he remember more than that there is a great deal of prejudice against some group?

Does the author assume that his is a lone, noble voice crying out against prejudice and discrimination or that he is one of a growing multitude who are determined to abolish these evils? (Ask any politician how much support a man can get by declaring that he and his cause are friendless?)

Will the average reader, or member of the audience, feel that he would rather defend and even share the fate of those against whom intolerance and discrimination are practiced than be among those who inflict visible hurt upon others?

Writers and producers are in a position to work most effectively to promote democracy. Before they can achieve real success, however, they must abandon the idea that prejudice persists only because it has not been sufficiently spanked in public and that it can be successfully beaten with any cudgel. There are drama, emotion, and all the elements of good fiction in the theme of racial and religious prejudice. The potentials for using these to advantage are abundant. But it requires much knowledge, deep insight, and consummate skill to abate prejudices through media which reach the general public.

GOVERNMENT OFFICIALS AND VOTERS

Have you any doubt about what the following lines mean?
"The right of citizens of the United States to vote shall not be denied or abridged by the United States or by any State, on account of race, color, or previous condition of servitude."
That is a forthright statement without any ambiguity. You know, of course, that it is the first section of the fifteenth amendment of the Constitution of the United States. Strange, isn't it, that almost fourscore years after its adoption there are in some sections of the United States several millions of adults who are certainly citizens (since not only they but also their parents and grandparents were born in the United States) but who because of race are not permitted to vote?

To be sure barring Negroes from the polls is not accomplished by any contravening laws explicitly mentioning Negroes. That would be unconstitutional. But poll tax, especially when unpaid poll taxes are cumulative, is a genuine barrier to people who barely eke out an existence. Naturally that bars many white people, too, in poverty-ridden poll-tax handicapped areas. In fact, when the percentage of actual voters in the poll-tax states is compared with the analogous percentage for free-election states, it appears that in Southern poll-tax states three out of four potential voters are kept from the ballot box. Political power thus becomes vested in a fraction of the citizenry, which is not exactly the way American democracy is supposed to operate.

There are indications, however, that the poll tax as a requirement for voting will be abandoned voluntarily by at least some of the states where it is still in effect. Federal action to abolish the poll tax as a voting requirement is unpredictable because of the filibustering tactic. The end of poll tax as a requisite for voting will not assure voting privileges to all. It will increase the number of Negro voters, as it has in North Carolina, Louisiana, Florida, and Georgia, where state action erased the poll tax. Subterfuges will, however, be used to restrain many Negroes from exercising the franchise in areas where their neighbors prefer to keep them disfranchised. One of the old tricks, "the white primary," may be a thing of the past. But there are others, including the "explain-the-constitution" examinations—oral ones—which make it possible for the examiner to reject a Negro professor of American history while conferring a passing mark upon a white ignoramus. The most formidable deterrent is "advice" not to vote. The tools of intimidation that lurk behind that "advice" are whips, brickbats, revolvers—in fact anything that can maim and destroy.

The "white primary" is a classic example of the way discriminators can develop a device that circumvents an established law. In six Southern states where some Negroes qualified as voters, despite poll tax and other impediments, the "white primary" was introduced. In those states every Democratic candidate was certain of election. By having the Democratic party organization in each of these states exclude Negroes from its ranks, the state officials accomplished their purpose without presumably violating the Constitution. (Note that the Fifteenth Amendment says, "the right . . . to vote shall not be denied or abridged . . . *by any State* . . .") Negro voters in those states had only two alternatives. They could vote for Democratic candidates in whose selection they had no part, or in futile protest they could cast their ballots for Republican candidates. Even the Supreme Court at one time pronounced the "white primary" legitimate. But in 1944 the Supreme Court reversed its earlier decision and declared that the exclusion rules of the Texas Democratic party were in effect the rules of the state and did in fact abridge the right to vote guaranteed by the Fifteenth Amendment.

The "white primary" has been abandoned reluctantly and only after it sustained further rebuffs by the Supreme Court. United States District Judge J. Waties Waring found in 1948 that officials of the Democratic party of South Carolina were keeping Negroes from participation in the primary. Acting on the petition of David Brown, a Beaufort County Negro, Judge Waring said, "The time has come when racial discrimination in political affairs must stop." To David Brown the judge made this memorable remark: "It's a disgrace and a shame when you must come into court and ask a judge to tell you you are an American."

The first of a man's prerequisites for the enjoyment of civil liberties is the right to cast a ballot. Those holding or seeking political office cannot afford to spurn a group of people who vote. Those who cannot vote may be treated disdainfully. Though in practice the franchise is still refused to many, we have made forward strides. As matters stand now, the voting privilege is not denied to any group on account of religion. Indians were once disqualified from voting in a number of states but they can now vote in all states. Provisions of the constitutions of New Mexico and Arizona which denied Indians the right to vote were in effect until voided by court action in 1948. At the inception of our nation practically all Negroes were slaves and could not vote. Woman suffrage is now taken for granted, although the first four generations of American citizens would have none of it. The trend in the United States has been to extend the privilege of voting rather than to restrict it. There is ground for an optimistic outlook.

To make your ballot effective in the fight against discrimination and on behalf of civil rights you will have to pursue the same methods and employ the very same measures you would to make your voice and vote count on any issue. Elsewhere we have discussed desirable laws. How to obtain the passage of laws is explained in books and pamphlets that inform the citizen about our form of government and his relationship to it. Some succinct advice is given in *Here's the Way to Secure These Rights* by Hanna F. Desser and Ethel C. Phillips:

> 1. *Plan to lobby—in a thoughtful and dignified fashion, of course, but with the definite objective of bringing pressure to bear for the enactment of your law.*
>
> *But be sure you know your state lobbying laws. Get them from the clerk of the legislature. Then find out from one of your lawyer friends how these laws have been applied and interpreted.*
>
> 2. *Don't spread your objectives all over the map. Hold your law to a few vital points. Stick to it until you begin to see results.*
>
> 3. *Draw in prominent leaders—as many as you can enlist —to sponsor your bill. "In union there is strength" was never truer than in pushing legislation.*
>
> 4. *Know what is happening to your bill after it is introduced. If there is a public hearing, see that you have spokesmen present with short but emphatic statements of support. Keep after your legislators to move the bill along—and, of course, to vote favorably on it. Watch committee hearings; attend them and speak up whenever you can. If changes*

are suggested, try to reach a workable compromise, for half a loaf is often better than none.

Suppose your bill is defeated the first time it is introduced. First of all, find out why. Then correct your mistakes and try again! Meanwhile, keep the issue before the public—and keep your group active.

5. Finally, follow through. When your bill is approved, signed, and sealed, your job is still not over. You must be on the alert to insist on forceful administration of the law, and ready to protect it from any future assault by those who opposed it at the outset.

To be sure the "you" in the above instructions can hardly mean "you" the individual. This is too tremendous a plan for anyone to attempt alone. Moreover, if you and you and all the other "yous" each went off on a personal tangent to secure a good law on the same subject, nothing but chaos would result. To enact legislation requires well-organized effort. Each of the five suggested steps requires a great deal of work, much of it necessarily by an organization. But "you" must make sure that it *is* done. Steps 4 and 5 are often too much neglected. Moreover, it is well to know that when the final test comes legislators will act according to what they believe the majority of their constituents wish, provided it is not out of line with what their own political leaders want. The need to arouse popular support is usually recognized. The need to get directly to the legislators and speak personally to them is often realized. But the advisability of also consulting the men who do not hold office but are powerful as party leaders is most frequently overlooked. It is highly desirable to obtain their favorable interest.

Writing to congressmen and state legislators is certainly helpful. But these elected officials did not win public office without learning something about public opinion and how it operates. A hundred telegrams all exactly alike or a thousand identical mimeographed letters do not command respect. The legislator who has received them says, "There was a meeting and these folks were excited by some speaker. They let out their emotions by signing this telegram or post card or letter. They haven't brains enough or else they haven't interest enough to formulate something of their own on the subject. They probably had a good emotional spree and by the time I get this, they've forgotten what it's all about."

Write a good letter, an individual letter. Or prepare a telegram of your own composition. That will indicate to your legislator that you are serious about the proposed legislation, that you have given it thought, that you can probably discuss it well enough to win many other converts. Moreover, you may happen to say something in your message—always make it brief—that will influence the recipient. Make it something his secretary will pass on even to a United States senator, busy as he is. That will have more weight with him than five pounds of identical post cards. Write only one line if you prefer, use a post card if you wish. But be an individual, expressing your wish to your elected representative. Don't make him think you are part of a made-to-order mob.

A considerable number of law-abiding people readily comply with any law if they are aware of it. But if the law is repugnant to the great majority of persons in an area wherein it is to be enforced, conformity is far less likely than where there are only occasional and sporadic objectors. Federal laws to which local citizenries take exception are, for obvious reasons, more likely to meet with resistance than those of state legislatures. With a whole population up in arms against a law, it may require sheriffs, bailiffs, or other warrant officers to prevent infringement.

In the main, however, laws designed to establish fair practices and to abolish unequal treatment based on race, religion, and ethnic origin are put into effect, not by force, but by persuasion, conciliation, and mediation. Whether such laws succeed in their purpose or fail depends upon the competence of administrators, rather than upon the police and the courts. When a law has been passed, you —and here again this means you in co-operation with others—cannot expect the desired results unless competent and well-motivated administrators are appointed. Interest in the securing of a law should not turn to apathy when the measure has been placed on the statute books. Organized effort is needed to ascertain that capable administrators are installed and that they receive proper backing. They may be seriously hampered by inadequate appropriations. It may be necessary for you or your colleagues to attend budget hearings. Administrators need aid and encouragement when they are willing and able to do their job properly. If they lack these qualities, they should be replaced by others. By all means, keep an eye on the enforcement of laws designed to secure civil rights.

As R. M. MacIver has pointed out in *The More Perfect Union,* "there is a large amount of particularly vexatious discrimination that depends not on the law but on the attitudes of officials. The law may be liberal but the interpretation of the law may be oppressive." To think in terms of passing laws and of obtaining desired court decisions and administrative rulings is indeed necessary in eliminating the most grievous effects of intolerance. But it is not enough. People occupying government posts, whether they be legislators, judges, policemen, or administrators, must be persons who ignore the race, religion, and ethnic origin of individuals and deal with them as human beings entitled to fair and equal treatment. Government officials must be able to speak and act without partiality. If anywhere in the United States racial and religious prejudice can be more baneful than in another, it is in the seat of government. It is proper for any citizen to demand of government officials that they be free of intolerance. One thing, however, he must remember: the citizen should not ask this on behalf of the members of his own group alone. He should be concerned about equal treatment and opportunity for all.

BUSINESS AND LABOR

The famous English philosopher and economist, John Stuart Mill, wrote: "Men might as well be imprisoned as excluded from the means of earning their bread." In the context in which this quotation appears it is apparent that Mill considered intolerance against racial and religious groups an outrageous injustice when it interferes with a man's right to earn. In the last analysis, the right to earn is the right to live. Obviously a man who cannot earn his food must either starve or steal. Since men are more inclined to risk imprisonment than to endure the pangs of starvation, keeping Victimians from earning a livelihood is certain to drive some into crime. Of all the disabilities inflicted by intolerance none is so devastating as disbarment from jobs and positions for which the Victimian is otherwise qualified.

Few Americans would knowingly and openly urge that economic injustice be inflicted upon a large part of our population. No one would even suggest that we put on relief rolls or drive into jails people who, were it not for racial and religious prejudices, would

be self-supporting citizens. But many Americans obdurately refuse
to work beside any but a white person. Others would rather reserve
all jobs they control for persons of their own racial, religious, and
ethnic background. Drawing these tight circles around themselves,
workers and employers are oblivious to the dreadful outlying area
of misery and poverty they create. The results of discriminatory
practices are a shameful denial of what all Americans so proudly
think of when we picture our country as a land of economic opportunity for all.

There is nothing inherent within our economic system which
makes it financially profitable for labor or for business to practice
discrimination. Actually, the system of free enterprise would operate *better* without any discriminatory practices. It is our mores, our
customs, and our antagonisms toward out-groups that cause white
people in some areas to insist on white persons, rather than colored,
as salesmen and fellow customers, as members of their labor unions,
as foremen, and in various other capacities. When white workers
refuse to work with colored workers it is seldom because of a devious plot on the part of the "boss."

When a factory owner refuses to employ Victimians, it is not because he is following instructions secretly issued by some industrial
association. Discrimination on the part of either business or labor
fundamentally is a social and psychological disorder operating in
the economic sphere.

How intolerance can be exploited by trouble-seekers on both
sides of an industrial dispute is well illustrated by an incident told
to me by Irving Salert of the Jewish Labor Committee. In a Kansas
factory employing about five hundred white workers and about
the same number of Negroes, a demand for increased wages was
met by an offer to raise the wages of the white workers without
raising the Negroes' wages. This was clearly an attempt to destroy
the local union by making its efforts effective for only one half of its
members. Nevertheless, to avoid the tension that would have resulted had they sought to keep the white workers from obtaining the
badly needed increment, the Negroes urged that the proposed
"settlement" be accepted. The white workers responded admirably.
They spurned the favoritism and rejected the offer. A strike ensued.

During the strike anti-Semitism flared up among the workers
some of whom in condemning the absentee owner of the factory
spoke vehemently against the whole religious group to which the

owner happened to belong. The local management meanwhile sought to estrange the workers from the union organizers by labeling the latter as "*Jewish* blankety-blanks."

When the strike was finally settled, appreciable gains had been secured for all of the workers, but their group prejudices had been considerably heightened. It requires only a grain of sense to realize that this vicious injection of prejudice against whole racial and religious groups did great harm to many people and was of genuine benefit to none.

It is only the fact that deep-seated antipathies against groups or a spurious sense of racial superiority are at least latent in the minds of large segments of the population that makes it possible for an agitator on either side of a labor dispute to appeal to prejudice. The prejudice is not created by the agitator; existing antipathies are exploited. They may be fanned to greater heat by unscrupulous rabble-rousers, but those who would find the source of all prejudice among labor in the alleged machinations of industrialists are simply ignoring the obvious facts or deliberately distorting them. The plain truth we must recognize is that agitation against Victimians among the working class comes from workers themselves more often than from employers. Certainly trade unions which still cling to discriminatory practices are not being induced by employers to do so.

There are excellent and evident reasons why labor and business should abandon prejudices and why the line between Victimians and non-Victimians should be abolished in factories, offices, stores, and all other places of employment. The adverse effect of discriminatory practices upon our national economy is, of course, a major reason that should influence both employer and employee. But from the standpoint of narrower self-interest, from the standpoint of the worker as a worker and of the businessman as a businessman, it is clearly advantageous to both to abolish discrimination based upon race, creed, and ethnic origin.

Any gain achieved for the workers by monopolizing jobs for their own racial or religious group is temporary and illusory. The top officials among labor leaders—those who guide the international unions—are fully convinced that discriminatory practices are highly hurtful to organized labor. The leaders of local unions are quite aware now that labor cannot afford intolerant practices. The rank and file of labor—like the rest of the population—still need considerably more education on this subject. Programs have been developed to show the worker in graphic terms the harmful effects prejudice has on him. The gist of the argument presented to labor through the channels of organized labor appears in an excellent cartoon booklet, *Discrimination Costs You Money,* prepared by the National Labor Service. In the booklet, which has been distributed in tremendous quantity, the fact that discrimination by workers is a boomerang is brought home to a new worker in the shop who objected to working alongside of Victimians. Al, the shop steward, enlightens the intolerant newcomer by recounting repeated failures to improve wages and working conditions as long as prejudice created conflict among the workers. Al tells him that victory was not achieved until all pulled together. In Al's words:

> *We didn't put our fight across*
> *With a Jim Crow union or restricted clause.*
> *We all helped you to sit in clover—*
> *Now you go home and think that over.*

The possibilities of using racial and religious prejudice as block busters to wreck organized labor, especially in times of economic recession, is sufficient incentive to labor organizers to take a firm stand against discrimination.

Since discriminatory employment practices are hurtful to organized labor, the question arises whether it is to the advantage of those who do the hiring to foster racial and religious intolerance among workers. An employer who exploits labor might think that it is—provided he is blind to the enormous disadvantages he creates for himself. If he employs Victimians and non-Victimians and plays the groups against each other, the fruits of prejudice are acrimony, dissension, and lowered morale among his workers, with inevitable lowering of productivity. If he employs only non-Victimians, he loses the possibilities of engaging for some jobs better-qualified men who happen to be Victimians.

My own observations in regard to employer attitudes on discrimination in employment lead me to believe that until a few years ago employers gave very little thought to the matter. Absorbed in the many other aspects of achieving success in their enterprises, they adopted a *laissez-faire* attitude in regard to the hiring or non-hiring of Victimians. Each employer's policies reflected the climate of opinion in his own area. Where prejudice was strong in the community, employment practices were discriminatory. Where public opinion was more enlightened, Victimians found greater employment opportunities. In general, the employer's policies reflected the local attitudes and tended to reinforce them—favorable or unfavorable—by establishing them in a more or less formal pattern. Since World War II, however, when acute shortages of labor and the federal wartime FEPC posed the problem sharply, and since the cumulative efforts of intergroup organizations began to take effect, businessmen have been forced to pay greater attention to problems of discrimination in employment. They can no longer remain neutral, indifferent, or non-committal.

Leaders of business are speaking out firmly today against prejudice, and their comments should be most helpful in the battle to end discriminatory practices. It is regrettably true that some mouth fine sentiments but end up with the old cliché "you can't legislate morality." But there is an expanding group of businessmen, especially in the states which have adopted fair employment legislation, who have taken admirable positions in such statements as these:

"The great majority of employers know that such discrimination is uneconomic, in that it results in an unsound use of man power and retards the development of purchasing power. . . . It weakens the position of the United States in the war of ideas between freedom and totalitarianism. . . . It [FEPC legislation] will strengthen the hands of those who believe in its purposes and will bring into compliance those few who do not." (Joint statement of Nelson Rockefeller, Henry R. Luce, Spyros P. Skouras, Beardsley Ruml, Herbert Bayard Swope, and others.)

"Businessmen have discovered that they have increased their business efficiency by broadening their area of employment selection." (William Castleman, president of The Little Business Men's League of America.)

"It is obvious that the biggest obstacle in securing fair employment practices throughout the state is getting minority workers past the office employment door. Once this is done, on the basis of proper qualifications for the particular job openings, it is up to these workers to make their own place on the work team. In our employment experience we have found that, given adequate ability and a friendly, willing personality, minority workers have no trouble in being fully accepted by their co-workers and in earning promotions to higher-paying jobs." (Ellsworth S. Grant, vice-president of

Industrial Relations, The Allen Manufacturing Company, Hartford, Connecticut.)

One of the points made in Mr. Grant's statement deserves underscoring. Legislation and public education on the subject can only open doors to economic opportunity for Victimians. The first few Victimians who step through each door that has been newly opened can do tremendous good or harm. They can either open that door much wider or bring about its partial closing. The Victimian who has adequate ability and a "friendly, willing personality" soon dispels the sense of strangeness in that spot, not only for himself but for other Victimians. A great many Negro men and women, as well as members of other minority groups, deserve the gratitude of all of us for the valiant job they have done through the sheer force of pleasant personality.

A case in point is that of a Negro girl who had been engaged as an assistant bookkeeper. She soon discovered that the woman she was to work for had been without an assistant for six months rather than let anyone but a white person serve at her side. At last the employer insisted that rather than have the books fall far behind despite the bookkeeper's working many hours' overtime, and since a tight labor market had prevented his getting a new white assistant, he would hire a competent Negro girl.

Three months later the bookkeeper took a long-overdue vacation. The clerical staff gave a little party on the eve of the vacation. Bidding her friends good-by, the bookkeeper kissed each of the girls. Without being at all conscious that there was any difference of color, and completely forgetful of her former prejudice and forebodings, she kissed her Negro assistant and thanked her heartily for making the vacation possible.

One of the useful tools in combating discriminatory practices is fair employment legislation. We have already discussed the methods and possibilities in this field. You may find it worth reviewing the paragraphs at the end of the chapter on "Discrimination in Employment."

If your contacts are among businessmen, urge not only individuals but business *organizations* also to take a firm public stand against discriminatory practices. If your state has a commission against discrimination it needs your assistance in its educational campaign. Offer to serve on one of the many committees that must function to make fair employment a reality.

If your connections and contacts are with labor, there is a wealth of material you can help to distribute and promote. There are excellent pamphlets, films, recordings, discussion guides, wall maps, and the like. Talk to labor officials about more intensive use of these. Help to make your trade and your union one in which discriminatory practices are frowned upon. But approach the matter pleasantly and good-naturedly when you are working on a personal level. You are an ambassador of a great cause, where genial ambassadors are needed. One can be very insistent and still be pleasant.

You have a stake in abolishing discrimination in employment. Whether you include yourself in the category of "business" or "labor," your first task in this connection is to recognize that *both* labor and business must make the fundamental principle of the American free-enterprise system a reality. Our system cannot achieve its full possibilities unless full opportunity is given to everyone to contribute to the utmost of his ability.

SOCIAL ORGANIZATIONS

The famous novelist, Pearl Buck, in an article which appeared in *Better Homes and Gardens* told of a "cultivated and imaginative man from Africa, black as coal and with a sense of humor as vital as electricity. He spent days with us this year and in our little community prejudice melted away like mist before sun." She adds, "One pleasant person from another land and race, coming into a community as a visitor, is worth a carload of books and a trainload of academic teaching. The human touch is the only way to cure prejudice."

The idea that "getting acquainted" diminishes intolerance is too broad an assumption. Like so many sweeping hypotheses about dealing with prejudice, this one is true only under certain conditions. A dull and unattractive African could not perform any service on behalf of interracial appreciation such as was done by Pearl Buck's visitor. A vibrant and friendly person does credit to any group.

The injury done to the individual as a result of discrimination should never be minimized. But how much greater is the loss to society! It is because congenial people can be given opportunity to become increasingly acquainted in certain organizations that it is such a pity to exclude worthy candidates on the ground of religion, race, or nationality.

A man is not inconsistent if he says, "I expect to be excluded from many organizations, such as professional associations, religious bodies, and clubs for which I do not have the occupational, educational, attitudinal, economic, or other qualifications. I am thoroughly willing to be rejected if my personal attributes or attainments do not conform to the organization's standards. But being kept out of an organization solely because of race, creed, or color, when these are not necessarily part of the picture, is a different and a grievous matter." Personal attributes are legitimate criteria, and may even include how one wears one's hair or manages a knife and fork, but to bar an entire group, some of whom possess all other qualifications, is clearly unfair and improper.

As long as people find greater conviviality with those more akin to themselves in social background, a blanket rule that race and religion should not enter into membership requirements will not be uniformly accepted. As matters stand now there are national organizations some of whose branches discriminate against certain groups while other branches of the same organization accept these same groups without question. One may well disagree with individual personal inclinations on this score, but one cannot disregard them.

If the bars of a voluntary organization are to be lifted, it can only be by the wish of the members themselves. A society without the right to a free choice of associates is not a free society. No sensible person would think of insisting that he has a *right* to a cordial reception everywhere. Only a painfully obtuse person could be happy in a club from which he would be rejected were it not legally forbidden to exclude him. Except in trade and professional associations, a fair membership practices law is simply unthinkable.

Fraternal bodies, service clubs, and similar organizations greatly influence the thinking of many millions of persons. The attitudes they instill in the public mind are most important. The very pattern of thought which serves as the basis of acceptance and rejection for membership—which in large measure reflects the prevailing mores—adds to the public's respect or disrespect for disadvantaged groups. A rigorous policy of exclusion strengthens all discriminatory practices. But, on the other hand, organizations which support and act on democratic principles provide an excellent opportunity for friendly association. Our concern with those organizations which practice discrimination should not cause us to overlook the splendid record of many civic clubs, luncheon clubs, veterans' posts, and other social bodies in bringing together people of diverse racial and religious backgrounds. The most serious aspect of racial discrimination by similar organizations is the loss of opportunity to build good will in the community.

Assuming that it is desirable to increase greatly the number of voluntary organizations which do not discriminate against racial and religious groups, four methods of working toward that end are conceivable. The first two require long-range effort; the others involve direct action of a more immediate nature.

1. The improvement of the status of excluded groups through greater educational and vocational opportunity will make increasing numbers of those groups acceptable for membership in various organizations on the basis of present standards. It should be noted, however, that there are already many members of all excluded groups who are thoroughly acceptable from every standpoint but who are nevertheless not admitted in many organizations.

2. The establishment of a far-reaching public educational program which would stress the advantages of association with people of other races and religions, rather than clannish exclusiveness. Obviously a program of this scope is a slow process, yet where social discrimination is deeply rooted in the customs and attitudes of large segments of the public, there is no way to get results quickly. There is no short cut to making reluctant people accept each other socially. In the last analysis social acceptance depends largely upon the ingrown attitudes of those who are to do the accepting. Those attitudes are part of complex social and psychological patterns. There can be no substitute for long-range education so long as it is necessary to remold basic elements of the individual and community mind.

3. It is always possible to create new organizations whose charters explicitly and unequivocally provide that there shall be no discrimination on grounds of race or religion. These new organizations, drawing together people who *do* welcome friendship with

those of other racial and religious backgrounds, can play a great part in further democratizing our nation.

The Anselm Forum of Gary, Indiana, has a long record of successful interracial and interdenominational effort in civic enterprise. It is a cross section of Gary's population, but it retains the right to select members on the basis of *personal* attributes.

"I would not miss a meeting of Anselm for anything," said a Greek-American member to me. "It gives me faith in democracy, a feeling that I am not rejected or despised because I did not happen to be born of a certain stock."

The members of Anselm have derived from their mutual experiences within the club a zestful interest in many things that the bored, self-contained, parochial-minded can never know. The story of Anselm Forum is described in a pamphlet available without charge from the Community Service Department of the American Jewish Committee (386 Fourth Avenue, New York). It should be read by anyone who is interested in the further development of non-sectarian, non-racial organizations.

4. What to do about the restrictive practices of existing organizations is one of the most difficult problems that confronts community-relations workers. They are faced with two general types of situations: organizations which totally exclude Victimians and organizations which have accepted one or a few members of a certain group but now either refuse membership to Victimians entirely or severely restrict their numbers.

Vincent G. is a member of a businessmen's luncheon club and as a matter of pride has maintained an almost perfect-attendance record. Not until four years after he had joined the club did it occur to him that none of his Jewish acquaintances were members. Looking over the roster, he discovered that the club contained no Jewish members at all. Discreet inquiry revealed, however, that there was no written rule against such admissions.

"It's simple enough," the membership chairman told him. "No Jew has applied for membership in the three years I've been chairman. There probably weren't any even before that."

"Perhaps," Vincent suggested, "knowing that none has been admitted keeps eligible prospects from applying."

"That's probably true," explained a charter member. "We started with a small membership that included no Jews, and it's been a habit to keep them out. We did blackball a few in the old days."

"But how about A. L. and H. C., for example?" Vincent probed, mentioning two of the most admired businessmen in town.

"Who says they'd want to join?" was the reply.

Vincent soon found himself in a squirrel cage. It was certainly fruitless—and might prove embarrassing—to urge the acceptance of two men who had not applied for membership and might decline an invitation to join. On the other hand, it was risky to obtain the applications of men who probably would be rejected. Vincent found A. L. and H. C. highly sensitive, prejudiced against the club because of what appeared to be a fixed policy of excluding their co-religionists, and determined not to court a rebuff. He proceeded through weeks of tactful negotiation to obtain private assurances from each man serving on the membership committee, as well as from the most influential members of the club, that A. L. and H. C. would be welcomed. Meanwhile he used his own persuasion and the intercession of others to convince A. L. and H. C. that they should join. Eventually he succeeded in getting two very desirable members into the club and in terminating the precedent of reserving the local chapter of an international businessmen's club for Christians only.

An indirect approach is often best if the discriminatory practices are unofficial. But where there is a written clause in the constitution or bylaws which excludes Victimians, an open discussion of the advantages and disadvantages of discrimination is unavoidable if that provision is to be repealed. Your fellow members should be made to realize the fact that their right to exclude people for *personal* characteristics remains inviolate but that each candidate should be judged as a *person* and not as a member of a certain group. The most effective way to make the point is to suggest as candidates Victimians who are highly respected in the community.

What about the Victimian who is asked to join an organization which has excluded Victimians or obviously limited the number in its membership? He certainly cannot justifiably say, "Admit every Victimian who applies or I will not come in." The organization does not accept every non-Victimian applicant either. Many a Victimian has said with dignity, self-respect, and propriety, "If it will be the practice of the organization to disregard the question of my racial and religious affiliation and that of future candidates, I shall be glad to join. But if I am to be an exception while other qualified members of my group will still be barred, I would rather stay out."

Everyone owes something to the racial or religious group of his origin. Some of his time and energy properly should be given to organizations for the welfare of his group. It is wrong, however, to devote one's entire energy to one narrow group and to neglect opportunities to meet and work with people of other groups in organizations with broader memberships. No one should feel that the organizations of his own group have a claim upon *all* of his time. Any tendency among any of the members of your own group to believe that there is something disloyal in associating with members of other groups need not greatly concern you. One simply *does* what one thinks is right and lets others determine for themselves where loyalty begins and ends.

Social discrimination, barring whole racial and religious groups in spite of the personal qualifications of individuals, will inevitably remain a perplexing problem for many years. This type of discrimination is not subject to legislative relief or can it be speedily eradicated by any other remedial measures. Elimination of unfair membership restrictions can only be done piecemeal and by long-range education. You can best hasten the process by working within the organizations to which you belong. You can also help by participating actively in social organizations which do not discriminate. These fellowships are splendid meeting grounds for people of different backgrounds. They perform a valuable function in broadening the vision and enlarging the horizon of their members. They create bonds of personal friendship which defy the bigots who would divide our citizenry and thus destroy our national unity.

PARENTS

Louise is troubled about the problem of prejudice. She wants her children to grow up unbigoted, unhampered by ill will against Victimians. She prefers that her sons and daughters cultivate a warm, kindly feeling toward people of all groups and that they judge each person in accordance with his own character. She has no cause to fear that they will be rejected or spurned. The group into which they have been born has a preferred status.

Irene, too, is worried about prejudice. Her ten-year-old daughter came home in tears because of derisive remarks some schoolmates made about Irene's people. Although the child walked away from her tormentors with her head up, she burst into tears as she related the occurrence to her mother. To Irene's fourteen-year-old son episodes such as this one are nothing new. He has already been abused physically as well as mentally by adolescent bigots on several occasions.

Obviously the problems created by prejudice are not the same for these two mothers. In some respects identical training cannot be given to both Louise's children and Irene's children if they are successfully to come through vicissitudes caused by prejudice. The dissimilarity is in a sense comparable to the different exercise required by a sickly boy and a robust, healthy one. Yet, whether a child is endowed with buoyant health or whether it has been puny since infancy, the basic rules of good health are quite the same in both instances. Similarly, a child's education on the subject of prejudice should include certain essentials regardless of whether it is more likely to run with hares pursued by prejudice or with prejudiced hounds. In fact, the Victimian child will become better equipped to meet tribulations and to come through spiritually unscathed if trained to abhor all racial and religious prejudice. He will then be less inclined to brood over prejudice as a grievous wrong presumably inflicted upon only his own group. The child who realizes that in some ways he, too, may be prejudiced against others and is taught to think clearly on the subject can better understand and bear whatever unfortunate rebuffs he may suffer.

It is often difficult for the parent to decide at what age a child should be taught about racial and religious prejudice. Many a parent has assumed that the subject should not be mentioned at all in the family circle until the child himself raises the question as the result of an experience involving prejudice. Recent studies have revealed, however, that children acquire prejudices at an earlier age than is generally realized. Mrs. Helen G. Trager, who conducted a joint project of the Philadelphia public schools, the Bureau for Intercultural Education, the Research Center for Group Dynamics of the Massachusetts Institute of Technology, and the Philadelphia Fellowship Commission, has refuted the assumption that children come to school at the age of six or seven with friendly attitudes toward all people and that they acquire prejudices only in their "middle years," nine, ten, and eleven. Among the six hundred children studied in this experiment, 43 per cent of the white children knew at kindergarten age that Negro children were not treated on a par with whites; by the second grade 73 per cent knew it. Negro children at that early age understood that when they were excluded from a game it was because they were Negroes.

Little children's conceptions and attitudes in reference to members of various racial and religious groups are, to be sure, confused and irrational, unless deliberate attempts have been made to educate them properly. The children are likely to reflect the stereotyped thinking of adults. And, as with most adults, there is considerable contradiction and ambivalence in their thought and conduct in respect to the members of various groups. In *Intercultural Education News* (fall, 1947) James H. Tipton reported the following incident which occurred in an elementary school during an outburst of anti-Negro feeling at Gary, Indiana:

"A little white boy came to the principal's office at the end of the day.

"Boy: 'I wanted to tell you that I won't be at school tomorrow. I'll not go to school with Negroes.'

"Principal: 'Why, Jimmie, don't you live in the same building with three Negro families? Aren't they friends of yours?'

"Jimmie: 'Oh yes, but that's different.'

"Just then a little colored boy came to the door and said: 'Aren't you ready to go home, Jimmie? I've been waiting a long time.'

"Jimmie: 'In just a minute, Eddie. You wait for me downstairs. I've got to finish talking to the principal.'

"In a few moments Jimmie and Eddie were walking home together, as great friends as ever."

In another school, during the same anti-Negro turmoil, two first-grade boys, one white, the other a Negro, walked up to the principal, hand in hand, saying, "We wanted you to know we're leaving school. We don't want to go to school with those coloreds."

There is no question that at home as well as at school children need guidance on many of life's basic problems. If they are to arrive at a wholesome understanding and proper attitudes in reference to the number-one problem of human relations—getting along well with members of out-groups—parental instruction must begin early. It is unfortunate if this instruction is delayed until it is necessary to undo already-acquired prejudices or if a Victimian child must receive it *after* a shocking impact has been suffered. Just as we have learned to begin sex education before the child undergoes a disturbing experience, so we have found that the subject of group relations can best be presented in a calm atmosphere undisturbed by aroused emotions. As sex education may begin with simple biological facts about the reproduction of flowers and animals, so the parent may well begin to explain racial and religious difference with stories about other peoples, pointing out that certain variations do exist and can be viewed wholesomely. In illustrative stories and incidents the parent can reveal to the child a fascinating panorama of human diversities amid essential unities. If the explanations are carefully made with cordial overtones, group differences among the child's playmates can be presented in an interesting, favorable light. But intelligent, planned home instruction is essential. The child is no more the gainer if he learns the group identities of his Catholic, Jewish, and Protestant associates along with some scurrilous ideas about the out-groups than he would be if he acquired his sex knowledge from guttersnipes. Positive, constructive information is far preferable to chance, chaotic, and often pernicious ideas. If the parent handles the problem himself, he can provide individualized instruction even better fitted to the child's need than can the teacher who must address herself to her whole class. Moreover, it is not merely the information that matters. Even more important is the warmth, good will, and kindliness in the parent's own manner that effectively and permanently broaden the child's horizon.

Parents should recognize that the child must go through a process of learning just when the group identification of an individual does matter and when it does not. Even mature people are often woefully mistaken in distinguishing between proper and improper use of group appellations. To my mind, the recognition of when it is appropriate and when it is inappropriate to attach group identity is *the* indispensable prerequisite for the avoidance of intolerant speech and conduct.

Dr. Julian Morgenstern, former president of the Hebrew Union College, tells the following incident:

"In the first year of my service as rabbi of the congregation at Lafayette, Indiana, in 1904, I would go to Logansport, Indiana, every other Sunday afternoon to hold religious school in the afternoon and services in the evening. In the religious school were two boys—twins—just eight years old at that time, who had a gift for saying and doing the most surprising things. When the train pulled

in at about two o'clock they would be on the station platform waiting for me.

"One Sunday afternoon they greeted me with the announcement,
'We have a dog. Uncle Fred gave us a dog.' Their joy was obvious.

"Two weeks later, when my train pulled in, there they were
again, accompanied by a third little boy from the religious school.
The faces of all three reached almost to their knees.

"'Hello, boys,' I said, 'What's the matter today?'

"'Our dog is dead.'

"The other little boy explained very soberly that Bounce Oppen-
heim's dog had been killed by a streetcar.

"With that, one of the twins looked up in my face very sadly
and said, 'A great many Jewish dogs have died lately.'"

Innocently using the name of a racial or religious group where
it does not belong is amusing in children, but a correct understanding of the scope of group affiliations and an appreciation of what
they do and what they do not signify is a necessary bit of mental
equipment which the child cannot achieve without assistance.

Any parent would do well to use as a concise guide in instructing
a child a brief pledge written by Judge Joseph M. Proskauer while
president of the American Jewish Committee. The pledge was
heartily endorsed by a number of religious leaders, including
Francis Cardinal Spellman and Bishop Henry St. George Tucker:

> *1. I will spread no rumor and no slander against any sect
> or race.*
>
> *2. I will never try to indict a whole people by reason of the
> delinquency of any member.*
>
> *3. I will daily deal with every man in business, in social,
> and in political relations only on the basis of his true in-
> dividual worth.*
>
> *4. In my daily conduct I will consecrate myself hour by
> hour to the achievement of the highest ideal of the dignity
> of mankind, human equality, human fellowship, and human
> brotherhood.*

By interpreting each of the four points of this pledge in terms
appropriate to the understanding of their children, mothers and
fathers can imprint the basic concepts which dispel racial and
religious intolerance.

To be fully effective, this instruction on group relationships must be part of a larger pattern. The *whole* of a child's life, and especially its relationship with its parents, has far-reaching effect on its attitude toward all human beings. The child on its way to becoming a maladjusted person is unlikely to be capable of congenial relationships with members of other racial and religious groups. Frustrations developed in early life often find outlets in virulent intolerance.

Intensive studies conducted at the Institute of Child Welfare at Berkeley, California, indicate that the most likely candidate for a life mired in bigotry is the child of authoritarian parents who is made to conform to rigid patterns for which no suitable explanation has been furnished. Forced to accept the parents' ironclad codes in an atmosphere where parental love is (or seems) absent, the child may develop a sense of insecurity. Or habit may implant in the child's character the inflexibility that characterizes its home life. But the resentment against mother or father or both, which dares not find direct expression, is frequently transformed into an inner hostility which finds outlet against members of other races and groups who are not able to retaliate, as the parents could.

To rear your child as a person whose relationships with outgroups are free of prejudice you should provide information concerning other racial and religious groups on a plane of friendly understanding. You should help the child to comprehend the distinction between individual and group responsibility. Apart from and beyond specialized guidance in these matters you should bestow visible affection upon the child and make it feel wanted and appreciated. Your wishes should be explained rather than imposed, and room should be allowed for flexible growth of the child's own personality. In brief, everything that contributes toward the development of a well-adjusted person furthers the child's abilities to build a sound, intelligent attitude toward all his fellow men.

THE POLICE

On June 20, 1943, a race riot suddenly flared in Detroit. Mobs of fifty to as many as ten thousand persons ranged the streets. Overnight thirty-four persons were killed, three hundred and nineteen injured, fifteen hundred and five arrested. A million man-hours of working time were lost to industry and two million dollars' worth of property was destroyed.

The rioting began when a white man and a Negro got into an altercation on the bridge to Belle Island. Their argument became a fist fight which might have ended then and there had it not been that tens of thousands of people were ready to believe the most fantastic and disgusting kind of rumors. Negroes were told that a Negro woman and her baby had been killed on the Belle Island Bridge. Whites far from the bridge were told that a Negro had raped a white woman there. These stories had no basis whatsoever in fact, but they were sufficient to excite the most brutal passions. In a senseless orgy of hatred, normally respectable citizens were soon smashing windows, looting stores, inflicting horrible injuries and death upon innocent persons of another race.

Many Detroiters had long expected such a riot to occur. Racial tensions had been mounting for several years. Friction between whites and Negroes had been accelerated by agitators of Ku Klux Klan mentality. There had been previous minor outbursts of violence. Danger signs were evident long before the riot, but they were not heeded, just as similar storm signals have been—and are being—ignored in other cities.

There are about twenty cities in the United States today where current conditions may lead to race riots. Is your city one of these danger spots? If you suspect that it may be, send for a pamphlet on *How to Prevent a Race Riot in Your Home Town* by Winifred Raushenbush, obtainable for ten cents from the American Civil Liberties Union, 170 Fifth Avenue, New York 10, New York. It contains some excellent suggestions.

Racial disturbances are caused primarily by unhealthy social conditions. Any farseeing program to prevent such conflicts must ultimately be concerned with eliminating the cause of trouble. To expect the police to maintain law and order among people subjected to unbearable living conditions is asking too much. But until fundamental improvements can be made, the police must be prepared to meet every emergency. There is genuine validity in these lines from a report of the Peace Officers' Committee on Civil Disturbances, which at the request of the governor of California investigated the Los Angeles "zoot suit" riots of 1943:

"Police can prevent riots. Not only can they prevent such riots

from occurring, but, should they occur, intelligent police methods can minimize their consequences. No agency of government can be more effective in furthering good race relations and in preventing riots than the police."

Without competent police the most trivial incident can be turned into a melee of grave proportions. When force *is* necessary, the police must be prepared to act intelligently and effectively. It is the police to whom all of us must look for the ultimate protection of our persons and our property when threatened by criminal action. In a democracy the police must serve the entire citizenry, enforcing the law equally, uninfluenced by the social, economic, or political status of any. And here is the crux of the matter as far as race relations are concerned: our police must be *impartial,* serving all citizens alike. A policeman who is intolerant toward any racial or religious group is a menace to the public safety.

A sheriff's officer presented to a grand jury a statement about crime on the part of the population of Mexican extraction in his county. This group of Mexican-Americans are segregated from their neighbors. Theirs is a poverty-stricken neighborhood. They are among the most wretched victims of discriminatory practices to be found anywhere in the United States. In explaining the crime rate, however, the officer glossed over these conditions. Instead, his report dwelt upon "biological" reasons for crime. It ascribed to Mexicans an inherent lust for blood, and a desire to kill which "has come down through the ages" from the time when the ancient Aztecs practiced human sacrifice. The same "biological tendencies" were ascribed in this report to Negroes and Filipinos.

What could be more appalling than to entrust to a man with such notions as these the security of Mexicans, Negroes, and Filipinos? How can one expect members of a racial or religious group to be law-abiding citizens if they have good reason to regard the local police as their enemies? If the police reflect the discriminatory attitudes prevailing in certain areas, if the police are to gather their concepts of races and of race relations from the gutter, if any brute can act as a sheriff, the outlook for law and order is dark indeed.

To dislike a racial or religious group and to join others in maligning that group are sorry and regrettable practices. They are something, however, which the law cannot prevent completely, any more than it can force anyone to stop disliking and defaming a relative. But a person who chooses to associate with hate mongers and to become allied with them certainly has no right to a job wherein he is expected to protect the entire public impartially. The obligation to be impartial is greater for sheriffs, policemen, judges, teachers, and other public servants than for others. There are many qualifications for a place on the police force, and one of these requirements should surely be freedom from racial and religious intolerance. Some cities now stipulate that requirement clearly in the qualifications for becoming and remaining a policeman. If the code of your local police lacks it, work toward having this stipulation added.

It is reassuring to find that since the Detroit, New York, and Los Angeles riots of 1943 considerable effort has been made by the police commissioners of a number of cities to improve the knowledge and conduct of the police in respect to racial, religious, and cultural groups. Intensive training for officers, based on reading, lectures, and discussion, has been introduced in some places. Social scientists, at first regarded with some distrust as theorists, have been welcomed as consultants. The problems that crop up in neighborhoods composed of persons of various races and cultures have been discussed at national and state conferences of peace officers, and a number of specific steps have been taken to provide instruction for members of police forces.

In August 1946 Commissioner Arthur W. Wallander of New York City instituted a new policy in the police department by adding an article to the *Police Manual of Procedure* to increase "the confidence, respect, and approval of the public." This code requiring "respect for the rights of each individual" calls for the obtaining of foreknowledge of trouble that is brewing by instructing commanding officers to keep in close contact with all organizations and persons "interested in promoting religious, racial, cultural, philanthropic, commercial, or civic welfare," and to keep files on the activities of both groups and individuals so concerned.

In 1947 the Chicago Park District issued a manual for use in the Chicago Park District Police Training School, *The Police and Minority Groups*. Its chapters are: "Worldwide and Neighborhood Aspects of Human Relations," "The Facts about Race," "The Social Situations in Which Tension Arises," "The Role of the Police Officer in Dealing with Tensions," "The Law and Administrative Controls as They Affect Human Relations," and "Illinois Statutes Affecting Group Relations." It contains a list of books, pamphlets, and films on human relations.

Typical of the text of this publication of the Chicago Park District are these lines: "Wherever there are found places or hangouts for street-corner gangs, one finds the natural setting for many racial incidents. Juvenile delinquents as a hardened and venturesome lot are more readily disposed toward violence and possess the daring that is requisite to the invitation of conflict. Areas of the city in which are found disproportionately large numbers of delinquents should be under constant police inspection for signs of racial tension. We must not close our minds to the tragic and inescapable fact that under present-day conditions the population of great cities such as Chicago, New York, Detroit, and Los Angeles can be transformed into mobs that will keep the community in a state of terror and disorder for considerable periods of time."

Indications of rising tensions are listed in a brochure prepared for the Youngstown (Ohio) police by the Intergroup Goodwill Council of that city:

1. *An* increasing *number of rumors, together with an* increase *in their sensational character.*
2. *An* increasing *number of incidents of violence or threats of violence. (Bus incidents, frictions in parks, et cetera.)*
3. Increasing *activity of race-agitating organizations, including groups seeking to exclude minorities from certain areas. (Protective neighborhood groups.)*
4. *Disintegration of relations between minority groups and police department. An* increase *in the number of charges and complaints of "police brutality" would be an evidence of this.*
5. *An increase in labor unrest.*
6. *Minority reaction to the increasing tension as reflected in the minority press.*

The role of the police in some neighborhoods is an extremely difficult one. Police are expected to maintain order in slums where people of different cultural backgrounds impinge upon one another and compete for crumbs under the most adverse circumstances. In such circumstances less intelligent and poorly educated policemen too often depend upon their night sticks and force to keep the populace from creating civil disorders. But where standards have been professionalized to a greater extent, the police are taught to approach the problem as friends of the people in their district. They form committees of citizens to co-operate with them. They encourage youth clubs and promote beneficial social activities. They consider good training courses for themselves a necessity, and they strive to understand the diverse type of people within the neighborhood.

To carry out their responsibilities the police need the sympathetic understanding of the citizenry. A wholesome relationship between the police and the public is essential, especially when agitators and tricksters seek to create disrespect for law and order by denouncing the police on fictitious or specious grounds and when they deliberately create adverse situations to embarrass the police.

You have a right to inquire about police standards in your community. You should be interested in the extent of education given to the police about such subjects as are presented in the publication of the Chicago Park District to which reference has already been made. Certain organizations to which you belong may well establish contact with the police and learn from them some of the problems with which they must cope in assuring equal justice for members of all racial and religious groups.

If a careful investigation indicates that the police force in your city is corrupt or so poorly trained or led that it is necessary to reorganize it, you should be prepared to help carry out such a program. You are more likely to find that the police in your city are trying to do a difficult job well, and that the proper encouragement from you, rather than criticism, will do far more to improve conditions. Your first duty is to familiarize yourself with the conditions and problems the police force is facing. You can best co-operate with them by seeing that they get the public support they deserve and the help they need in handling these situations.

RESEARCHERS

Our present knowledge of the nature of racial and religious prejudice has been derived mainly from observation and from copious experience in dealing with it. It is not so complete and accurate as it should be. By carefully planned studies and controlled experiments, scientists should be able to obtain more accurate information than we now possess. To do so, they must *check, recheck, and double-check their work.* The application of the scientific method

292 PUNISHMENT WITHOUT CRIME

in social studies is not so simple and direct as it is in the physical and biological sciences. Intolerance is not a germ that can be isolated in a laboratory. Unlike a stable chemical element, prejudice cannot be reduced to a pure form and made to yield the same unvarying results under carefully controlled conditions. Prejudice, as we have seen, is a highly complex mental, emotional, psychic, and social phenomenon. It cannot be put into a test tube or examined under a microscope. It cannot be laid bare by a scalpel.

Investigations have been carried on for a much longer time in the field of physical sciences than in the social sciences. It is only within the past decade that serious investigations of genuine intensity have been made to study racial and religious prejudices scientifically. Many of the experiments have been fumbling, and some, to say the least, have been questionable. Beginnings are never easy, and we can only urge a maximum of patience, forbearance, and sympathy in considering the work being done by researchers specializing in the study of group relationships. We very badly need concrete, verifiable information; the search will bring highly valuable results, provided sufficient skill is employed.

In 1947 the Social Science Research Council published a truly remarkable bulletin of one hundred and fifty pages, *The Reduction of Group Tensions*, by Robin M. Williams, Jr. The author makes some excellent suggestions. He also lists one hundred and two propositions that currently serve as hypotheses in dealing with group relationships—for example, "Intergroup hostility and conflict are the more likely . . . as a result of economic depression, prior cultural conflict, or various types of social disorganization."

Just how true is that statement? Practically everyone assumes that economic depressions intensify antagonisms between *racial* groups in the depressed area. But do they? Proof that leaves no reasonable doubt has never been furnished. Why not make such a complete, thorough, and penetrating study on this one matter that we shall thereafter really *know* the truth and its ramifications? It might cost a quarter of a million dollars to take one hypothesis out of the realm of common-sense finding and either disprove it or establish it in the area of scientifically verified data. But from then on we would have something solid in a sea of shifting probables. Dr. Williams has listed more than a hundred propositions—some of them more probable than others. Thus far none has been thoroughly subjected to sufficient testing to eliminate every legitimate doubt.

From time to time certain tenets will be fully explored by research. We should not, meanwhile, abandon any pragmatic hypothesis which is the best we have found empirically. Our workable knowledge for combating intolerance is far superior to snap judgment, popular notions, and uninformed opinion. As Robert M. MacIver has written in *The More Perfect Union* (Harper & Brothers, 1948):

> *The wisest general can never have absolute assurance that his plan of campaign will work. It is the very essence of strategy to go by the best indications available and never to flinch from making decisions because there is always a possibility that they will go wrong. If the scholar does not accept the same limitation, then the guidance he is qualified to give in matters of social strategy will be lacking. He must be content to follow the lead given by his experience, his knowledge of social situations, his analysis of probabilities, and he must not let his very proper longing for complete verification have a paralyzing effect on his social wisdom.*

In other words, we must do the best we can with the knowledge we now have. If, when, and as, genuinely scientific findings disprove what is now accepted as true, we should *then* alter whatever opinion or method is shown to be faulty.

There is a tendency to confuse the solidly constructive work of the social-science researchers with the superficial "findings" of those who make polls of public attitudes only in order to publish their outcome in the public press together with some comments. A distinction should always be drawn between the results of sporadic polls and the sound body of verifiable data which is laboriously compiled by skilled investigators on many aspects of prejudice. As Dr. Samuel H. Flowerman, director of the Department of Scientific Research of the American Jewish Committee has said, "There is altogether too great a disposition to lump together all social science into the category of public-opinion polling—and to point to the failure of polls in predicting the outcome of the 1948 election. Social scientists who have been working intensively on problems of prejudice have increasingly shifted their sights away from surface polling techniques. To argue against social research as being tantamount to polling operations is hence of limited validity and usefulness.

"Shifts are taking place away from concern with attitudes [which have been taken to mean verbal expressions of like or dislike] to concern with such concepts as group dynamics, group membership, group pressures, social role, social perception, cultural values, et cetera. Studies dealing with the level or extent of prejudice against a particular group as measured by attitude questions on polls are giving way to studies of the formal and informal social structure of community life, social disorganization, and its effects upon inter-group relations, et cetera."

A recent experiment conducted at the University of California admirably illustrates the differences in technique and intent between a "study in depth" and a superficial-attitude poll. The work, which required several years, was done by four social scientists: R. Nevitt Sanford, Else Frenkel-Brunswick, T. W. Adorno, and Daniel Levinson. Arangements were made for the researchers to distribute lengthy questionnaires covering various types and aspects of prejudice to groups of students, Rotarians, Kiwanians, public-health nurses, prison inmates, factory workers, and others. To encourage complete frankness, the questionnaire was answered anonymously but each person was asked to put some identifying designation, other than his name, on the questionnaire he submitted, so that he could by reference to that symbol identify his own paper later. Having scored the questionnaires, the investigators selected those which, on the basis of the answers they contained, indicated persons who were among the 25 per cent most prejudiced. They similarly chose those which had come from the 25 per cent of the examined group who appeared to be least prejudiced. By returning to the same audience (a class, a club, or the like) and by inviting to their office the persons whose papers bore such-and-such identification symbols, the investigators brought in men and women whose scores were markedly higher or lower than the average. Not all of the "highs" and "lows" were summoned for further study. By a process of selection among the two thousand who had filled out questionnaires only several hundred were chosen as the subjects for the study.

The purpose of the project was to determine as accurately as possible the basic personality differences between the "highs" and the "lows." Painstaking attempts were made through various methods, including interviews, to learn which general personality traits accompany prejudice and to analyze the relationship of the other characteristics to intolerance. Intensive work was done on every phase of a well-defined inquiry. The findings of this study have been prepared for publication in a book, *The Authoritarian Personality*, which forms a valuable contribution to our knowledge of racial and religious prejudice. Such a study as this reveals clearly the essential differences between the scientific technique and sampling of public attitudes about prejudice which sometimes passes for research.

Even the best of modern techniques for measuring prejudice are not entirely satisfactory. The researcher who is interested in something more than intriguing the public by announcing what such-and-such percentage of the population presumably thinks about a certain group faces an initial handicap because there are neither precise instruments with which to measure prejudice nor accurate, standard terms in which to express his findings. Many professional workers who are familiar with the practical problems of prejudice are not as yet satisfied that the devices used to determine the nature and extent of prejudice in individuals and in groups of individuals are sufficiently valid and reliable. It is undoubtedly true, however, that the crudity of present measurement techniques does not make them worthless. Even though the means of measurement and the techniques of social-science experimentation are very far from perfect, they are the best methods available today. We should not reject them merely because they are as yet inadequate. Even modern medical diagnosis and therapy have serious shortcomings, but nobody refuses the help of his doctor on the ground that medical science still has not achieved perfection.

It is heartening to find that within the past four or five years more studies and much better studies than ever before have been made of various aspects of racial and religious prejudice. The increasing utilization of modern scientific techniques is owing largely to the fact that several national community-relations agencies (notably the American Jewish Committee and the Commission on Community Interrelations of the American Jewish Congress) as well as some universities (including the University of California, Chicago University, Purdue University, and the University of Michigan) have recognized the validity and importance of this type of social-science research. Some highly commendable work has also been done in this field at the Massachusetts Institute of Technology.

As Dr. Williams has pointed out in *Reduction of Group Tensions*, prejudice, in a general sense, is an inevitable and universal feature of social life, but "there is a great difference between 'prejudices' against social positions such as employers, ministers, labor leaders, radio commentators, professors, landlords, et cetera, on the one hand, and prejudices against racial or cultural groups on the other." The latter type of prejudice he correctly described as "a negative attitude which violates some important norms or values nominally accepted in the culture." In other words, prejudice against people because of an activity in which they are engaged—hiring people, renting houses, publishing newspapers, et cetera—is one thing. But prejudice against a group whose members perform many different functions in society—which include employers and employees, land-lords and tenants, merchants and customers, et cetera—is a quite different thing. We know far too little about these wholly irrational prejudices. Because of the intricate and variable nature of prejudice, because each of its complex elements is dependent upon many psychological and environmental factors, any reliable, accurate diagnosis is a colossal undertaking. If we are to find effective therapies, we must utilize every source of sound information.

What is actually occurring today is that the researchers are at the same time and often by the same experiments learning the facts about prejudices and also how to measure those prejudices more reliably. We have good reason to expect from their efforts increasingly dependable results. From their studies there emerge some findings which have immediate value to those engaged in the day-to-day struggle with prejudice. Other findings cannot by any stretch of the imagination be turned to immediate account, although in the long run they may well be of even greater value. When, for example, we learn by scientific study that a confirmed anti-Negro bigot, instead of revising his opinions, merely resents a motion picture in which a Negro is the hero, we can put the knowledge to some account. At least we know that a certain technique will not help with certain people. But when we are told that a study indicates that in the main people in the highest financial and lowest financial brackets are more anti-Semitic than those in the middle brackets, no practical application of that knowledge suggests itself. Especially is this true when one realizes that in each of the three brackets there are individuals who are violently anti-Semitic and others who have no antipathy toward Jews. The person who must face the problems of fighting prejudice wants to know what it is that makes certain individuals deviate from the average reaction of people who otherwise are very much like him. He also wants to know, concretely and practically, what he should do as a practitioner to reduce the extent of prejudice. But no matter how urgently we need specific, applicable information, we should not deny to the researcher the time he needs to make a conscientious scientific study—the only kind which will suffice.

In recent years polls and polling techniques have had such spectacular publicity that any consideration of research must include some discussion of their relation to the scientific method. If for no other reasons they should be scrutinized because of the discredit which certain misuses of polling reflect upon conscientious researchers and because of the considerable social damage they do under the guise of informing the public.

Factual polls have highly legitimate uses. They merely and simply report the facts about some particular situation. Factual polls do not attempt to reveal people's thinking, nor do they pretend to uncover the reasons for people's attitudes. They can describe what people *do*. In connection with a well-planned campaign, a factual poll on discrimination may well be used to publicize the handicaps endured by Victimians. Even when so used, however, a poll should be confined to specific, concrete facts pertinent to the issue. The discovered facts should be presented in order to stimulate action, to secure passage or enforcement of a law, change an administrative practice, or obtain some other positive result.

Attitude polls, on the other hand, concerning the unpopularity of racial or religious groups, serve no beneficent purpose. The techniques are fallacious and the results are highly misleading if divulged to the public. Two social scientists, H. J. Eysenck and S. Crown, made an experimental and methodical study of national stereotypes and published the results in the *International Journal of Opinion and Attitude Research*. They found that whereas stereotyped replies to questions concerning group stereotypes presumably indicate a great amount of stereotyped thinking on the part of the respondent, that is not necessarily the case. When challenged to reply to a question to which he has no answer, the subject falls back on a stereotype he has heard about, even when he does not believe it to be accurate. Asked whether or not he believes a certain stereotype to be true, despite the fact that he has never seriously accepted it, he may well say, "Yes." Confront people suddenly with absurd questions about the Turks, the Chinese, the Hottentots, or any other group, and they will come up with absurd answers.

The replies to public polls on attitudes of groups of people depend largely on how they are framed or how they are worded. You need only ask, "Would you take a Victimian into your home as a boarder?" to get an 80 per cent negative response and draw the conclusion that people dislike Victimians. But ask, "Are Victimians entitled to decent treatment?" and you will get a better than 80 per cent in the affirmative, from which you might justifiably conclude that the Victimians are not greatly disliked after all. The simple and undeniable fact that the polls overlook is that people imply different things even when they furnish the same answer. One person may hate Victimians worse than poison and yet be so law-abiding that he would not disturb the hair on the head of one. Another may barely dislike them but be the hothead who throws his words and his fists against almost anyone, including Victimians. How can two such "attitudes" be added together so as to make a total which means anything?

It can hardly be denied that publicizing scurrilous *questions* about a racial or religious group in the public press is a serious injury to that group. Whatever the "facts" which the poll may offer as a result of the questionnaire, the suggestion planted in the mind of the reader is dangerous and damaging. During World War II a similar method was consciously and deliberately employed by the Italian Fascists when they attempted at Hitler's behest to stir up anti-Jewish feelings among the Italians. The Italian-Christian public was completely devoid of anti-Semitism and *would have scorned openly anti-Semitic propaganda*. But slyly and with considerable success some Italian journalists, by merely asking insulting questions about Jews, were able to plant invidious ideas in people's minds. How can the American public fail to be affected by the questions and statistics it reads in the polls?

I have contemplated taking a poll concerning a certain agency which publicizes unpopularity polls about groups. I would ask in my questionnaire, "Do you think that this agency rigs its figures to suit the people who pay for their polls?" "Would you trust its figures or do you consider them dishonest?" Not all of the answers would be favorable to the polling agency. But regardless of the answers, publication of the questions would teach publicizers of such polls something they have refused to recognize about the effect of derogatory polls on public opinion.

If the unprejudiced portion of the public would or could pursue a different course of action by being told in the newspapers that a certain group is suspected and scorned by 39 per cent of the population (whereas they might otherwise have thought it was 29 or 49), it might somehow make a bit of sense to publish such polls. But the programs for promoting better human relationships are inevitably the same for you and for your neighbors regardless of such an annual poll figure concerning any group. What can you do differently, except perchance that you may find your job of breaking down barriers all the harder if people say, "Oh, those Victimians! Lots of people hate them! It's been proved by a survey!"

Scientific research, on the other hand, is a positive, constructive force. If it is intelligently applied with an eye to methods of reducing racial and religious intolerance, we shall surely be enabled to secure better results in our efforts to reduce its extent. Every well-established and thoroughly validated bit of fact will make the discovery of further facts more feasible. Meanwhile the practitioner must continue to place considerable faith in his own experimental knowledge. The practical strategist should not be expected to accept an idea merely because it has been labeled "scientific research." Practitioners who have had training in scientific methods are as skeptical of flimsy explorations and of skewed deductions as any researcher could be.

The most useful approach to fighting prejudice—which is, after all, a social phenomenon—is the blending of efforts of the social scientist and the social practitioner, for neither alone can effectively deal with the social problems of prejudice. Perhaps together they can, within a more rational framework, forge more useful and effective techniques for diminishing the harm of prejudice.

Assuming that you are not a social scientist, what can you do to help those engaged in research on prejudice against racial and religious groups?

You should discourage poll takers who publicize adverse attitudes toward specific racial and religious groups. All groups are entitled to equal respect and none should be a recurrent object of a poll's disrespect. *Facts* concerning discriminatory practices, on the other hand, are useful since *direct specific* measures can be taken to eliminate them. These facts should be used to prevent and eliminate actual malpractices and never publicized in the vague hope that they may somehow do some good.

You should reject pseudo-scientific findings based on inadequate investigations. Beware of broad, sweeping conclusions about group relationships based upon trivial experiments. Require that "scientific findings" be exact and precise.

You should encourage intensive studies employing valid research methods. Be patient in awaiting results of such studies, for they require a vast amount of work and considerable time to complete. Familiarize yourself with the best-known concepts concerning group relationships and use the best methods of coping with prejudice that you can currently obtain. Be thoroughly willing to modify an opinion or a method of combating prejudice whenever scientific research furnishes grounds for doing so.

CHAPTER 5

Bystanders, More or Less Innocent

A publisher (whom we shall rename "Harning") questioned the patriotic loyalty of Victimians. With what he considered to be admirable fairness he said in a lengthy editorial that *some* of the specific group are loyal Americans and then railed against the presumably disloyal Victimians. To his surprise a shower of rebuking letters from members of the group he cited struck his desk. Some flayed him. Some canceled subscriptions. One correspondent confined his entire message to two words: "Drop dead." The virulence of these Victimians spurred Harning into more slashing attacks. He printed the stupid letters with a scorching rejoinder. Immediately his "Letters-to-the-Editor" column turned into a debating platform in which Victimians were denounced and defended on the score of patriotism and in regard to other personal attributes.

Harning, a wealthy, well-entrenched political kingpin and the owner of the only newspaper in the immediate vicinity, became too incensed to listen to reason. In the course of the controversy he was able to issue figures indicating that neither circulation nor advertising suffered from the dispute. It was the local Victimians who suffered while Harning's ego waxed fat on the proud assumption that he was manfully defending freedom of speech. To defeat a man through the columns of his own periodical is even more difficult than punching him in the nose with his own fist. In this instance the situation was made even more difficult since there was no other way to reach his readers without resorting to direct mailings at tremendous expense. Harning was very fair in one respect. He published pro-and-con letters without partiality. There did appear a few splendid letters from non-Victimians but these were completely overshadowed by anti-Victimian epistles and the blistering effusions from overwrought Victimians which did more damage to their cause than the malicious ones.

Several Victimians who had long been on the friendliest terms with Harning held lengthy but fruitless conversations with the embattled publisher. Their pleading was based, as were the defensive letters, on the assumption that what Harning was doing was wrong because his opinion about Victimians was wrong. They argued that Victimians are not disloyal or lacking in patriotism. Harning replied acidly that he was not indicting all Victimians. He had accused only *some* of them. Harning's real mistake (which some vaguely sensed but none stated clearly) was that he had aroused suspicion and malice against *all* Victimians, good and bad alike, by the very nature of his attack. Had he named individuals and said, "These people are disloyal," he could not properly have been accused of spreading intolerance against the group. But since he named no individuals and did not limit his accusation to specified readily identifiable persons, his accusation was, in effect, an attack against the group. Obviously it was quite impossible for each Victimian to come before the public and prove that this broadside accusation did not apply to him. And yet there was no other way to answer Harning's allegations. It was not Harning's intention, in fact, to indict the whole group. He felt that he had made that clear and that those he was attacking were open to criticism. He overlooked the fact that unless an accusation carries with it some ready means of distinguishing the sheep from the goats, it is inadvisable to make it publicly. "Name names and call your shots" is a legitimate request.

In any event, the letter-to-the-editor writers missed the main issue by a mile and argued about the loyalty of Victimians as though all were patriotic or as though all were unpatriotic, while Mr. Harning insisted on his right to free speech, overlooking the fact that he was raising a questionable issue in (to say the least) a tactless way. The chorus of nitwit eloquence reached a crescendo in a full page of letters before some sensible Victimians decided to take this matter out of the center of public interest by shifting attention to other matters. This they did by writing letters to the editor on various matters and launching some new newspaper controversies. With plenty of other letters to publish, Mr. Harning was wise enough to put into his wastebasket all further communications on the qualities of the Victimians as well as the bouquets and brickbats directed at him.

I have told this story here because of one significant episode in it. Two weeks after Harning's editorial had started this Battle of the Bilge, a Victimian attended a meeting of clergymen. For two hours they insisted that the Harning controversy was altogether his problem and in no way theirs. They saw no reason why they should become involved in it. Finally they asked, "What can any intelligent person want in reference to this flow of nonsense except that it should cease as soon as possible? If individually or collectively we issue statements it would only increase the torrent of absurd correspondence."

The clergymen were quite right in preferring not to prolong the public controversy. But they had failed to grasp the essential question. Having been shown the basic issues, they received the matter differently.

"Yes," they said wholeheartedly. "This is *our* problem and one we should not dodge. Tell us what to do. We want to do our share toward ending this ridiculous attack on a group of our fellow citizens."

Specific incidents, properly employed, provide opportunities to interest bystanders. They can be utilized to arouse people who evidently feel that racial and religious prejudices do not impinge upon their own lives and therefore require no attention on their part. But merely publicizing an account of an incident will not accomplish that. The clergymen in this case knew full well what had been going on; they had read the newspaper daily. Someone had to prove to them—and mind you, these were ministers, men sensitive to public issues—that this called for action on their part, that this was not just one more interesting story. When aroused to a recognition of their responsibility they planned a continuous program to improve group relations in their city.

Even among thoughtful, socially minded people there are many to whom intolerance presents no challenge and who think "someone" ought to do something about it, but not they.

That racial and religious prejudices ultimately injure us all (although the harm done directly to some exceeds the indirect harm to others) is not a sufficiently dynamic concept. We must also face the fact that intolerance cannot be eliminated if only those who feel its direct impact undertake to combat it. This is as logical as the proposition that a man's property would not be safe if he alone, and not the community, sought to protect it. There should be a sense of mutual responsibility for the eradication of racial and religious prejudice, no matter whom it directly victimizes, comparable to the sense of responsibility we feel for the security of our neighbors against the threat of crime.

How far can we expect our neighbors to go in the struggle against prejudice? In a Florida city a community-relations agency was determined to engage a Negro secretary. In the office building where she was to work no other Negroes were employed. Since this girl could not use the washroom designated for white women only, the organization built a washroom for her. It was difficult to meet this and other problems created by Jim Crow legislators who would have frowned upon the employment of a Negro woman as a secretary in a lily-white office building. But how much further should the community-relations agency have gone in its policy of equal treatment for people of all races? Should the young woman have been urged to resist the restrictions by violating them? Should she have insisted on using the hitherto only available women's washroom? I think not. Some good was certainly achieved in this instance without going to an extreme whereby more would have been lost in the battle of public opinion than could have been gained. Valor is not enough in combating intolerance. Wisdom is a valuable—some say it is the best—part of valor.

Some individuals and organizations are ready and even eager to go all out on fighting crusades against well-established practices which reek of social and religious intolerance. Others, like the proverbial people who are "against sin," are quick to condemn intolerance provided they are not required to take a stand in reference to actual instances of intolerance. These more hesitant folk are anxious not to lose the good will of customers, neighbors, or friends whose prejudices they fear to step on. In their advertisements, national advertisers do not picture Negroes playing the ordinary roles of smokers, drinkers, housewives, bathers, et cetera, even though some of these advertisers would gladly do so as far as their own feelings in the matter are concerned. But there is the prejudiced element in the population to be considered! Catering to the wishes of the intolerant makes many a person a silent partner in discriminatory practices, though he has no personal liking for these subtle cruelties.

In enlisting recruits for the struggle against intolerance it is unwise and unrealistic to characterize each person as "for the elimination of racial and religious prejudice" or "against" it. Nor is it possible to force a person to commit himself by "signing on the dotted line." Insisting merely raises the question: "Which dotted line?" There are a whole series of lines, representing numerous shades of opinion, and these lines very often cut across social groups and organizational affiliations. One may be prejudiced against one racial or religious group and not against others. A woman may belong to the Daughters of the American Revolution and not be prejudiced against Negroes even though the D.A.R. has barred Negro artists from its Convention Hall. A subscriber to an organization which is dedicated to the eradication of prejudice may be a member of a social club which excludes Victimians. There is no measure of thought and action on matters of prejudice by which one can determine an individual's attitudes as one would grade apples. The subject is far too complex.

Think of a few of your own friends, and ask yourself on which of the following lines each of them would be willing to sign:

I am opposed to racial and religious intolerance.

I would voice my objections to any of my acquaintances if he uttered an intolerant statement.

I wish that there were no discrimination in employment against persons because of race or religion.

I employ persons of races other than my own as readily as I employ persons of my own race.

I would like to see a national fair employment law passed to forbid discrimination.

I am willing to spend several hours each week in a door-to-door campaign to obtain signatures for a fair employment practice act.

I would as readily stop at a commercial hotel which is open to people of all races as at one whose clientele is limited to white people.

I would as readily patronize a resort hotel open to people of all races and creeds as one whose guests are exclusively of my own race and creed.

I shall urge the owner of the resort hotel I patronize to accept guests without regard to race or religion.

You can expand this list indefinitely. There are generalities to which almost everyone would assent and specific proposals wherein the gamut of opinion runs from a vigorous "yes" to an equally vigorous "no" with many shades of half-hearted uncertainty between.

In the battle against intolerance some people go along readily on certain projects but not on others. Even among the would-be saints there are shades of difference in respect to what they will and will not do and in the extent to which they will accept certain leadership. Even when wholehearted in their condemnation of intolerance, some people are inhibited by caution or fear of exacerbating the prejudices of others. They will not change in a day from passive well-wishers into ardent crusaders, although in due time many of them may become much more active. Enlisting allies involves obtaining from each person the maximum amount of aid that that person is willing to render. This is not enrolling people in a political party. It is more nearly comparable to building a national movement on behalf of mental health. No one organization takes care of all aspects of an undertaking of such magnitude and complexity.

Of all the mistaken strategies for enlisting the public in the battle against prejudice none is more certain to fail than what I would call "the pious exaggeration." To announce publicly that prejudice is growing in extent and to publicize an alleged increase in the number of people who hate one group or another is as fatuous as it is dangerous. That does not make bystanders want to take up the cudgels. It makes them believe they are better off staying out of it. Certainly merchants are less inclined to employ Negro sales-people if they have been led to believe that anti-Negro prejudice is rife in their neighborhood, and especially if they are told that it is increasing. You may rely upon the bigots to exaggerate the extent of prejudice. That justifies their own attitudes. You can also let them build their own bandwagon without assistance from those who wish to diminish intolerance.

To enlist others in the anti-intolerance ranks we should furnish whatever evidence is available that intergroup friendships are growing, that intolerance is on the way out, that the wave of the future is carrying us toward a more just and equitable relationship. Intolerance should be branded as an unworthy and often loathsome survival from the past, something to be sloughed off as we become more civilized. Meanwhile, before the goal is achieved we cannot afford to spurn whatever honest co-operation can be obtained from those less active than ourselves. The arena of public opinion is vast and, since there are still not enough workers willing to practice in their own daily lives unequivocal equality unmarred by racial and religious prejudice, we should welcome allies who go part of the way with us. That includes many who do not feel prepared to strike as hard as we are willing to strike now at specific abuses —provided, of course, they do not attempt to tie our hands. This is not a controversy wherein each person is 100 per cent friend or else 100 per cent foe. Most people are at present to some extent intolerant and to some extent opposed to intolerance. Unless we are willing to move ahead with scouting parties, advance units, front ranks, rear ranks, and even a rear guard, we shall have a tiny force of insignificant strength.

Rather than reject and antagonize well-intentioned laggards, we should persuade people to move upward in the scale of interest and effort. We shall enlist more recruits by encouragement than by denunciation.

While I am opposed to alarmist outcries about the prevalence of prejudice, I would urge utmost publicity for specific instances that call for rectification. Events which no decent person would condone and which reveal the disgraceful results of intolerance can be used effectively, especially if workers in every community are prepared to tell others what they can do to remove the underlying causes of these shameful incidents. For example, it is well worth publicizing the story of the fifty boy scouts of New York City who had won a trip to Washington, D.C., but who lost their cherished opportunity to visit their nation's capital because no Washington hotel would house a mixed group of whites and Negroes. The boys, true to their scouting ideals, refused to separate into segregated hotels. To reveal instances of fellowship between members of the various groups encourages others to enter into similar comradeship. To draw the curtain from obscure lives and homes crushed by intolerance is beneficial if the impact arouses a desire to terminate the evil. Wailing about the suffering of *millions* is relatively ineffective. It is the difference between announcing that a thousand men have been killed in battle and telling of the life and death of just one of them. Specific issues properly presented to the public, setting forth steps to be taken to eliminate intolerance of one form or another, are bet-ter than a vague message urging good will in broad, vague terms. I do not say that a well-worded message with a good illustration is valueless unless it proposes specific action to be taken, but I do say that a definite suggestion on which the reader can act is better. "Let's all be friends" is less cogent than "If a Victimian is a good ballplayer, let's have him on our team."

Any attempt to interest the particular individuals with whom you are in contact in eradicating intolerance should begin with finding out first what the other person's attitude is. A period of explorative questioning should precede the statement of your own views. It is necessary to begin where the other fellow is when we seek to convey our own enthusiasms. If he is an incorrigible bigot, don't waste your breath. If he is at all sympathetic, you may, if you exercise some patience, lead him nearer to your own views.

PART FIVE

New Instruments—New Hopes

CHAPTER 1

Community Relations Organizations— Their Purposes

Three scientists were working together in a laboratory one midnight at the crucial moment when years of experimentation on physostigmine were brought to culmination. This was the test by which they would learn whether they could synthesize a drug for the treatment of glaucoma, an eye disease for which there had previously been no satisfactory relief. If the natural crystals of physostigmine in one tube and the synthetic crystals in another melted at the same temperature, their long labors would not have been in vain. While the three men waited breathlessly, the crystals in both tubes melted with the thermometers registering exactly the same.

As reported by Paul de Kruif in an article in *The Reader's Digest* (August 1946), "Old Professor Blanchard, white man from the Deep South, Josef Pikl, the German colleague, and Percy Julian, the Negro, threw their arms around one another. Their eyes were dim with happiness."

When men of different races, religions, and nationalities achieve an objective by their common efforts, even their most ingrained prejudices melt away and are forgotten in the adventure of creative travail. The primary problem is to get individuals of varying backgrounds to work together amicably. Because Dean Blanchard was undeterred by the racial prejudice of some of his colleagues he was able to recognize Julian's unique abilities, invited him to De Pauw to guide senior students, was instrumental in raising money for

Julian's research. Humanity has profited by Julian's discovery. It has profited just as tangibly by Blanchard's integrity—by the straight thinking that made Julian's work possible.

The history of science and art furnishes examples of a fine and productive spirit of co-operation. As individuals, thousands of workers in many fields have submerged petty prejudices in order to achieve a common goal. And although we have appreciated the manifest advantages to society which grew out of such co-operation, we have been incredibly slow in recognizing the benefits which we might reap by *systematically* fostering better group relations between the members of various racial and religious groups. The damaging effects of prejudice too often go unnoticed by those not directly victimized. In recent years, however, and chiefly in the United States, there has sprung up a network of organizations designed to deal with the problems of group relations which had hitherto been solved only by chance and circumstance—or, more often, left unsolved. These organizations—more than 90 per cent of which have come into being since 1935—have already demonstrated that organized effort, planned programs, and methodical procedures are remarkably helpful not only in preventing destructive clashes but also in creating a vital and productive co-operative spirit in the community.

The term "Community Relations" has come into vogue only within the last few years. The very concept is comparatively new. Borrowing as it does from several of the older sciences and arts, community relations has some of the characteristics of each and cannot properly be classed with either group. Most accurately defined, it is a *social methodology*, a flexible set of principles and practices enlivened by a purpose.

The *community*, as it is used in this context, is composed of people with a common interest based on proximity or shared experiences. The community may be as small as a village or as large as a nation. For practical purposes community-relations activities are conceived as national, regional, and local. The "region" is generally a state and the "local" is usually equivalent to a city.

Excellent statements of purpose have been issued by community-relations agencies. From among these I quote a portion of *The Credo*, issued by the Committee for the City and County of Henderson (Kentucky):

The Committee is more than an organization. It is a faith in the ideology of democracy. It is a physical embodiment of the belief that men and women—citizens of the same community—can assemble from different interests and occupations, from different racial stocks and religions, from different political affiliations, from different social and economic positions, and by subordinating special interests to general interests, can thereby achieve a richer, fuller community life than is otherwise obtainable. It is the belief that our biggest problems are held in common—disease and health, ignorance and enlightenment, poverty and prosperity, bad and good government, the conditions of housing, availability of recreational facilities, adequacy of public buildings, development of needed civic enterprises. All of these are problems and projects in which all citizens hold a common responsibility and for which solutions can come through community-wide co-operation. We propose now to get the facts about our community, to put together the blueprints for a greater city and county, and to work together to bring our visions and plans into reality. God helping us, we shall not fail.

Stated in their broadest terms, the objectives of one intergroup agency resemble rather closely the objectives of any other. The Board of Community Relations of the City of Buffalo is charged "with the task of helping to eliminate the reasons for conflict between groups and to foster the spirit of democracy in keeping with the traditions which have made this country great."

The Buffalo organization is part of the government of the City of Buffalo. It functions under the authority of city ordinances and has the advantages and disadvantages of all bodies financed by government officials. The intergroup organizations established by municipalities have greater official authority than do the voluntary private agencies working for the same purposes. As long as those in political control are favorable, their income is more readily obtainable than that of agencies dependent on voluntary contributions. Tax-supported agencies have presumably a more official and hence more effective approach to government departments, bureaus, and personnel.

Groups functioning as part of the governmental setup are not,

however, so free to criticize the political administration which supplies their funds and appoints their policy makers. If the political
leaders are adverse to the aims of the organization they can often
prevent the achievement of those very purposes which community-
relations bodies should serve, and still point to the agency as proof
of their interest in combating discrimination. Undoubtedly there is
ample room and reason for both types of intergroup agencies—the
voluntary and the government-maintained. In a number of large
cities both types now function in constant co-operation.

The organizations designed to improve group relationships have
grown up in topsy-turvy fashion. Their programs and policies vary,
their specific interests vary, and they do not always agree upon
methodologies. To classify these agencies into neat categories is
impossible. Some work on a national scale; some devote their efforts
to a state or region; and others serve a single city. There are agencies
composed solely of members of one racial or religious group, as well
as non-sectarian and interracial organizations of mixed membership.
Some concentrate on education and some on social action. Some are
highly specialized while others have a very wide range of activities.

Margaret Hickey in *The Ladies' Home Journal* of December 1947
credited "262 local communities, 34 state commissions, and 118
national or state agencies" with effort "to improve racial or religious
understanding." The number of local agencies has grown since then
and is constantly increasing.

National community-relations agencies under the auspices of particular racial or religious groups have come into being as the direct
result of intolerance suffered by members of those groups. Some of
the national agencies have set up local branches. These branches of
national agencies outnumber the purely local intergroup agencies.
The former have the advantage of a close and constant contact
with members who fully appreciate their value and more readily
contribute to their support. These agencies not only carry on educational programs within their own groups but also attempt to inte-
grate their group into the larger community. If they are to be
effective at all, they must keep their gaze on the *entire* public, not
merely their own part of it. They cannot operate successfully without
bringing members of their own groups into friendly contact with
members of other groups. Intensive work in the field has convinced
all groups that defending Victimians against intolerant attacks is

not half so important, and its effects are not nearly so lasting, as the defense and promotion of those principles of democratic life which assure security and justice for *everyone*.

A local Victimian community-relations agency recently received a phone call from a man who wanted to know whether it was interested in defending people wrongly accused by a member of their group.

"We certainly are," was the reply.

"I am running for re-election to office in a suburb of this city," said the man. "It happens that two years ago I was invited to speak at a meeting of an organization that was new then and which seemed on the surface to have good purposes. I made some inquiries and learned nothing unfavorable about the organization. A few of the members of the organization were personally known to me as decent citizens. At the meeting I was horrified to hear a tirade against your group by a visiting speaker. I had already delivered my talk. I could not get the floor again, so I stalked out in indignation. So did my friends. Today everyone knows that that organization is a hate-fomenting outfit. To have one's name associated with it is a political liability. In order to defeat me an opposing candidate has reprinted a newspaper article which announced that I was to speak at that meeting. I am being falsely accused of being hostile to your group. Can you help me? Will you help me?"

Within forty-eight hours the community-relations agency had investigated and had learned that the candidate for re-election was a broad-minded, unprejudiced person. Using its moral influence among the Victimians of that suburb, the Victimian community-relations agency by telephone and by word of mouth was able to counteract the ill effect of the misleading reprint that was being circulated as a handbill. While the community-relations agency would never participate in a political contest by endorsing any candidate, it did authorize this one to say in addressing audiences wherein Victimians were present that his record had been examined and that no evidence had been found of prejudice or unfairness against members of that group.

The ideals for which community-relations agencies strive are sufficient to recommend them to any thoughtful person. The actual accomplishments of these groups are, however, even more convincing proof of their value than their statements of purpose. Often their activities are too little appreciated simply because a large part of their work is not, and cannot by its nature be, publicized without lessening its value. They have allayed dangerous fears, stimulated civic improvements, and harnessed for communal progress valuable resources previously squandered. Their most laudable successes are seldom fully recognized because their efforts are usually merged with those of other organizations. Their influence has often been greatest when it was least dramatic. What man is a hero in the eyes of his neighbors because he prevented a fire? A conflagration that never occurred makes no exciting headlines.

It is inspiring to think of a group of people without fear, anxiety, or alarm forming and maintaining an organization to improve group relationships. Imagine a group of Americans getting together and saying to one another, "It's mighty nice the way people of various races and religions live together in our community. We have no disturbing cases of friction here; there has never been an outbreak of violence due to prejudice in our city. Yet, all things considered, conditions could be better. Greater co-operation between members of the different groups, better understanding of each other, and opportunities for mutual helpfulness should be cultivated. What if intolerance is not rampant in our midst? Let's proceed now to build greater friendships and to work for still better relationships. Let's not be satisfied with having fulfilled a large part of the American dream. Let's try to make the whole dream come true."

That *would* be splendid. Actually, it rarely, if ever, happens. Here and there an idealist recognizes a social need long before it becomes a critical necessity. But unless there has been a recent startling event or unless there have been unmistakable portents of danger, the proponents of well-organized and consistently sustained community-relations activities often encounter complaceny and apathy. Their proposals are countered with such remarks as, "Why look for trouble? Why waste funds and energies? Let well enough alone. What are you worrying about?" On the other hand, if those who are proposing the new organization can point to a disturbing incident or two, they may meet with enthusiastic response: "Great idea! Let's go!" And then in a very short time, as the disturbance fades into the past, a cloud of indifference settles upon the rank and file. The few earnest toilers look in vain for traces of the evanescent public interest.

About nine years ago I spent half a morning urging an influential citizen to sponsor the formation of a local community-relations organization among the members of his religious group. He insisted that such an organization would have very little, if anything, to do because there wasn't any "trouble."

"Look at it this way," I urged. "A man does not work to build financial assets only when bankruptcy is imminent or when things are going badly for him. It is by improving his economic situation right along that a man avoids bankruptcy and offsets his losses. Community relations need bettering all of the time and not only when spiritual insolvency arrives or is in the offing. There is plenty of constructive work to be done toward bettering community relations every day of the year."

I made no headway. Wishful thinking had convinced this man that intolerance was virtually non-existent in his city. He would not be budged from that cherished notion.

When I left him I went into a second-rate stationery store. On an improbable chance I asked for a copy of a hate sheet that had a large national circulation at that time. The stationer eyed me a moment and then fished a copy out from under his counter.

"I don't like this paper," he told me furtively, "but a few of my customers ask for it."

I visited about a dozen other magazine shops. In three of them I was able to buy the hate publication. Nowhere was it on display, but copies were available. I returned to the man's office with the magazines under my arm. He was horrified and carefully noted the names and addresses of the stores where I had made my purchases. That three little newsdealers had sold a few copies of an objectionable periodical was of insignificant consequence compared to the scores of better reasons for fostering a local community-relations agency. But to the local bigwig this was (as I expected) of paramount importance.

Without any urging he now summoned some of his friends to meet me that evening. They were similarly impressed. I used the opening provided by the hate sheets to outline what I considered far more cogent reasons for a community-relations program. But all that really seemed to concern these men was how to stop the trickle of that hate publication into their city. They kept on reverting to that one subject. It was as though I were trying to tell them about erecting a power plant to utilize the flow of a nearby river and all they were willing to think about was the spill from the drain of one little roof.

That occurred some years ago. Today there is greater receptivity for long-range community-relations programing. Yet in most places the desire to annihilate any suddenly bothersome thorn exceeds the attention paid to whole thickets of ever-present brambles. What wondrous opportunities go by default daily!

I dwell upon this peculiarity of the public mind toward matters involving group relationships because it has a profound effect—and a hurtful one—on the progress of group-relations agencies and especially upon the propaganda used to justify their existence. First, the idea that community-relations programs are necessary only to combat *bad* situations prevents the establishment of local agencies with adequate staffs and year-round programs. Civic leaders insist that there isn't enough trouble. A few influential individuals can be entrusted with the job of bringing the occasional outspoken bigots to account. If it's only "cops and robbers" that needs playing, volunteer players who enjoy the excitement are willing and ready, even though the results they achieve are sometimes questionable. Second, a childish sense of achievement resulting from clashes with hostile individuals or groups often makes it necessary to use a scare technique in raising funds for community-relations agencies. A constructive job of bettering group relations day in and day out has far less appeal to prospective contributors than spectacular instances of tilting with enemies. In order to get the support of some groups in the community incidents of animosity are sometimes exaggerated, with complete disregard of perspective, and members of minority groups are needlessly agitated. Third, since community-relations agencies are appreciated most when they seem to be rushing about stabbing villains, rather than building friendships, great professional devotion to the cause is required to concentrate on unobtrusive matters of genuine (but not thrilling) social profit. As long as the public lacks a desire to lay up favorable assets in community relations and desires only the calm, peaceful serenity of gradual deterioration, the promotionally minded will be able to capitalize on individual instances of intolerance even when these are of comparatively little consequence.

Community-relations agencies should certainly deal with instances of overt prejudice whenever they occur. They should take them in stride. They need to keep track of professional troublemakers and agitators in order to hold these schemers in check. I am not attempting to minimize this aspect of their work. But overemphasis upon this, the negative phase of their program, is a costly mistake. Cleaning out occasional weeds is by no means the major purpose of community relations. The chief job is to plant, cultivate, and nourish strong, healthy vegetation that will crowd the weeds out of existence. Just as a department store needs a complaint department, the community-relations agencies need knowledges, skills, and personnel to take care of misdeeds and of miscreants who foment or take advantage of group prejudices. But no department store considers its major purpose to be the maintenance of a complaint department. Community-relations organizations should not be content with meeting emergencies from day to day. Rather, they should be engaged in dynamic undertakings that will bring about large-scale improvements. The daily accomplishment will be necessarily small, but the aggregate of gains in the course of even a few years should be impressive.

How well community-relations agencies will accomplish their purposes will depend largely upon the special skills developed by professional workers who are proficient in their specialized fields of endeavor. A needed step in the direction of bringing together the workers of various agencies was taken in November 1947, when the National Association of Intergroup Relations Officials was founded. It will not be enough, however, for individual professional community-relations workers to meet in an association. The agencies they represent also need to become more united than they have been in planning, in programing, and in accomplishing in unison the broad objectives to which all of them are dedicated.

Largely because the community-relations agencies are comparatively new in the field, some of them are beset by difficulties and disappointments. Eventually they may well gain recognition as an integral part of the community structure, as fully as worthy of support as any other social organism of our democracy. Meanwhile they must have the faith expressed by Charles W. Ferguson in *A Little Democracy Is a Dangerous Thing:* "I believe that democracy is educative, that it will provide the schooling the mass of us need, that it offers the training field for social advance, that even if the first fitful attempts at democracy should fail, later ones will find the people better prepared." Believing in the power of democracy to overcome the obstacles of indifference and ignorance, every community-relations worker should make certain that he brings to the service of democracy the greatest amount of knowledge, ability, and zeal that he can muster.

CHAPTER 2

The Possibilities of Community Relations Organizations

I had a phone call one afternoon from a student. He was, I am sure, a serious and unselfish young man, probably in his early twenties. I fear that I disappointed him.

"Seventeen of us who are taking summer courses at Columbia," he explained, "have formed a club to fight prejudice. We want to do something to abolish discrimination. A speaker at our meeting yesterday told us to consult you for help."

"What sort of help is it you wish?" I inquired.

"We want to do something. Not just study the subject or discuss group relationships. So far all we get is literature, and we're told to go out and educate other people. That's not what we want. We want to *do* something about prejudice."

I put as much friendliness as I could into my voice. "What do you mean by doing something?"

"That's why I'm calling you," he replied. "We don't know what to do. What would you suggest?"

At that point I was about to offer to send a skilled consultant to the group to explore with them the concrete problems within their immediate environment and to help them discover a project they might tackle directly. But the student forestalled that by saying, "We want no more speakers or discussions. We've had enough talk. Tell us what to *do*."

"Is it your opinion," I asked, "that educating ourselves and others is of no consequence?"

PUNISHMENT WITHOUT CRIME

"No. I guess that's useful too," he said haltingly, "but it's not the purpose of our club. We want to do something beyond that stage. We want results."

"Have you found out," I asked, "whether there are any discriminatory practices against racial and religious groups which injure or harass some of your fellow students? How about an inquiry to determine conditions in regard to their obtaining rooms, places to eat, or——?"

"No," he cut in, "that's just dawdling. We want to do something on a bigger scale than that. We want to attack the whole problem of prejudice."

I groaned inwardly. "Perhaps you can break the restrictive covenants around Harlem. How about selling some of the houses you own in the restricted area or how about inviting members of minority groups into the restaurants you run?"

"We don't own any houses or restaurants," was, as I expected, his reply.

"If you don't control an institution or situation," I said, "you can alter it only by influencing the people who do. That always requires educational efforts such as you say do not interest your group. Except for practicing in your own lives the things you advocate there is nothing much you can do that does not begin with obtaining a hearing for your views and getting them accepted."

He thought a moment before asking, "But isn't there some project you can suggest that we can undertake? We need something that will show results in a few weeks. We're only summer students."

"It seems to me," I replied, "that you came to Columbia because you do believe learning is essential. I can't understand your assuming that where intolerance is involved education is pointless. Of course if you wish to explore this further with me I might discover some job that might satisfy your group. I suggest that you come to my office for an hour."

He thanked me most graciously, but I never heard from him again. He had found my attitude unsatisfactory. What he wanted was a program for an immediate, smashing victory over intolerance —a program in which such prosaic tasks as inquiry, study, and discussion would be wholly unnecessary. Saint George slew his dragon without addressing meetings or listening to speeches, didn't he?

As a matter of fact, had I been able to talk to the young man for a while it is possible that we *could* have discovered a satisfactory project for his group—a situation in their own immediate environment which they could have altered quickly and decisively by their own conduct and example. Certainly we could *not* have found any outlet for this little group which would have had the momentous impact which they hazily hoped to achieve. They might have been persuaded to undertake some action which might serve as a catalytic agent, a precipitant, a model for other groups.

But no matter what course of action they might have chosen, the members of the group would have had to alter their thinking. They would have had to abandon the adolescent idea that somewhere there was one vital spot where they could attack prejudice and by their own heroic efforts forthwith destroy a huge block of it. The action of individuals may be of tremendous importance, but only in so far as it influences the action and thinking of others. To be effective on a large scale, a program or an activity or an idea must reach out to an ever-expanding circle of people. That extension of the effect can be achieved by any or all of the usual methods of communication—personal contacts, meetings, newspaper articles, radio programs, books, films, et cetera. Whatever the process by which it is attained, the problem is always to reach more people and persuade them to accept and act on certain ideas. Among community-relations workers this process of reaching out to widening circles of people and convincing them to promote democratic ideas and programs is called "education."

As one example of the educative process we cite the efforts made to acquaint people with the religious practices of other groups. The use of this type of education in community-relations activities is not to convert or proselytize anyone. Its purpose is to remove suspicions, fear, and contempt stemming from ignorance of the religious life of those whose religious institutions we do not normally visit. A score of processes have been employed to banish hurtful attitudes that result from not knowing the customs and practices of religious fellowships other than our own. Visiting a church or synagogue is the most direct and simple technique. But there are many who for one reason or another never happen to have that experience. Even for those who get a brief firsthand acquaintance with a neighboring religious institution supplementation is highly desirable. What could be more logical than to publish such books as *One God*, (by Florence Mary Fitch), in which ceremonies of Protestants, Catholics, and Jews are pictorially described? The book suggested a radio program which reached a far larger audience. But the radio program had only voice and sound effects. Why not a motion picture with its visual advantages? A motion picture having been made, why not televise it? And how much more educative the book or the motion picture becomes when accompanied by an intelligent discussion. Hence discussion guides are recommended. There are many instances where first a story appeared in a magazine, then a comic book was based on it, followed by the use of other media to bring home to more and more people, in more and more impressive ways, the lesson embodied in that story.

Although education is the major activity in community-relations work, it is not the only one. Beyond that there is something else known as "social action"—the application of forces greater than persuasion to a specific, limited target in order to establish a definite change in social practice. For example, the attempt to convince more and more people to open the doors of opportunity to non-whites in areas of employment formerly closed to them is rightly classified as education. It involves the use of one or more of the education techniques. But if you frame a specific piece of fair employment-practice legislation and press for its adoption, you embark upon a program of social action. When it is no longer a case of persuasion alone but involves an attempt to put a new law on the lawbooks or to change an old one or to win a court decision or an administrative ruling, social action is involved. Social action begins when the public is told, "Here is our proposal. We are asking the legislature . . ." Most authorities agree that before social action is attempted there should be a program of education to enlist considerable public opinion in favor of a proposed measure.

Where it is likely that the introduction of an FEPC measure will encounter inevitable defeat it is wiser to introduce a bill calling for a study by the legislature of the extent of discriminatory practices in employment. Similarly before urging fair education practice laws it may be better to have the legislature undertake to study the situation. There is less resistance on the part of state legislators to investigate such problems than to enact laws for their eradication. We note with regret that even requests for inquiries on discrimination have in some instances been rejected by legislatures. But such requests have better likelihood of passage than the statutes for which they are intended to pave the way. When a study has been made, the findings can be used to educate the legislators as well as the public.

At this stage most of the energies of those working in community relations necessarily are devoted to education. That doesn't imply that the workers are confined to advocating platitudinous principles of co-operation. Every agency has found that merely talking about "good will" and leaving its very meaning vague no longer satisfies any but the half-hearted. One specific practical application of the Golden Rule is more rewarding than endless repetition of the phrase, "Do unto others as thou wouldst have them do unto you."

I recall an interracial dinner held in a hall of a large Harlem church almost twenty years ago. The whites drifted in and took seats together while the Negroes clustered around other tables. I shall never forget that dinner because of an episode I witnessed at the counter where the cloaks of the visitors were being checked.

The men taking the wraps at the checkroom were Negroes and I daresay that they thought they were merely showing a proper courtesy to the white men and women, as a token of appreciation, when they deliberately ignored Negroes who were waiting and gave immediate attention to every white person who entered.

A Negro who had evidently been waiting a long time asked plaintively, "Won't you please take my coat?"

"We'll get around to you," he was told while several white persons who had just come in were beckoned to step up to the counter. This at a dinner to promote fair and equal treatment!

It would be an error, however, to write off "get-acquainted" programs and "good-will" gatherings as devoid of value. The mere fact that a Negro and a white minister exchange pulpits of a Sunday morning does some good. If you doubt that, try to imagine its happening in certain localities. No one can seriously deny that many a person's social status has been raised by his being invited to the home of a distinguished leader in the community. Social contact and purely educational programs are quite inadequate without supporting social action and direct efforts to terminate specific forms of discrimination. But they *are* decidedly beneficial. Those who insist that getting Victimians and non-Victimians together is of itself not at all valuable are underestimating the results of personal contact. There are no social calipers that can measure the aftereffect of an hour of intergroup fellowship. Yet what hate monger would be glad to hear that those he has been trying to drive apart have decided to spend a sociable hour together? A genuine demonstration of friendship between groups should never be despised.

The case for long-range social education was well stated by Lawrence Scott in his column in *The Call*, of Kansas City, Missouri: "A race relations institute, a race relations clinic, or even a small week-end seminar may not be impressive in its immediate results, but these are the plateaus of preparation necessary if there are to be continued inclines of progress. Even the smallest gesture of good-will becomes a part of the total pattern of social progress, just as even the smallest gesture of ill-will adds weight to the social lag and reaction."

A promising technique used by community-relations agencies is the community audit or survey. Although surveys are a comparatively new type of activity in this field, they are now generally considered an essential part of the work. This opinion is based upon the very sensible idea that before trying to eliminate discrimination in your town you should know what the situation is. Obviously a project in educating the local community may well lead to social action.

In June 1947 the Southern Regional Conference reported that as a result of two years of investigation and other efforts by Negro and white leaders in Jacksonville, Florida, sixty-five concrete improvements were made. They inquired into the health, housing, transportation, law enforcement, recreation, and welfare services available to the city's Negro population. Here are some of the accomplishments the follow-up committee reported as a result of friendly co-operation between members of both races in finding out the facts and "doing something" about them: Facilities were opened at the City Health Department to provide equal care for the dental needs of Negro and white children. A dental trailer now visits schools to care for the emergency cases in low-income families, both Negro and white. One hundred and twenty blocks in Negro residential sections were hard-surfaced. Garbage collection was started for the first time on twenty-five streets occupied by Negroes. Traffic and street lights were added. Bus service in the Negro area was increased 35 per cent. Pay of Negro teachers was equalized with that of whites beginning with the fall term of 1947 and three Negroes were placed on the salary schedule committee.

These are only some of the accomplishments in Jacksonville but they indicate what may result from a community survey provided a good committee or agency turns the acquired information to account.

Elsewhere in this book we have discussed the reasons for believing that you cannot improve matters by announcing the results of inquiries about people's *attitudes* toward presumably disliked groups. Usually when I say that it does more harm than good, someone replies, "But everyone knows it anyhow," and I answer, "Then why waste your breath telling them?" On the matter of pointing out the appalling conditions resulting from intolerance, where there are concrete tangible *conditions* to alter, I would be the first to say, "Let the public know!" Comfortable citizens are too often oblivious to what is happening in the slums; they do not feel the bruises and gashes inflicted by discrimination. They should be told. They should be convinced with carefully verified facts, not half-convinced with guesses. It is the job of community-relations agencies to make the complacent understand how the deprivations of Victimians are deleterious to the *entire* community, including their own part of it. They should be made to realize that rats breeding in filthy slums in their city spread disease to wealthier homes as well as hovels; that uncollected waste on the other side of the tracks may start a fire that will burn the handsomest houses in town.

Community-relations organizations are primarily public-opinion molders. The well-equipped agencies use many of the methods employed by public-relations and advertising agencies. A great deal of valuable information is freely available on the simple mechanics of getting one's message effectively to the greatest number of people. For example, it can be determined whether a particular message can more effectively be conveyed by radio, or in a magazine article, or in a film, or in a pamphlet. It can be shown that not only the media but also the manner of presentation is tremendously important. A community-relations agency cannot afford to stumble about blindly, trying to find its own answer to questions of this sort when expert advice is obtainable. Today most community-relations agencies are well aware that enough people cannot be reached for the accomplishment of their purposes without resort to media of mass communication. How much is done with radio broadcasts, films, film strips, pamphlets, news articles, and the like, depends upon how much funds and what personnel are available to produce these or to put to use the products of other agencies.

A community-relations agency which employs its funds and resources to best advantage can never afford to ignore the quality in terms of craftsmanship of an item offered for publication or promotion. A playlet which elicits high praise in the school where it was written does not necessarily warrant the cost of printing in the hope that it will be used elsewhere. Six radio transcriptions which had won applause when presented on a local station were sent to me in the hope that my agency would undertake the expense of making recordings to be sent to many other communities for use in their radio stations. But while it was true that these radio programs were as admirable as amateur actors could make them and while they were appreciated as the product of home talent, the dramatic quality of the voices, the sound effects, and the music were inferior in quality to what professional actors and expert musicians furnish. Had we sent copies of these recordings to radio station managers who would judge them by the high standards of other transcriptions furnished to them they would have been rejected. A community-relations agency is in competition for public attention with innumerable others who likewise seek space in the public press, time on the radio, and use of other channels. It is not enough to have a good message. It must be presented in the best forms that talent and skill can supply.

The preparation and distribution of "literature" is still one of the most important aspects of community-relations work. "Literature" is nothing more than information put in printed form for convenience in transmission—the same information that might otherwise be presented in a speech or a conversation. As used by community-relations agencies, "literature" means anything printed or mimeographed or reproduced by any process in quantity. If it is on paper and intended for wide distribution, it is classified as "literature." The term includes articles on any subject, reports of scientific investigations, handbills urging passage of a law, or just about anything which takes the place of talking to someone in person. A piece of "literature" may be good, bad, or indifferent, just as an interview or a speech may be. To be prejudiced for or against the use of "literature" in community-relations work would be as absurd as being for or against conveying ideas except by spoken words.

However useful the printed word may be, community-relations agencies cannot afford to rely solely upon "literature" or any of the other impersonal means of transmitting ideas. In the improvement of human relations it is necessary to bring people together. A good speaker can influence each of the people who hears him more than will a mere reading of his speech. A discussion in which all present participate will stimulate greater thinking than will an address. A personal conversation is more likely to persuade than will a phone call. Along with the extensive coverage which requires use of mass media, intensive work must always be done in direct personal contact on the friendliest terms achievable. The most fruitful personal associations developed by a community-relations agency are those among its own most intensely interested workers.

An alert community-relations organization knows the special interests and abilities of its own workers. Its committees are composed of those persons most able to render service. Whether it be a committee on housing, legislation, research, youth, recreation, employment, educational practices, public health, or whatever, accomplishment depends upon what the members of the committee can contribute by reason of their training, their experience, their contacts, and their grasp of the problems. The local agency is often in need of people who know something about labor, about public education, about playgrounds, transportation, about almost anything that affects human relationships. It cannot always search out the best qualified person. It will take the agency a very long time, and perhaps forever, to learn of your interests and experience. Don't wait to be discovered. Inform the chairman or the secretary who you are and how you can be of most help. Learn all you can about the agency and at the same time tell its representative about yourself.

No matter how well staffed and no matter how large its membership, no community-relations agency can score appreciable gains if it depends only on its own facilities. Its principal jobs are accomplished with and through the numerous well-established organizations of every kind that exist in every community. To an intergroup organization the improvement of human relationships is of first, foremost, and primary concern. Labor unions, veteran organizations, women's clubs, luncheon clubs, chambers of commerce, school boards, religious bodies, and a host of other organizations consider the relationships between racial, religious, and ethnic groups important, but their own reasons for existence are to serve certain other major purposes. Yet all of them can contribute directly and indirectly toward the realization of the goals of the community-relations agencies. Moreover, they have constituencies, publications, channels for reaching audiences, and the mechanisms by which education and social action can be carried on. It is by building friendships with the leaders and the staffs of many organizations and by winning the sponsorship of these organizations for meetings, conferences, seminars, forums, legislative proposals, and social action, that the effective community-relations agency accomplishes most of its work.

Community-relations agencies invite selected people to confer on matters in which they can be particularly helpful. The local agencies send strategic persons to seminars and workshops conducted at institutions of higher learning. The ultimate goal is to influence the rank and file, to get out to the public at large, to enlighten those who are uninformed or misinformed.

Fifteen years ago, when I was rabbi of Sinai Temple in Mount Vernon, New York, I was much impressed when some veterans came to me and said, "Rabbi, we were thinking of holding a good-will meeting but changed our plan. Some very fine people would tell each other about good will. But those who would be at the meeting don't need to be told. Instead, we've taken the names of the people we figured we would want to speak at that meeting. You are one of them. We've spoken to the superintendent of schools and he has consented to have speakers talk about good will at all the assemblies in all the schools that week. Instead of getting together we're going to scatter into the schools. Here's your assignment."

That was quite an innovation in those days. Today most schools plan and conduct their own brotherhood programs during Brotherhood Week in February. The amount of program material for such occasions has increased enormously with the passing years, with the National Conference of Christians and Jews spearheading the movement.

The effectiveness of community-relations agencies has increased greatly in the last few years. New methods and techniques are constantly being developed to meet new problems and a growing spirit of co-operation is making a wider experience available to all groups. Today there is a tremendous amount of excellent program material available where there was but the scantiest sort a few years ago. There is a better understanding of objectives and a firmer grasp of problems. A capacity for realistic self-criticism is indicative of a vigorous approach to the situation, and a remarkable expansion of the types of activities shows an increasing ability to cope with changing problems. Most important of all there is a growing realization of the infinite possibilities in the field and of the necessity for constant co-operative work toward the ultimate achievement of the democratic ideal.

Needless to say you can be of greatest help to a community-relations organization by joining it, by serving on its committees, and by influencing others to do likewise. If you are not already aware of whether there is in your locality such an organization as a Council for Unity or a Council for Democracy or a Community Relations Council or a branch of a national organization with which you might wish to affiliate, you can obtain that information from the American Council on Race Relations, 4901 Ellis Avenue, Chicago 15, Illinois. The Council publishes a Directory of Agencies in Intergroup Relations, which includes the names and pertinent information concerning national, regional, state, and local agencies.

CHAPTER 3

Sum and Substance

In 1854 Abraham Lincoln said, "Most governments have been based practically on the denial of the equal rights of men. . . . Ours began by *affirming* those rights. *They* said, some men are too ignorant and vicious to share in government. Possibly so, said we; and by your system you would always keep them ignorant and vicious. We proposed to give *all* a chance; and we expect the weak to grow stronger, the ignorant wiser; and all better and happier together."

Abraham Lincoln never assumed that the founding fathers of our country had completed the task of giving practical application to the concept that "all men are created equal." We cannot today assume that we have freedom for all men. The slavery which Lincoln knew has passed into history, but millions of Negroes are deprived of basic civil rights. Millions of other Americans are likewise denied the full privileges which are nominally theirs. As late as 1948 it required an act of Congress to make Japanese aliens, of whom 85,000 were long resident in the United States, eligible for American citizenship. The process of conferring even elementary rights upon some segments of our population has been, and remains, an incomplete and a tortuous one.

We like to think of the history of the United States as a steady upward movement toward universal freedom. That is an oversimplification. The status of many racial and religious groups has varied greatly from time to time and place to place. Intergroup relationships have been marked by favorable developments in one period and retrogressions in others. But viewed as a whole, the movement has certainly been toward a more broadly democratic society. Although at times adverse developments temporarily obscured gains or swept them away, the general *direction* has been encouraging. In 1928, when a resurgence of the Ku Klux Klan had been quashed, George Thompson Fry correctly reported in the July issue of *Reader's Digest* that "decade by decade, over the whole land, the conflicting elements have softened their hatreds. . . . There is less bigotry than in any former age." Mr. Fry buttressed this opinion with substantial facts. His statement at the time was certainly well founded. It is even more true today. We now complain bitterly of situations which had been formerly accepted as inevitable.

How far we have advanced and how much of our progress is permanent it is difficult to say. The canvas is too vast and the factors too involved for accurate and reliable judgments. We can only conjecture the rate at which the distinction between Victimians and non-Victimians in daily life is disappearing and project that rate tentatively into the future. Some years from now historians will know how accurately the Report of the President's Committee on Civil Rights, or the civil-rights planks in the platforms of political parties, or fair employment legislation mirrored the sentiments of our day.

It is difficult even to arrive at precise standards by which progress can be judged. For people north and south of the Mason and Dixon Line, who believe that segregation is of itself totally ruinous in the relationships of whites and colored people, no gains made by Negroes within its confines can compensate for the humiliation and degradation of segregation. A new school for Negroes, however handsome and well equipped, is to some minds a stigma and a defeat. Between those who, on the one hand, abhor segregation but believe it wiser from a practical standpoint to make progress for the present within its limitations and those, on the other hand, who insist that segregation must be the first line to attack, there are disputes concerning any gains for Negroes on a segregated basis. Some will never compromise or even negotiate. Others would agree with Walter Lippmann that "in diplomacy, when the stakes are life and death, the problem of the maker of policy is to select not the best objectives that could be desired but the best that can be realized."

There are those who are convinced that the establishment of the basic human rights is impossible of achievement wherever lives are plagued by prejudice and that adequate gains will never be obtained except by replacing our present economic and social order with radically new economic and social patterns. A few seem to believe that nothing short of violent revolution can bring freedom from intolerance. The average American rejects this philosophy and is thoroughly convinced that the most desirable changes can be made by adhering to the fundamentals of the American way of life.

Since even men of highest good will cannot in all matters agree on what is a genuine advance and what is an unworthy palliative in the field of group relations, it is useless to attempt a precise and mathematical enumeration of current assets and liabilities. Not even the passage or defeat of desired legislation can be considered a reliable barometer, for there is always the possibility of new progress or retrogression within a brief space of time. What *is* significant is the extent of firm determination on the part of men and women of good will to advance the democratic ideals of our nation. To have lost a fight here and there, to have only half remedied a situation that cries out for change, need not dismay us.

As Justice Meier Steinbrink, national chairman of the Anti-Defamation League of B'nai B'rith, said on May 6, 1948, "That we have a great distance to travel should discourage none of us, for we have already come a long way toward achieving real democracy." Whatever be the temporary gains or losses of those who desire the establishment of civil rights both in law and in life, there can be no fatal failure unless it be a failure to press on with wisdom and with courage.

No matter what may be the day-to-day or month-by-month situation of the forces working against intolerance there can be no doubt that we are today seeing the development of powerful social forces arrayed against one another. An intense interest has developed in intergroup relationships and a deeper concern with the well-being of all groups. In dozens of spheres of activity organizations have been created and programs have been developed to reduce prejudice, to eliminate discriminatory practices, and to establish better group relationships. Among clergymen, teachers, labor leaders, industrialists, the police, and other government officials, there are now many stanch advocates of fair practices in dealing with all people in the various phases of human existence. Innumerable parents are taking positive steps to insure that their children will be free of intolerance, and many civic leaders are determined that in their communities every individual shall enjoy full opportunity to achieve his full potentialities, regardless of racial, religious, or ethnic origin. Far more than ever before artists and writers—journalists, novelists, dramatists, scenarists, motion-picture producers, radio broadcasters, cartoonists, and others who provide the intellectual fare of our nation—are finding significant themes in the problems of prejudice. Everywhere there is a new realization of the importance of establishing genuinely democratic relationships among all groups and all peoples.

Nor are we alone here in the United States in our determination to provide for and insure the rights of the individual. The free peoples throughout the world are moving forward toward new freedoms. As a concrete demonstration of that desire, the General Assembly of the United Nations on December 10, 1948, adopted the Universal Declaration of Rights which in thirty articles sets forth the basic, inviolable rights of the individual. Article 2 makes it unmistakably clear that the Declaration is directed against the abridgement of those rights by intolerance, whether practiced by governments or by individuals. This article reads: "Everyone is entitled to all the rights and freedoms set forth in this Declaration, without distinction of any kind, such as race, color, sex, language, religion, political or other opinion, national or social origin, property, birth, or other status." Our nation is obligated to secure those rights for everyone within our borders.

In the tradition of America, each of us has a personal share in eradicating prejudice at its roots. Those roots are enmeshed in the fabric of our lives and we must know how to cut them without destroying more of good than of ill. But the eradication of prejudice and of the discriminatory practices it breeds is not something we may do or not do as we please. Each passing year finds us as a nation increasingly threatened by discord at home and required to answer to other nations, who are asking, "What are you doing about the unequal treatment of your citizens?" The challenge cannot be evaded, for it is being flung at us on every hand.

Unlike totalitarian governments we cannot look to a clique ruling our destinies and say, "We hope you will take care of this for us." True to the American way of life, we must solve some parts of the problem as individuals, each in his own sphere. We will not sacrifice cherished liberties and transfer to the control of government officials the whole area of human relationships. True it is that flagrant violations of human rights require effective action on the part of civil authorities. Clearly there is a need to strengthen the Civil Rights Division of the United States Department of Justice and to create similar agencies in the various states. Laws to abolish certain forms of discrimination likewise have a proper place in the struggle against intolerance. But in the final analysis it is not the government, it is *we*—every individual one of us—who must eliminate the innumerable snags and barbs in group relationships and free our communities of the snide and brutal tricks that prejudice plays upon all of us.

It were best if each of us, out of religious conviction and a sense of moral obligation, were to set himself firmly against those practices in American life which create so much of discord and misery. The appeal to conscience should never be neglected. With some people that appeal is always, and with all people it is sometimes, very powerful indeed. But even those who cannot be moved by the plight of others, even the most smug and the least altruistic, must be awakened to the issue and made to realize that from the standpoint of self-interest alone they share this problem and must take part in its solution.

Simply stated the question is, "Shall we allow bigotry to undermine our democracy? Can we suffer the ghastly social losses inflicted upon the most mistreated and still remain a vigorous and confident people?" It is hard to see how anyone can shrug off the matter. In terms of what intolerance does to all of us, whether we reckon ourselves as victims or victimizers, the danger is real and imminent. Prejudice has gotten into the warp and the woof of our existence. In every aspect of our lives it creates maladjustments, which are all the worse because we are frequently unaware of them.

Intolerance is a constant drain upon the individual and the nation —not something that injures us only at the time we feel the sting of bigotry and discrimination. At this very moment an agitator may be blowing upon the sparks of dormant prejudices which in due time may flare in a riot costly to you and to me. Right now it may well be that a statesman in another nation is saying, "The United States! Why should we place faith in her? She cannot even protect millions of her own citizens from mistreatment because of the color of their skins!" Today it is certainty that many children and young people who would have become splendid citizens are being turned into delinquents and criminals as a result of prejudice.

It is not surprising that racial and religious prejudice has been termed America's Number-One problem of today. It is not something far off. It is at your door every day. Ignoring it certainly will not help. Intelligent handling of it is thoroughly possible. But of this you may be sure: in a very real sense the struggle for inter-group harmony and for better human relationships is the struggle to defend the American way of life. It is not the fate of someone else that is at stake here. It is our very own fates that are being decided. What will *you* contribute to that momentous decision?